Finding Love

The Salty Key Inn Series
Book - 3

Judith Keim

BOOKS BY JUDITH KEIM

THE HARTWELL WOMEN SERIES:

The Talking Tree – 1
Sweet Talk – 2
Straight Talk – 3
Baby Talk – 4
The Hartwell Women – Boxed Set

THE BEACH HOUSE HOTEL SERIES:

Breakfast at The Beach House Hotel – 1
Lunch at The Beach House Hotel – 2
Dinner at The Beach House Hotel – 3
Christmas at The Beach House Hotel – 4
Margaritas at The Beach House Hotel – 5
Dessert at The Beach House Hotel – 6
Coffee at The Beach House Hotel – 7
High Tea at The Beach House Hotel – 8 (2024)

THE FAT FRIDAYS GROUP:

Fat Fridays – 1
Sassy Saturdays – 2
Secret Sundays – 3

THE SALTY KEY INN SERIES:

Finding Me – 1
Finding My Way – 2
Finding Love – 3
Finding Family – 4
The Salty Key Inn Series Boxed Set

THE CHANDLER HILL INN SERIES:

Going Home – 1
Coming Home – 2
Home at Last – 3
The Chandler Hill Inn Series – Boxed Set

SEASHELL COTTAGE BOOKS:

A Christmas Star
Change of Heart
A Summer of Surprises
A Road Trip to Remember
The Beach Babes

THE DESERT SAGE INN SERIES:

The Desert Flowers – Rose – 1
The Desert Flowers – Lily – 2
The Desert Flowers – Willow – 3
The Desert Flowers – Mistletoe and Holly – 4

SOUL SISTERS AT CEDAR MOUNTAIN LODGE:

Christmas Sisters – Anthology
Christmas Kisses
Christmas Castles
Christmas Stories – Soul Sisters Anthology
Christmas Joy

THE SANDERLING COVE INN SERIES:

Waves of Hope – 1
Sandy Wishes – 2
Salty Kisses – 3

THE LILAC LAKE INN SERIES

Love by Design – 1
Love Between the Lines – (2024)
Love Under the Stars – (2024)

OTHER BOOKS:

The ABCs of Living With a Dachshund
Once Upon a Friendship – Anthology
Winning BIG – a little love story for all ages
Holiday Hopes
The Winning Tickets (2023)

PRAISE FOR JUDITH KEIM'S NOVELS

THE BEACH HOUSE HOTEL SERIES

"Love the characters in this series. This series was my first introduction to Judith Keim. She is now one of my favorites. Looking forward to reading more of her books."

BREAKFAST AT THE BEACH HOUSE HOTEL is an easy, delightful read that offers romance, family relationships, and strong women learning to be stronger. Real life situations filter through the pages. Enjoy!"

LUNCH AT THE BEACH HOUSE HOTEL – "This series is such a joy to read. You feel you are actually living with them. Can't wait to read the latest one."

DINNER AT THE BEACH HOUSE HOTEL – "A Terrific Read! As usual, Judith Keim did it again. Enjoyed immensely. Continue writing such pleasantly reading books for all of us readers."

CHRISTMAS AT THE BEACH HOUSE HOTEL – "Not Just Another Christmas Novel. This is book number four in the series and my introduction to Judith Keim's writing. I wasn't disappointed. The characters are dimensional and engaging. The plot is well crafted and advances at a pleasing pace. The Florida location is interesting and warming. It was a delight to read a romance novel with mature female protagonists. Ann and Rhoda have life experiences that enrich the story. It's a clever book about friends and extended family. Buy copies for your book group pals and enjoy this seasonal read."

MARGARITAS AT THE BEACH HOUSE HOTEL – "What a wonderful series. I absolutely loved this book and can't wait for the next book to come out. There was even suspense in it. Thanks Judith for the great stories."

"Overall, Margaritas at the Beach House Hotel is another wonderful addition to the series. Judith Keim takes the reader on a journey told through the voices of these amazing characters we have all come to love through the years! I truly cannot stress enough how good this book is, and I hope you enjoy it as much as I have!"

THE HARTWELL WOMEN SERIES:

"This was an EXCELLENT series. When I discovered Judith Keim, I read all of her books back to back. I thoroughly enjoyed the women Keim has written about. They are believable and you want to just jump into their lives and be their friends! I can't wait for any upcoming books!"

"I fell into Judith Keim's Hartwell Women series and have read & enjoyed all of her books in every series. Each centers around a strong & interesting woman character and their family interaction. Good reads that leave you wanting more."

THE FAT FRIDAYS GROUP :

"Excellent story line for each character, and an insightful representation of situations which deal with some of the contemporary issues women are faced with today."

"I love this author's books. Her characters and their lives are realistic. The power of women's friendships is a common and beautiful theme that is threaded throughout this story."

THE SALTY KEY INN SERIES

<u>FINDING ME</u> – "I thoroughly enjoyed the first book in this series and cannot wait for the others! The characters are endearing with the same struggles we all encounter. The setting makes me feel like I am a guest at The Salty Key

Inn...relaxed, happy & light-hearted! The men are yummy and the women strong. You can't get better than that! Happy Reading!"

FINDING MY WAY- *"Loved the family dynamics as well as uncertain emotions of dating and falling in love. Appreciated the morals and strength of parenting throughout. Just couldn't put this book down."*

FINDING LOVE – *"I waited for this book because the first two was such good reads. This one didn't disappoint.... Judith Keim always puts substance into her books. This book was no different, I learned about PTSD, accepting oneself, there is always going to be problems but stick it out and make it work. Just the way life is. In some ways a lot like my life. Judith is right, it needs another book and I will definitely be reading it. Hope you choose to read this series, you will get so much out of it."*

FINDING FAMILY – *"Completing this series is like eating the last chip. Love Judith's writing, and her female characters are always smart, strong, vulnerable to life and love experiences."*

"This was a refreshing book. Bringing the heart and soul of the family to us."

THE CHANDLER HILL INN SERIES

<u>*GOING HOME*</u> *– "I absolutely could not put this book down. Started at night and read late into the middle of the night. As a child of the '60s, the Vietnam war was front and center so this resonated with me. All the characters in the book were so well developed that the reader felt like they were friends of the family."*

"I was completely immersed in this book, with the beautiful descriptive writing, and the authors' way of bringing her characters to life. I felt like I was right inside her story."

<u>*COMING HOME*</u> *– "Coming Home is a winner. The characters are well-developed, nuanced and likable. Enjoyed the vineyard setting, learning about wine growing and seeing the challenges Cami faces in running and growing a business. I look forward to the next book in this series!"*

"Coming Home was such a wonderful story. The author has a gift for getting the reader right to the heart of things."

<u>*HOME AT LAST*</u> *– "In this wonderful conclusion, to a heartfelt and emotional trilogy set in Oregon's stunning wine country, Judith Keim has tied up the Chandler Hill series with the perfect bow."*

"Overall, this is truly a wonderful addition to the Chandler Hill Inn series. Judith Keim definitely knows how to perfectly weave together a beautiful and heartfelt story."

"The storyline has some beautiful scenes along with family drama. Judith Keim has created characters with interactions that are believable and some of the subjects the story deals with are poignant."

SEASHELL COTTAGE BOOKS

A CHRISTMAS STAR – *"Love, laughter, sadness, great food, and hope for the future, all in one book. It doesn't get any better than this stunning read."*

"A Christmas Star is a heartwarming Christmas story featuring endearing characters. So many Christmas books are set in snowbound places...it was a nice change to read a Christmas story that takes place on a warm sandy beach!" Susan Peterson

CHANGE OF HEART – *"CHANGE OF HEART is the summer read we've all been waiting for. Judith Keim is a master at creating fascinating characters that are simply irresistible. Her stories leave you with a big smile on your face and a heart bursting with love."*

Kellie Coates Gilbert, author of the popular Sun Valley Series

A SUMMER OF SURPRISES – *"The story is filled with a roller coaster of emotions and self-discovery. Finding love again and rebuilding family relationships."*

"Ms. Keim uses this book as an amazing platform to show that with hard emotional work, belief in yourself and love, the scars of abuse can be conquered. It in no way preaches, it's a lovely story with a happy ending."

"The character development was excellent. I felt I knew these people my whole life. The story development was very well thought out I was drawn [in] from the beginning."

THE DESERT SAGE INN SERIES:

<u>*THE DESERT FLOWERS – ROSE – "*</u>*The Desert Flowers - Rose, is the first book in the new series by Judith Keim. I always look forward to new books by Judith Keim, and this one is definitely a wonderful way to begin The Desert Sage Inn Series!"*

"In this first of a series, we see each woman come into her own and view new beginnings even as they must take this tearful journey as they slowly lose a dear friend. This is a very well written book with well-developed and likable main characters. It was interesting and enlightening as the first portion of this saga unfolded. I very much enjoyed this book and I do recommend it"

"Judith Keim is one of those authors that you can always depend on to give you a great story with fantastic characters. I'm excited to know that she is writing a new series and after reading book 1 in the series, I can't wait to read the rest of the books."!

<u>*THE DESERT FLOWERS – LILY*</u> *– "The second book in the Desert Flowers series is just as wonderful as the first. Judith Keim is a brilliant storyteller. Her characters are truly lovely and people that you want to be friends with as soon as you start reading. Judith Keim is not afraid to weave real life conflict and loss into her stories. I loved reading Lily's story and can't wait for Willow's!*

"The Desert Flowers-Lily is the second book in The Desert Sage Inn Series by author Judith Keim. When I read the first book in the series, The Desert Flowers-Rose, I knew this series would exceed all of my expectations and then some. Judith Keim is an amazing author, and this series is a testament to her writing skills and her ability to completely draw a reader into the world of her characters."

THE DESERT FLOWERS – WILLOW – *"The feelings of love, joy, happiness, friendship, family and the pain of loss are deeply felt by Willow Sanchez and her two cohorts Rose and Lily. The Desert Flowers met because of their deep feelings for Alec Thurston, a man who touched their lives in different ways.*

Once again, Judith Keim has written the story of a strong, competent, confident and independent woman. Willow, like Rose and Lily can handle tough situations. All the characters are written so that the reader gets to know them but not all the characters will give the reader warm and fuzzy feelings.

The story is well written and from the start you will be pulled in. There is enough backstory that a reader can start here but I assure you, you'll want to learn more. There is an ocean of emotions that will make you smile, cringe, tear up or outright cry. I loved this book as I loved books one and two. I am thrilled that the Desert Flowers story will continue. I highly recommend this book to anyone who enjoys books with strong women."

Finding Love

The Salty Key Inn Series
Book - 3

Judith Keim

Wild Quail Publishing

wildquail.pub@gmail.com
www.judithkeim.com

Published in the United States of America by:

Wild Quail Publishing
PO Box 171332
Boise, ID 83717-1332

ISBN# 978-1-959529-96-5

Dedication

This book is dedicated to those who are willing to put their hearts at risk by loving deeply.

CHAPTER ONE

REGAN

Opening Day! Regan Sullivan hurried across the grounds of the Salty Key Inn, stopping a moment to gaze at the bougainvillea recently planted around the pool's perimeter. Lifting a blossom-laden branch, she studied the vibrant pink color of the petals and drew a deep breath, embracing its beauty. No matter how often people tried to capture color like this in fabric or paint, they could never quite succeed. Mother Nature always won.

Sometimes Regan felt as if she was in a tropical painting. Nothing quite as exotic as a Paul Gauguin, but alive in scenery she liked a lot better than what she'd been used to seeing in New York City or her hometown of Boston.

In the sky, streaks of pink broke through the early-morning gray, promising another hot, early September day along the Gulf Coast of Florida. She focused on a nearby hibiscus whose pink blossoms were opening to the sun and thought about all the changes in her life. Growing up, she would never have dreamed she would be part owner of a hotel. She'd already begun to think of her life in two sections—before Uncle Gavin's will, and after.

The far-fetched challenge their Uncle Gavin had given her and her two sisters, Sheena and Darcy, was like something out of a novel. They were to live and work together for one whole year to restore the hotel and get it up and running. If they met that requirement, they'd each inherit a third of his sizeable estate. It sounded wonderful, but in reality, it was no easy matter. The three of them living together, working together, and coming up with creative ideas to accomplish this were real challenges.

She moved on, still thinking of her situation. Their uncle had wanted this experience to be a life lesson for each of them. At the bottom of the letter he'd left for her, he'd written an ambiguous message: "Beauty is in the eye of the beholder." When Regan had read it, she'd been upset, thinking he'd been referring to her appearance, which she felt was the only thing people noticed when they met her. Now, she was beginning to suspect Uncle Gavin had had something entirely different in mind.

A flash of blue caught her eye. She stopped and glared at the peacock hurrying toward her. "Petey! No!"

The pesky peacock who ruled the hotel grounds stopped mid-rush and looked at her. Regan had learned if you remained strong, Petey was all squawk and no fight. Tail drooping, he turned away.

"Hi, Regan!"

She caught sight of Brian Harwood and returned the wave he gave her before he entered Gracie's, the restaurant at the hotel. Drawing a deep breath to stop her racing heart, she vowed to keep her promise to herself to avoid getting involved with him. No matter how attractive she found him, she was sure he was someone who would hurt her. He looked like a poster boy for Florida with his sun-streaked hair, tanned, buff body, and dark, friendly eyes that drew people in. Women all but drooled over him, and he almost always responded with interest, proving to her he was Trouble with a capital T.

Regan unlocked the door to the hotel's reception office and hurried inside. The official opening of the Salty Key Inn was about to take place, and she wanted to be on top of things because Sheena was dealing with issues in her family, and Darcy was writing her weekly column for the *West Coast News*, a local newspaper.

Regan went right to the computer to check the reservations system. They were able to open only the twenty ground-floor rooms in the Egret Building. The twenty rooms on the top floor of the building would remain unfinished until they had enough revenue to complete them. The eight suites in the separate Sandpiper Suites Building, where she and her sisters were now temporarily living, would be the last rooms to be renovated.

Her eyes scanned the list of people due to arrive for the Labor Day Weekend. Fifteen couples were taking advantage of the special renovation rates for the whole weekend. For a stay of two nights or more, they'd receive a discount off their room rate for two nights anytime within the next four months, when Uncle Gavin's challenge would end, and she and her sisters would find out what the rest of their lives might be like.

Regan's cell rang. She checked caller ID and smiled. *Moses Greene.* In a very short time, Mo had become one of her best friends. They'd met when he'd helped her select furniture for the hotel. Colorful and sweet, he was a very talented interior decorator. She hoped to be his business partner one day.

"Hi, sweetie," he said. "I called to wish you and your sisters a successful weekend at the hotel. It should be a good beginning. By the way, Bernice is excited about having her business up and running for you."

"She's doing a great job," Regan said. She and Mo had talked his cousin, Bernice Richmond, into opening a cleaning business to handle the housekeeping at the hotel.

"You're going to the Keys for the weekend as planned?" Regan asked him.

"Yes, I figure it's time to get out and meet some new people.

After the holiday, I've got a busy schedule coming up. Sheena's mother-in-law has been promoting my business, and I have a number of houses to work on."

"Let me know when I can help. Hopefully, after the holiday, things will settle into a calmer routine with fewer guests."

His soft chuckle came through the phone. "I think you're supposed to hope for more and more business at the hotel, not less of it."

Regan clapped a hand to her chest, and then laughter burst out of her. "Gawd! Sheena and Darcy would kill me if they'd heard what I just said."

"Kill you for what?" said a voice, and Regan turned around to face Darcy.

"Gotta go, Mo," Regan said. "Have fun, and call me when you get back. I'll want to hear all the news."

"Deal," said Mo, and he hung up.

"What's going on?" Darcy's blue eyes penetrated Regan's violet-blue ones challenging her for an answer.

"I told Mo I hoped things would settle down here at the hotel, and he reminded me as a hotel owner, I shouldn't want that."

Darcy shook her head, tossing her red curls playfully. "I know how you feel. Between the newspaper work and trying to organize a small wedding, I sometimes wish ..."

"Sometimes wish what?" Sheena entered the office.

Regan and Darcy exchanged amused glances. *Sisters!*

"Well?" Sheena prompted, smiling at them.

"I sometimes wish this whole challenge was over. I'm busy with other things, and so is Regan," said Darcy.

Sheena studied each of them and sighed. "Okay, pep talk time. We have to focus. We're down to four months to meet the challenge of getting the hotel up and running and pulling in some revenue. You know, and I know this could mean a lot of money to us if we succeed. More than that, we can make this hotel the kind of place Uncle Gavin envisioned. I, for one, want to stay on and help run the hotel if, and right now it's a big IF, we can pull this off. Don't let anything keep us from making this happen. Agreed?"

Chastised by the determined tone in Sheena's voice, Regan nodded. Her big sister was sometimes bossy, but she had a good heart, and they all had good reasons to want to beat the challenge. For Sheena, it would be to help her husband Tony set up his own plumbing business in Florida and to help educate their two teenage children, Michael and Meaghan. For Darcy, it would be the chance to write a novel and to have a nice life with her fiancé, Austin Blakely. And for herself? Regan would go into the interior-decorating business with Mo, combining her childhood wishes for recognition of her skills and acceptance for who she was as a person.

"Okay, then," said Sheena. "Let's see who we're talking about as guests." She looped a lock of auburn hair behind her ear and looked over the list. "Sorry, Darcy, but your old roommates from Boston are still coming. I thought you told them not to."

Darcy's lips formed a tight line of disapproval. "I tried to tell them to wait until we've had time to do more renovations, but nobody can tell Alex Townsend anything. I'm sure she wants to come here just to make nasty remarks. You know what a snob she is."

"It's important our guests understand we're in transition, working to make the hotel better," said Sheena. "You've made that clear in our advertising campaign, Darcy."

"But you don't know Alex like I do," griped Darcy.

"Nicole Coleman is nice though," Regan said, offering Darcy a tidbit of encouragement.

"She's the whole reason I roomed with them in Boston."

Darcy's long sigh spoke volumes. "I guess we'll have to do our best with Alex."

"Now that Sheena is here, let's grab a cup of coffee," Regan said to Darcy. "It's going to be a busy day."

"Bring me back a cup," said Sheena. "I think I'm going to need an extra jolt of energy. With Randy Jessup ending his summer stay with us, Michael and Meaghan are at each other, fighting over every little thing. It all has to do with their being nervous about entering new schools, not that they're about to admit it."

"No worries. I'll bring coffee back for you," said Regan, thinking Sheena was a saint to have allowed Michael's friend to spend the entire summer with her family.

The phone rang, and as Sheena answered it, Regan and Darcy dashed out the door.

As they were about to enter Gracie's, Brian was leaving. He smiled at Darcy. "Congratulations on your engagement. Austin is a great guy. I'm happy for both of you."

Regan watched a flush creep up Darcy's cheeks. At one time, Darcy had thrown herself at Brian, even going so far as to proposition him. Now, it seemed so foolish.

"Thank you," said Darcy. "I'm a very lucky woman."

Brian grinned at her. "And talented too. I read your newspaper columns, you know."

The look of surprise on Darcy's face was telling. Regan squeezed her sister's hand, proud of all she'd accomplished.

Brian's gaze swept over Regan, causing goose pimples to do a tap dance across her shoulders. "Heard you and Chip were at The Pink Dolphin last night. Sorry I missed you. I wanted you to meet Jill."

"Jill?" Regan tried to hide the frown she felt forming.

"She's an old girlfriend of mine who's moved back here. We're together again."

The pit in Regan's stomach filled with acid. She told herself it was nerves from their opening weekend, but as Brian continued on his way, she felt the sting of tears.

Darcy elbowed her. "What's the matter?"

"I think it might be allergies. I love all these new flowering bushes, but it's a little much," Regan replied, surprised by how easily she'd just lied.

After Regan and Darcy returned to the registration office, Regan forced herself to push away thoughts of Brian with a girlfriend. This weekend was what she and her sisters had worked so hard for. They were, as of this morning, another big step ahead on their way to meet the challenge.

"Remember," Sheena was now saying, "each guest is to be treated as if he or she is the most special one we have, exactly like the hospitality consultant told us."

"I can do it for everyone but Alex," said Darcy glumly.

"This is a good lesson for all of us," Sheena said. "Some guests will be easy. Others, not so much. You, Regan, are used to dealing with all kinds of different people from your job as a receptionist in New York. Right?"

"Yes, but it means so much more now. If we don't succeed, we'll have given up an entire year trying to earn the rest of Uncle Gavin's estate and keep the hotel."

"But, Regan, the year so far has definitely not been wasted. Think of all that's happened to each of us," said Sheena.

Regan's gaze shifted to the sparkling diamond ring on Darcy's finger. She glanced at Sheena, happily making notes on a sheet of paper. She thought of her interior design work with Moses Greene. "You're right. It's been time well spent, after all."

"The earlier phone call was from Blackie Gatto, wishing us

luck," said Sheena. "He's going to try to stop by sometime this weekend to see how things are going."

Darcy cocked an eyebrow at Sheena. "Bet he just wants to see you. Is Tony going to be around?"

Sheena glared at Darcy. "Not that again. You two know our relationship is strictly business."

"I think he's attracted to you," Regan said. "But I know you're not interested in him or anyone because Tony and you together? Hot. Really hot."

Sheena's cheeks turned a pretty pink. With her trim build, auburn hair, and hazel eyes, she didn't look like the mother of two teenagers. But then, she'd had her children young.

Darcy smiled at Sheena, "You two really are good together. I hope Austin and I will be as happy after so many years of marriage."

"I have a very definite feeling you will be," said Sheena, her eyes gleaming with affection. "He's perfect for you."

Standing by, Regan felt excluded. She hadn't found the perfect one for her and wondered if she ever would. She'd already decided to stop seeing Chip Carson. He'd been belittling her after she'd tried to explain to him even if it seemed very old-fashioned of her, she was not about to go to bed with anyone until she was ready to commit to a life with him.

At the sound of someone approaching, all three sisters turned to greet their first guests.

Regan hurried to open the door for the woman standing beside a man with a metal, prosthetic leg. Regan beamed at them with all the excitement she felt. "Hello! Welcome to the Salty Key Inn. You must be Sgt. Thomas Jansen and Cynthia."

"Please. Just Tom and Cyndi," Cynthia said, smiling. Of average height and build, she had a pretty face and short, blond hair. Even handicapped by his leg, Tom stood tall and straight and looked at Regan with a steady, blue-eyed gaze. His short dark hair cut close to his head added to the image of a military man.

Regan held the door while Tom walked into the office, followed by Cyndi. Observing Tom's seemingly easy use of his leg, Regan felt a lump form in her throat. Tom and Cyndi were one of two military couples taking advantage of their special discount program for military members. The other couple, from Atlanta, would arrive late in the afternoon.

As they'd practiced earlier, Sheena checked in the guests, Darcy took care of the luggage, and Regan walked them to their room, where she made sure they had plenty of ice and offered to help in any other way.

Soon, a stream of people arrived to take advantage of a full day at the hotel. Since there had been no previous guests, rooms were available for early check-in. Busy with other arrivals, Regan didn't notice Alex and Nicole right away, but as she stepped into the registration office, she recognized them immediately. Nicole was a pretty girl with long, blond hair, which offset the dark, straight locks on Alex's taller head. Both wore high-end, fashionable clothes and nice jewelry more suited to an upscale resort.

Sheena, who'd never met them, asked cheerfully, "And who do we have here?"

"Alex Townsend and Nicole Coleman," Regan said, giving them a smile. "Welcome to the Salty Key Inn."

"When Darcy told us the hotel was in transition, she wasn't kidding," scoffed Alex. "This place needs a whole lot of fixing up."

"Ah, yes, you must be Alex. Let's get you checked in," said Sheena, unable to hide her scorn.

As she was entering their information on the computer, Darcy came into the office.

Darcy's look of dismay transitioned into a smile Regan knew was forced. "Hi, Nicole! Hi, Alex!"

As Darcy reached out to give Nicole a quick hug, Alex let out a shriek. "Oh my God! You're engaged? Let me see that ring."

A look of envy crossed Alex's face as she studied the three large diamonds winking at her from Darcy's ring finger. "Nice, very nice."

Nicole threw her arms around Darcy. "I'm so happy for you! Who's the lucky guy?"

"Someone I met here at the hotel," said Darcy, smiling happily.

At that moment, Brian stuck his head into the office. "How's everything going?" He smiled at Alex and Nicole and turned to Sheena. "Need me to do anything?"

Sheena shook her head. "Thanks, anyway. We're set for the moment."

Brian gave her a little salute and left the office.

"Wow! He could help me with anything he wanted," said Alex, staring at him through the window. "Talk about a hottie! What is he? Some kind of handyman?"

Regan surprised herself by rising to his defense. "He's a successful businessman who owns his own construction company."

Sheena cleared her throat. "I think we're all set here. Ready to go to your room?"

Nicole and Alex looked at each other and nodded.

Regan and Darcy led them to the specially reserved, ground-floor, corner room facing the pool. At the thought of hearing them criticize her creative decorating, Regan couldn't stop the nervous flutter in her stomach. She could tell from the stiffness of Darcy's shoulders she, too, was worried about their reactions.

Regan slid the key card into the lock on the door, opened it, and stood back.

"Oh, how nice!" said Nicole, as she walked into the room. "I love furniture done this way."

"Thanks. Using chalk paint on furniture to give it an antique look is something I love to do," said Regan, feeling relief wash over her.

"Very quaint," Alex said. "And we're close to the pool. Cool. I want to try out my new bikini. Especially if there are handsome guys around like the one we saw."

Regan fought off unpleasant images of Alex and Brian together. "Our access to the beach is right across Gulf Boulevard, and beach chairs and towels are available at the pool." She picked up the ice bucket and said, "Two complimentary bottles of water are in the small refrigerator. I'll get you some ice."

"The Key Hole, the bar next door, offers discounts to our guests," said Darcy. "Just show them your guest card."

Regan left them, filled the ice bucket, and hurried back to the room.

"Is he cute?" Alex was asking Darcy, again studying her ring.

Darcy glanced at Regan.

"Austin cute? He's a doll, and one of the nicest guys I've ever met," Regan said. "Show her a picture, Darcy."

Darcy reluctantly pulled her phone out of her pocket and began scrolling through photos.

Nicole and Alex leaned closer. In the photo, Austin smiled back at them, his bright-blue eyes shining beneath a shock of dark-brown hair.

"Wow," said Alex. "He's so handsome." She nudged Nicole. "Maybe we'd better stay here longer than a weekend."

Nicole gave Darcy a warm smile. "I really am happy for you.

Best wishes to you both."

"Yeah," said Alex. "I'm surprised by how fast it happened, but I'm pleased for you. Good job!"

Regan drew herself up. "Darcy and Austin's relationship is very sweet, very real. They'll be doing a lot of traveling in the future."

"Really?" Alex crossed her arms over her chest and studied Darcy.

Looking uncomfortable, Darcy nodded. "We're going to honeymoon in Europe."

"Wow! A lot of big changes for you," said Alex in a condescending tone Regan found irritating.

Regan took hold of Darcy's arm. "We'd better get back to the office." Using her professional, smooth voice, she turned to their guests. "Enjoy your stay, and let us know if we can do anything else for you."

"Thanks," said Nicole. "Glad to be here."

Alex didn't respond, but went to the sliding door, opened it, and stepped onto the small patio outside.

In the hallway outside the guestroom door, Darcy let out a puff of breath. "Alex is going to drive me crazy. I already can't wait until she leaves."

"Me too," said Regan. "She's enough to make anyone go mad."

They hurried back to the office to help Sheena. Now that they were truly open for business, Regan wondered what other kinds of problems they'd face. They'd already learned the hotel business was full of surprises. Some good. Some not so good.

CHAPTER TWO

SHEENA

Sheena checked off the last of the names on the reservations list with a sense of satisfaction. Fifteen couples had been assigned their rooms with no glitches. Better yet, they'd all seemed pleased with their accommodations. Everyone, that is, but Alex Townsend, who had one of the best rooms in the hotel. She'd complained that to get to the pool, she and Nicole had to walk too far. Now, Alex was complaining there was a problem with the air conditioner.

She looked up as Darcy came into the office. "Get the latest issue with Alex settled?"

"Brian helped me check out the air conditioner in their room. He told them it's working fine, but they shouldn't run it and keep their sliding door open, that it messes up the system. Alex was so glad to see him I'm sure that won't be her only complaint about it."

"She's something else. I had no idea she was so difficult." Sheena gave her a sister a steady look. "I hope you didn't act like her when you were together."

"I hope so, too," said Darcy. "Is everyone else checked in?"

"Regan is with the last couple, the military veteran from Atlanta and her husband."

Darcy sank into a chair with a sigh that reverberated in the room. "Is this how it's going to be every day?"

"Things will smooth out," Sheena said, hoping she was right. The tension in her shoulders felt like iron claws.

"How about taking a break and going over to The Key Hole?"

Sheena looked at her watch. "Let me check in with the kids, and if everything's okay, I'll join you. The office closes in minutes. Who's turn is it to handle off-hours calls?"

"Regan's," said Darcy. "Thank goodness. I want nothing more to do with Alex."

Regan came into the office, glanced at the clock on the wall, and sank into one of the chairs. "Am I glad this day is almost over!"

"You two go ahead to The Key Hole," said Sheena. "I'll be along later."

Earlier in the day, Sheena had made sure Meaghan showed up for her shift at Gracie's. The restaurant had become a local favorite, and they needed all the help they could get. Michael, she knew, was working on the landscaping for Gavin's, the new restaurant she and her sisters were building on the property. It would replace the little pink house where she and her sisters were to live together for the entire year before a fire destroyed it.

Tony walked through the office entrance. "Hey, hon! How'd it go?" He smiled at her, affection lighting his brown eyes.

His dark curly hair had grown longer, and she found she liked it that way. In jeans and a T-shirt that showed the benefit of his working with Brian in his construction business, he looked ... well, adorable.

Sheena's lips curved happily. "It went well, but it's going to take a while for us to get used to always being available to our guests and their constant demands." She shook her head. "I met Darcy's old roommate, Alex. No wonder Darcy was nervous about having her here."

"That bad, huh?"

"Afraid so, but it's a good lesson for all of us—learning how to deal with fussy guests."

"Thought you might like to stop over at The Key Hole," said Tony, arching an eyebrow and smiling. "Michael and Meaghan are fixing sandwiches, and then they're heading down to the beach. They promised to be back by dark."

"Sounds good," said Sheena. "Give me a minute. I just want to be sure the phone system is switched over to the emergency line."

After checking the phones, Sheena locked the office door behind her and stepped into the balmy air. She wondered if she'd always feel their guests were like her family, needing her attention. She'd come to Florida to find herself, but it apparently didn't mean she could change all that much with her new role.

CHAPTER THREE

REGAN

At The Key Hole, Regan sat in an over-sized booth with Darcy, glad for the opportunity to be away from the hotel. She'd no sooner settled in her place when her cell phone rang. She checked caller ID and let out a sigh. It was the hotel line.

"The Salty Key Inn," she said, wondering why she had to be the first one to handle the emergency line. She listened and then drew in a calming breath, "We'll have fresh towels for you tomorrow morning, Alex. No problem."

"What now?" said Darcy, narrowing her eyes.

"Alex and Nicole want to be sure we'll give them fresh towels every day. I explained that to them earlier. I think they're purposely making trouble for us, and I don't understand why." She looked up and waved to Tony.

He came over to their booth and slid onto the red-vinyl-covered bench opposite them. "Sheena will be here any minute." He turned his attention to Darcy. "She said your old roommate is causing a problem."

Darcy gave him a glum look and nodded.

At the sound of people entering the bar, they all turned.

Sheena entered, followed by the two young women they'd just been talking about.

"I wish they'd just go away," murmured Darcy as Alex and Nicole approached.

"And who's this handsome guy?" Alex said, smiling as she openly assessed Tony in a way that felt awkward to them all.

"That's Tony Morelli, my husband," said Sheena, sliding in beside him.

"Oh," said Alex, softly. "Sorry."

"Nice place," said Nicole looking around.

"Quaint," said Alex, and then, seeing Brian enter the bar from the kitchen, she hurried to him.

"See you later," Nicole said and walked over to the bar.

"Quaint?" said Regan. "Is everything here 'quaint' to Alex? What a crock!"

"Apparently, Brian isn't," said Sheena. She leaned in close. "I had no idea anyone could be so irritating, Darcy. How did you ever put up with her?"

A teasing smile Regan knew well crossed Darcy's face. "I thought living with my sisters for a year was going to be difficult, but after rooming with Alex, who knew how easy it sometimes could be?"

Regan joined in the laughter, but out of the corner of her eye, she continued to watch the way Alex was throwing herself at Brian. He, of course, was smiling and nodding at whatever Alex was saying. When he noticed Regan staring at them, Brian gave her a helpless shrug.

Regan stiffened, and then told herself Brian's behavior wasn't her problem, it was his girlfriend, Jill's.

Regan relaxed as the barroom filled with conversation, diverting her attention from Alex, who'd taken a seat at the bar next to Nicole after Brian disappeared into the kitchen again.

When their drinks came, Sheena lifted her glass of white wine. "Here's to the Salty Key Inn!"

"I'll drink to that," said Tony, clicking her glass with his mug of beer.

"It looks like we're off to a good start," said Sheena, tucking a strand of auburn hair behind an ear. "Regan, you're taking calls tonight, but I'll take over first thing in the morning."

"And I've agreed to take over from you on Sunday morning," Darcy said to her. She looked up and smiled as Austin walked through the door, followed by Chip Carson.

Austin slid into the booth next to Darcy and Regan. Chip sat down opposite them, beside Sheena, and smiled a greeting to everyone.

"You celebrating or commiserating?" Austin asked, after giving Darcy a kiss.

"A little of both," said Darcy. "Things are going well, except for dealing with my ex-roommates."

Austin put an arm around Darcy's shoulder. "Don't let them bother you, honey. You and your sisters are doing a great job here."

Regan studied the looks of love exchanged between Austin and Darcy and knew she was right to hold out for a man who'd look at her that same way. Chip was fun to be with most times, but he wasn't the guy she was waiting for.

The appearance of Alex and Nicole at their table interrupted Regan's musing.

"We wanted to meet your fiancé," said Nicole sweetly. She smiled at Austin. "I'm Nicole Coleman, and that's Alex Townsend. I'm so happy for you and Darcy."

He rose to his feet. "Thanks. I'm one lucky guy."

Alex openly assessed Austin. "I'd say she's one lucky gal." She turned to Chip. "And who are you?"

Chip's eyes swept over Alex and lingered. "Chip Carson. I'm with Regan."

"Not exactly. We're not together," Regan said, not wanting anyone to get the wrong impression.

Alex's eyebrows lifted. "Oh?" She turned back to Chip. "Well then, maybe *we* can get together sometime."

###

Regan returned to the suite she was sharing with Darcy too tired to think of going out with Chip or anyone else. She hadn't liked the way he'd assumed, because he'd wanted it, they were "with each other," implying the wrongs things about their relationship.

With everything quiet at the hotel, Regan decided to go for a swim in the pool. Her father, Patrick, had insisted all the Sullivan girls learn how to swim. Regan had fought it at first and then had found it a good way for her to unwind. And when she'd turned out to be an excellent swimmer, she'd enjoyed it even more.

Regan donned a swim suit and then slipped out the door and crossed the hotel grounds in the dark, grateful for the privacy and quiet.

She opened the gate to the pool, set down her towel down on a chaise lounge, and slid into the water, gasping a bit at its relative coolness. Soon, her limbs were slicing through the water in sure, even strokes.

After swimming several laps, Regan pulled herself up onto the pool steps and sat, catching her breath. Then, wrapping a towel around her, she headed back to her suite feeling like a new person.

In her suite, she took off her bathing suit and studied herself in the full-length mirror. She wasn't at all prudish about being naked and liked the idea of finding a sexual partner, but she was determined to do as her mother had asked by being sure of that man before doing anything like going to bed with him, and then, only if she was willing to marry him. That's why she had no intention of seeing Chip again.

Later, lying in bed, Regan stared up at the ceiling. She longed not to feel alone when her sisters seemed so settled.

Darcy knocked on her bedroom door and entered. "Hi. Thought you'd want to know after you left The Key Hole, Chip asked Alex out. I didn't want you to be caught by surprise when you heard it and wind up being hurt."

Touched by her concern, Regan sat up and faced her sister. "It's okay. I'd already made up my mind Chip isn't for me. But, honestly, I wish he wouldn't be with someone like Alex. She's only going to hurt him."

Darcy nodded and sank down onto the bed. "I think you're right. She's very selfish. She didn't think twice about leaving Nicole alone. Austin and I asked Nicole to sit with us." Her features softened. "I'd forgotten how nice Nicole is when she's apart from Alex. And later, Brian joined us. His girlfriend had plans for the night, so it turned out to be a pleasant evening."

"I bet he and Nicole got along very well," said Regan, trying to sound as if she didn't care.

"They're both nice people, but no sparks," said Darcy, giving her a long look before rising. "Guess I'd better get to bed. It's another busy day tomorrow."

After Darcy left the room, Regan lay in bed hugging her pillow, wishing it was a warm, breathing guy who loved her.

The next morning, Regan rose early, slipped on a pair of shorts and a T-shirt, grabbed her sandals, and headed to the beach.

Walking along the sand and feeling the wind in her long black hair, the nagging thoughts that had kept her from a healing sleep evaporated into the air. Today was a new day, a good day, she reminded herself. She was free to concentrate on helping her sisters meet Uncle Gavin's challenge and then, if they were lucky, she'd be able to work with Mo.

Regan looked up to see Cynthia Jansen walking up the

beach toward her. She waved and waited for her to approach. "Good morning! How are you? How is everything at the hotel?"

Cynthia's smile brightened her features. "Oh, my, things are great! The beds are comfortable, and you've made everything easy for Tom and me. I appreciate getting a break like this."

"Are you headed back to the hotel? If so, and if you don't mind, I'll walk with you. Gracie's should be open now, and they have the best coffee and breakfast ever."

Cynthia's soft laugh rippled in the air. "Sounds wonderful." There was a silent strength to her Regan found interesting.

"Is it difficult to live with someone who's been through so much in battle? I've often wondered how some women carry on while their men are away fighting."

Cynthia studied her with hazel eyes that seemed to reach inside her. "Funny you should ask that. I'm thinking of writing a book about it, but I don't know where to begin."

"My sister Darcy might be able to help you," said Regan. "She writes a column for the local newspaper. Someday, she's even going to write a novel—something light and romantic."

"Really? It would be very helpful if I could talk to her about it."

"I'm sure she would be happy to hear what you have to say. Her columns are about various people she meets."

They left the beach, crossed Gulf Boulevard, and entered Gracie's. Regan now recognized some of the early-morning regulars who sat at the tables. Taking Cynthia's arm, she led her over to the corner table that was the family's favorite.

Lynn Michaels, one of the eight people Gavin had more or less rescued, all of whom now lived at the hotel, came over to them carrying a pot of coffee and two mugs.

"Coffee?"

Regan turned to Cynthia.

"Yes, thank you," Cynthia said. "Black."

"Same here," said Regan. "Lynn, this is Cynthia, one of our hotel guests."

Lynn bobbed her head. "Nice to have you here with us. The girls are doing a great job to make this hotel the way their uncle wanted."

Cynthia glanced at Regan.

"It's a long story. I'll tell you later."

Darcy walked into the restaurant, saw them, and came over to their table.

Regan reintroduced Cynthia and said, "Cynthia wants to write a book about her experiences as a military wife."

"Please call me Cyndi," she said. "And if you have the time, Darcy, I'd love to talk to you about it."

"Sure," said Darcy.

Regan checked her watch and got to her feet with a little sigh. "I've got to open the office. See you later."

Walking across the grounds to the registration office, which sat by the swimming pool, Regan noticed Alex leaving Chip's jeep, wearing the same outfit she'd worn last night.

Hurrying toward the office to avoid a conversation with her, Regan was stopped by Alex's cry of "Wait!"

Regan sighed at being caught and turned to Alex.

"Hey, I wanted to talk to you," said Alex. "I know you've been dating Chip, and I just want you to know it's nothing serious between Chip and me–just a vacation hookup."

Regan hid her distaste. "Believe me when I say it doesn't matter to me. As I said last night, Chip and I aren't together."

Alex shrugged. "Okay, thanks. See you later."

Regan watched Alex walk away, more certain than ever she was right about breaking it off with Chip. *Vacation hookup? No, thanks.*

Inside the office, Regan checked the computer. Two couples were arriving that day for the rest of the Labor Day weekend.

A knock sounded on the door. "How're things going?" asked Bernice, stepping inside. "Everything okay with the housekeeping?"

"You're doing fine, though we did have one complaint about towels for Room E-110. We need to be sure there are plenty of clean towels there every day." Regan couldn't help rolling her eyes. "The two women staying there are Darcy's old roommates from Boston, and they're very hard to please."

Bernice clucked her tongue. "Always one or two fussy ones. Don't worry. I'll make sure they get plenty of towels and washcloths. I've hired a new worker, and she's good."

"Thanks. Let us know if you need anything."

"I think you're low on pool towels," Bernice said. "People tend to put them in the basket at the end of a swim and reach for a new one when they return to the pool. We could use more beach towels, too."

"Okay, I'll talk to Sheena about it. Thanks for letting us know," Regan said and watched Bernice hurry away.

Sheena arrived a few minutes later. "How are we doing?"

"Good, so far. Bernice is recommending we get more pool and beach towels. Can we afford to do that?" They'd spent almost all of the one hundred fifty thousand dollars Uncle Gavin had left them to get the hotel up and running.

Sheena shot her a worried look. "I hadn't budgeted in that expense. Hopefully, we can buy a few more towels after everyone pays for this weekend. It's going to be difficult to take care of everything and raise enough money to finish the twenty top-floor rooms in the Egret building. And then we have to try and complete the eight Sandpiper Suites."

Regan was glad Sheena had the role of managing the

finances. She was content to oversee decorating the rooms.

A guest walked into the office. “Can you tell us how we’d go about arranging a fishing trip?”

Regan had recently picked up some brochures from companies at St. John’s Pass. Smiling, she handed one over. “Here you go. All the information is here.”

After the guest left, Sheena said, “Go ahead and have breakfast. I’ll handle the office for a while.”

As Regan was about to leave the office, Blackie Gatto arrived, accompanied by a man Regan didn’t recognize.

Sheena beamed at Blackie. “I’m so glad you could make it. I wanted you to see what we’ve done since you last visited. We’re officially up and running, though there’s a lot more work we need to do.” She turned to the other man. “And Arthur, nice to see you again.”

Sheena indicated Regan with a wave of her arm. “Arthur, this is my sister Regan. She’s the one who’s been overseeing the refurbishing of the rooms. And Regan, this is Arthur Weatherman. He owns several restaurants in the area.”

“Nice to meet you.” Regan smiled and headed for the door.

“Hold on,” said Blackie. “I wanted Arthur to see some of the rooms you’ve renovated and thought you could show them to us.”

Regan paused and nodded. “Sure, I can do that.”

As she said the words, Regan wondered why Sheena and Blackie exchanged satisfied smiles.

CHAPTER FOUR

DARCY

Darcy left the restaurant with a promise to meet with Cyndi again. Her mind was spinning. Cyndi had agreed to let her use some of the information about her own life in a column for the local newspaper. Darcy, who'd likened many people and their actions to those of angels, thought Cyndi was another perfect subject. More than that, she was intrigued by the idea of writing a non-fiction book with Cyndi about the commitment military families make to each other and the country. First, she needed to talk about it with her editor at the paper.

As Darcy walked to the registration building, Meaghan rushed out of the Sandpiper Suites Building and ran toward the restaurant.

"Hi," Darcy called to her.

Meaghan waved as she ran by. "I'm late! Talk to you later."

Darcy waved her on. Meaghan worked as a bus girl at Gracie's. Reluctant at first to help in any way, Meaghan had changed from a spoiled teenager into a nice kid who was learning earning money wasn't as easy as she'd thought. Darcy admired Sheena and Tony for making their children work at the hotel. It had done both kids some good.

Her thoughts flew to Austin. He would, she was sure, make a great father. They'd talked about having children and had agreed to wait a while after they were married so they could travel whenever they had time. In the meantime, they were enjoying being engaged and planning a wedding. Sometimes, Darcy felt as if she were in a dream. Austin was the perfect man for her, and he loved her like nobody else ever had.

As Darcy approached the office, Regan, Blackie Gatto, and another man—a stranger—emerged.

"Hi," called Regan. "I'm going to show them some of the guest rooms. Want to join us?"

Darcy shook her head. "No, thanks. I promised to meet Austin to go over some decorative designs for the restaurant."

"Okay, see you later," said Regan.

Darcy left Regan leading the men toward the Egret Building and entered the office. "Who's with Blackie and Regan?"

Sheena gave her a sly smile. "Arthur Weatherman. He owns several casual seafood restaurants. When Blackie learned about Arthur wanting to redecorate some of them, he thought of Regan. We're hoping he likes what's she's done to the guest rooms enough to hire her to do his restaurants."

"Wow! Does she know this?"

Sheena shook her head and lifted a finger to her lips. "Don't mention a word of this to her. She'll find out if she gets the work. Otherwise, she doesn't have to know. I wouldn't want to hurt her feelings."

"Got it." Darcy gave Sheena a thumbs-up, pleased by how she and her sisters had formed a real bond over the past months.

"You're meeting with Austin about Gavin's?" Sheena asked her.

"Yes. He's already said he'd carve the sign for Gavin's. He's going to match the logo for the restaurant with a stylized capital G and an insert of the rest of the letters, underlined with simple lines signifying waves. But he's also agreed to create some fancy decorative carvings to enhance the paneled walls inside, and we want to come up with a design to use on signage inside. He loves doing that kind of work when he's not practicing his dentistry."

"How's that going?"

"His partner's patients love him. But then, so do I," said Darcy with enough feeling to bring a smile to Sheena.

"You two make me happy," said Sheena. "I'm sure Mom would be thrilled for you too."

Darcy sobered. "Yeah, too bad she died so young and before she knew how the three of us have pulled together to try to beat Uncle Gavin's challenge."

"Strange how it's worked out," said Sheena thoughtfully.

Their conversation ended with the arrival of new guests, a young couple Darcy thought might be on their honeymoon.

While Sheena checked them in, Darcy handed them brochures and told them about the special offers from surrounding businesses.

She'd just finished showing them to their room and getting them settled when she heard voices in the hallway outside the door.

"Nicole, you've got to come with me. I want to see if I can get Brian to go out with us."

"No, I'm here to relax and have fun, not hunt down guys. I'm going to the pool."

Their voices grew dimmer as they obviously moved away.

Darcy paused for as long as she could and then turned to the couple who had eyes only for each other. "Have a nice stay, and let us know if we can do anything for you."

She left the room and hurried out of the building, hoping not to be delayed by either Nicole or Alex.

Standing at the construction site of what would be the

restaurant they'd decided to name Gavin's, Darcy could well imagine what it would look like one day. She and Austin had gone over the plans, and she had spent many hours discussing the project with her sisters.

Built of concrete blocks with a stucco finish on the outside, Gavin's was going to be a fairly small restaurant with an elegant Old Florida feel inside and excellent food, just like their uncle had envisioned. Beadboard stained a rich, dark-brown on the walls would be offset by high, white ceilings throughout the first floor. Austin and his woodworking skills would be put to use enhancing the wood paneling. The letter G was to be carved into the wood in several places: behind the bar; at the entrance; and on the doors of the small private dining room. Guests would sit in chairs covered with a bright, printed fabric Regan and Mo had chosen to complement the commercial carpet in various shades and patterns of blues and greens.

Reviewing the plans once more, Darcy was relieved the proceeds from the insurance settlement following the fire were paying for it, though, once again, they'd had to be very careful about costs.

"You think December 15th is a reasonable time to get everything done?" Darcy asked Austin.

He thought a minute and then nodded. "The exterior walls and roof are already up. The interior will take longer, but I think it's doable. I'll start carving the plaques today."

"You understand why I have to stay at the hotel this entire weekend, right?" She sometimes escaped to his condo.

He lifted her chin and kissed her. "No problem. We'll make up for lost time this week."

CHAPTER FIVE

REGAN

Regan took Blackie and Arthur to a room facing the garden. "We've tried to keep the theme to a casual, beach look with the sand-colored carpets, the furniture, and the soft goods. Most of the furniture was cleaned and then painted with blue chalk paint to give it an old look. With a little scouting around, we were able to get the rest of the furniture for reasonable prices."

As she talked, Arthur kept his gaze on her, making her uneasy. "How much do you think you saved by doing this?"

"Several thousand dollars for each room. You understand we're on a strict budget, right?"

He nodded. "Indeed. I knew Gavin Sullivan, and generous as he was, he wasn't about to waste a penny. Neither am I."

When there was nothing more to be said, Blackie spoke up. "Thanks for showing us what you've done. Very impressive, Regan. Gavin always liked that you appreciated beautiful things."

Regan hid her surprise. She hadn't known Gavin, yet he seemed to have known a lot about her and her sisters. Sheena thought it was because Gavin and her mother had exchanged letters and, later, photos. Still, it put her ill at ease.

Still wondering at Blackie's remark about Gavin, she led the men back to the registration office.

Sheena met them. "Now, may I show you what we've done down by the bay and what we're doing with the restaurant?"

Both men nodded. Sheena left with them, leaving Regan to handle the next guests. After they'd registered and Darcy had shown them to their room, Regan looked up the financials they'd recorded on the rooms renovation. She'd answered honestly when she'd said they'd saved thousands on each room. Even buying second-hand furniture was expensive.

Chip showed up as she was tallying numbers. "Hi, Regan. Thought I'd let you know I took Alex out last night. Didn't think you'd mind."

"Not at all," Regan said. "Besides, I've decided not to date anyone for a while. You and I have different ideas about things, and I'm becoming busier with the hotel. And I hope to be working part-time with Mo on various projects."

"That loser?"

Regan gave Chip a steady look. "Hey, please don't criticize him to me. Mo is my best friend. I love him like a brother. He's talented, and he's very kind." She gave him a narrow-eyed look that sent a clear message to him.

"Whew! Why are you so touchy?" His lips curled with disdain. "Maybe you should relax, go with the flow, and be more like Alex. She's a lot of fun."

"Never," said Regan. "Now, please excuse me, I'm busy."

Sheena returned to the office in time to see their standoff. Frowning, she said, "Am I interrupting anything?"

"Not at all," said Regan. "Chip was just leaving."

"You're messing up a good thing, Regan," Chip said, turning away from her. As he exited the office, he let the door slam behind him.

"What was that all about?" Sheena asked her.

"I'm ending the relationship with Chip for good. He wants what I won't give him. In fact, he told me I should be a lot more like Alex."

"And what exactly does he mean?"

"Besides spending the night with him? I can only guess what so-called 'fun' she gives him. Alex says it's just a vacation hook-up."

Sheena placed a hand on Regan's shoulder. "I'm proud of you for being exactly who you are. And, to be honest, I've never quite trusted Chip. Not after someone drugged you at his roommate's party."

Regan nodded but couldn't hold back a sigh. Would she ever find the right guy for her?

"Blackie and Arthur want to talk to you about something," said Sheena. "Oh, here they come now."

Regan watched with curiosity as Blackie and Arthur entered the office.

"Is there somewhere where we can talk privately?" Arthur asked Sheena.

"Why don't I leave?" Sheena said, gathering her purse and all but racing out the door.

"Well, then," said Arthur, when the three of them were alone. "Let's all sit down. I've got a serious proposition for you, Regan."

Confused, Regan glanced at Blackie.

He gave her a reassuring nod. "It's a very intriguing idea. Listen to what Arthur has to say."

Regan gulped nervously and lowered herself into one of the four chairs in the office.

Blackie sat beside her, facing Arthur.

"As I'm sure many people have told you, Regan, you're a very beautiful woman," Arthur began.

"I thought you were interested in what I'd done in the rooms, how I'd decorated them," she responded with dismay.

"I am, I am," said Arthur. "My proposition is two-fold. First of all, I'd like you and your partner to submit ideas for renovating my six seafood restaurants in the 'Florida's Finest

Restaurants' chain I own. I like what you did and, even better, I like your attitude."

Regan's eyes widened. "Really? That would be wonderful."

"And?" prompted Blackie.

Arthur drew a breath and beamed at her. "And I'd like you to become my spokeswoman, the face, so to speak, on my new advertising campaign for Florida's Finest Restaurants."

"Me?" Regan didn't know what to say. Arthur had already acknowledged her skill at decorating, so he saw more in her than her face. Still ... she hated the idea of putting herself on display.

"It could be a very nice source of income for you," Blackie reminded her. "I'd help you set up the contract and handle the money for you. It would be an ongoing endeavor."

"I couldn't possibly do anything like that for a while." Regan clasped her hands together as her mind spun. "I'd have to wait until business at the hotel settles down. I promised my sisters to do everything I can to help us succeed."

"Very admirable," said Arthur. "It will take some time for our marketing department to do their work, so I don't see that as a problem. We'd begin sometime after the first of the year, which is still four months away."

"Thank you so much for the offer," said Regan, still stunned by the turn of events. "I'll talk it over with my sisters and get back to you."

Arthur stood. "Fine, young lady. I'll wait to hear from you. But don't wait too long. There are others I can use, but I want you for the job. You'll give a refreshing, new look to all I'm doing."

Blackie stood and placed a hand on Regan's shoulder. "I think your uncle would be very proud of you."

Regan nodded, remembering his quote to her. "Beauty is in the eye of the beholder." *Had he ever suspected something like this would happen to her?*

As soon as the men left, Sheena came into the office. "Well?"

Regan told her about the opportunity to bid on redoing Arthur's restaurants, and then she paused.

"Is that it?" Sheena asked, giving her a knowing smile.

"He wants me to be the face of his restaurant chain, like some models do for perfumes and other products." Regan gave her sister a penetrating look. "You knew about this?"

Sheena's look of satisfaction was telling. "Blackie and I talked about it. You'd be perfect for both."

Elation replaced her lingering surprise. "I've got to call Mo. He'll be so excited!"

Sheena laughed. "Go ahead. I'll stay here in the office. I want to work on financials anyway."

Regan felt as if she were floating a few inches above the grass as she raced to her room in the Sandpiper Suites Building. Her mind whirred with ideas. If she and Mo could gain a reputation for doing commercial properties, the opportunities in Florida might be endless.

To calm herself, she fixed a cup of coffee, sat at the kitchen table, and then punched in his number on her cell.

He picked up after several rings. "Hello?"

"Am I disturbing anything?" she asked in a teasing voice.

"Nope," he answered. "It's been a disappointing trip."

"Why? Aren't you meeting new people like you wanted?"

Mo let out a long sigh. "I realize I'm not over Juan. I just want to come home."

"Oh, I'm so sorry," Regan said. Juan had broken up Mo's relationship with him a couple of months ago, deeply hurting Mo. "Well, I've got good news for us. You know Florida's Finest Restaurants chain? They want us to bid on redoing six of their restaurants!"

"What? How'd that happen?" Mo's excitement formed a smile on her face.

"Blackie Gatto introduced Arthur Weatherman to me, and I showed him the rooms we did. And guess what? He wants to feature me in advertising for his restaurants. Nice, huh?"

"Very nice, sweetie. A beauty like you? People will love it and you. That does it. I'm coming home. We'll celebrate together."

"I was hoping you'd say that. Can't wait to see you!"

"What about Chip? Won't you want to celebrate with him?"

"I'm through with Chip. It's over." Regan waited for a beat or two for Mo to say something.

"Good," he finally said. "To be truthful, I never really liked him."

Regan bit the corner of her lip. What was wrong with her? Sheena hadn't liked Chip, and neither had Mo. Why hadn't she seen what they had? No wonder she'd never find the right man. Apparently, she was horrible at seeing them for who they really were.

CHAPTER SIX

DARCY

Darcy sat in her office looking over the designs she and Austin had come up with for the restaurant. It pleased her she was engaged to a man who was so creative, even though his professional practice of dentistry would provide them a secure future.

She thought of her earlier conversation with Cyndi Jansen. She was already thinking of ideas for the newspaper column she'd write about her. She wished she could talk to Nick Howard, her old mentor at the newspaper, about the idea of writing a book with Cyndi. Even weeks after his death from cancer, she missed him like crazy. Not a day went by she didn't talk to him in her mind, seeking the wisdom he'd always shared with her. Nick had known her dream was to write a novel about ordinary people in extraordinary situations, but now, faced with someone's true story of such a situation, Darcy worried she might not be equal to the task. A column was one thing, a novel another. And an entire non-fiction book, still another.

Regan came into the office in a rush. "Hi! Did you hear my good news?"

Darcy noticed the look of joy on her sister's face. "What now?"

Regan took a seat and filled her in on the proposal Arthur had made to her. "What do you think?"

"It's great," said Darcy. "I'm happy for you, but I'm

wondering what it's going to mean for our challenge. If you are in business for yourself and I'm writing my novel, that leaves Sheena with the hotel. I know she says she wants to stay with the project, but is she going to be able to handle it alone? I think it's time to start looking for a hotel manager who can work for us in January after we meet the challenge."

"How about Casey Cochran? He did a great job of consulting with us. He'd be perfect."

"I agree, but I wonder if we can get him to do it. He's so good he might want to manage something bigger, fancier."

Regan waggled a finger at her. "You never know until you try."

Darcy couldn't stop the laugh that escaped her lips. After suffering from being made to feel stupid most of her life due to a learning disability, her baby sister was becoming more and more sure of herself.

"While you're here, Regan, I want your advice on my wedding colors. Most Valentine's Day weddings would feature red, or pink, or both. I want something different. How about all white?"

"For the flowers? The gowns? What?"

A thread of excitement curled and expanded through Darcy's insides. "I thought you, Sheena, and Meaghan could wear white dresses in any style you want. I, of course, will have a long, white dress, nothing too fancy but still ... a wedding dress. The flowers can be an assortment of white roses, tulips, lilies, and anything to give them texture. Their leaves will add some green color."

"And what about the guys?" asked Regan.

"They can wear gray slacks, white shirts. What do you think?"

Regan gave her a thoughtful look. "It could work nicely with the only touches of color being dove-gray and the green in the flowers' leaves. But, as you said, you'd want to have lots of texture for interest. It would be understated, but very nice."

"Because the wedding will be at sunset on the beach, I want nature to be part of the ceremony."

"Yes, I like it!" Regan beamed at her.

"I can't believe it's me having this wedding," Darcy gushed. "Austin is perfect for me, and I get not only him but a chance to travel and to write." She felt the sting of tears and blinked rapidly to keep them from filling her eyes. "How could I be so lucky?"

Regan gave her a quick hug. "He's lucky too. Remember that, Darcy."

She nodded, but Darcy knew of the two of them, it was she who had much more reason to be thankful.

After Regan left the office, Darcy's thoughts turned once more to Cyndi Jansen. They'd agreed to meet the next morning for an interview for the newspaper article Darcy wanted to write about her. Cyndi had mentioned PTSD and how it was affecting her life with Tom, and Darcy wanted to learn more about it.

Online, Darcy read there are many ways PTSD can affect someone's everyday life. Some of the most common symptoms of PTSD included recurring memories or nightmares of the event, sleeplessness, loss of interest, numbness, anger, irritability, or constantly being on guard. Sometimes, these symptoms wouldn't surface for months or even years after the event occurred or after returning from deployment. They could also come and go, persist, and disrupt one's daily life.

Darcy continued reading and learned servicemen and women might have felt as if their lives or the lives of others were in danger or they had no control over what was happening. While in the military, they may have witnessed people being injured or dying, or they may have experienced physical harm themselves.

Lost in thought, Darcy remembered the conversation she'd had with Austin's grandfather about serving in Vietnam. He'd mentioned the man who'd saved his life had committed suicide. Was that a result of PTSD? She wondered if anyone had even addressed those issues with him back then?

Chip Carson came into the office. "Thought we'd better schedule a tune-up on the computer system for next week, to see how things are going since you're up and running."

"Good idea," said Darcy, glad he was on board with their IT systems.

He sat down in a chair and faced Darcy with a troubled look. "Guess I blew my opportunity with Regan, huh?"

She studied him and felt a need to protect her sister. "In reality, as she told me, you two were never on the same wavelength about a lot of things. Besides, you didn't waste a minute asking Alex out."

Chip gave her a sheepish look. "C'mon, give me a break. It's a holiday weekend. I wanted to go party." A satisfied smile curved his lips. "And Alex likes to party."

Darcy clucked her tongue, feeling old resentments against Alex building inside her. She pushed them away and focused on keeping her relationship with Chip professional. "Why don't you meet with me Thursday afternoon to discuss the computers?"

He stood. "Okay. See you then." He started for the door, stopped, and turned around. "You Sullivan sisters sure are particular."

Darcy couldn't help the sense of pride that filled her. "Guess so." It had taken Uncle Gavin's challenge, living and working together, to give her and her sisters a chance to know each other. Better yet, they were learning they liked each other. For that, Darcy would always be grateful.

The day passed without any crises beyond running out of pool and beach towels and needing more beach chairs. As Darcy stood behind the swimming pool counter with Sheena, checking their towel supply, she kept an eye on Cyndi and Tom Jansen lying in chaise lounges beside the pool. She was surprised to see his prosthesis tucked under the chair and his damaged leg exposed for all to see.

Sheena noticed her staring and nudged her. "Makes you appreciate what some people go through to help protect our country, huh?"

Darcy nodded.

"Here comes Alex," said Sheena in an undertone.

Darcy turned her attention to Alex, who was wearing a bikini that was hardly there. On her, it looked good, but it seemed to Darcy the skimpiness of the suit was a little like an advertising campaign.

Alex sidled over to them and leaned on the counter. "Hi, Darcy. Just wanted you to know Chip has asked me out again. Hope your little sister won't be mad at me." Her look of concern was barely manufactured.

"No, she won't mind at all. I guess Chip didn't mention she dumped him," said Darcy with pleasure.

Alex's eyebrows shot up. "Because of me?"

"No, because Regan has realized she has very little in common with him. But I'm certain the two of you will have a good time together."

"Oh, well, I wanted to be sure," said Alex. She turned and walked away, her hips rolling in a seductive walk that emphasized her bare buttocks.

"Good heavens," said Sheena. "Is she for real?"

Darcy gave her sister a grim look. "That's her, worse than she's ever been. I wonder what Nicole is doing, left on her own."

"She was talking with Cyndi and Tom Jansen earlier. It seems Cyndi's brother is coming in this afternoon. Alone."

"Do you think? ..."

Sheena laughed. "Yes, Cyndi told me she asked Nicole if she was free this evening to double-date with them. I'd love to see Alex get her comeuppance. Until now, she hasn't seemed to care one whit about Nicole."

Darcy chuckled. "If there's any justice, he'll at least be a nice guy."

CHAPTER SEVEN

SHEENA

Sheena left Darcy and headed over to the suite her family was sharing. She and Tony were about to build their own house in a neighborhood not far away, but it wouldn't be completed until after the New Year, which was perfect timing. Then, she would be free to stop living at the hotel as Uncle Gavin's will required.

Crossing the lawn of the hotel, Sheena thought about her children. At seventeen and handsome like his father, Michael was pushing to be considered an adult. In reality, he was a teenager with raging hormones and a lack of common sense. But he was a good kid if she didn't count the two summer episodes with drugs and alcohol with his friend, Randy Jessup. But with school beginning and a chance to be on the football team, Michael had decided it was more important to do sports than to get into trouble.

Meaghan waved to her from the pool, where she was swimming with a new friend. Her children were allowed to use the hotel pool when guests were not using it. Smiling, Sheena waved back, happy to see her daughter settling nicely into her new life in Florida.

A combination of both her parents—with Tony's darker skin tones, hazel eyes, and Sheena's auburn hair—Meaghan was turning into a beautiful young woman. Three years younger than Michael, she was becoming the sweet girl she'd once been. Away from wealthy friends in Boston who thought they were entitled, Meaghan had learned a lesson about working hard for things. Sheena had Gracie to thank for that. No one who worked in Gracie's restaurant was allowed to sluff off work, and with the restaurant so busy, even a busgirl like Meaghan had to prove herself.

Sheena opened the door to the suite and stopped in surprise. Michael and a young girl she hadn't met were lounging on the small couch Sheena had rescued from another suite.

"What's going on?" Sheena asked, subtly inhaling for signs of cigarette smoke or worse.

Michael jumped to his feet. "Hi, Mom! We're just hanging around, watching television or whatever."

The whatever, Sheena could see, was the making out that had obviously been going on. Sheena studied the small, red-cheeked, brown-haired girl who was wearing shorts so tiny Sheena could almost see her crotch. "I'm Michael's mom. And who are you?"

"This is Kaylee Kendall," said Michael, smiling at Kaylee in a way that spelled teen trouble.

Sheena extended her hand. "Nice to meet you, Kaylee. It's a nice day for the beach. I suggest you two go on outside and enjoy the day."

Michael glared at her privately, and then a sheepish smile crossed his face. "Okay. C'mon, Kaylee." He held out his hand. She took it and got to her feet.

"Nice to meet you, Mrs. Morelli," Kaylee said sweetly as Michael hurried her out of the room.

Sheena watched them leave, thinking it was time for another talk with Michael.

Sheena was putting together the lasagna that was Tony's

favorite when he walked through the doorway.

"Hi, hon! What's for dinner?" he asked, coming over to her and giving her a kiss. When he stepped away from her, he eyed the lasagna and smiled. "M-m-m."

"Thought you might like it," she said, giving him a warm smile.

He grabbed a beer out of the refrigerator, opened it, and sat down at the kitchen table. "What's new? The hotel doing well?"

Sheena set down the spoon she'd been using. "The hotel is running smoothly. But, Tony, I think we need to talk to Michael again about sex. I happened to come home for a minute this afternoon, and he and a girl named Kaylee Kendall had obviously been making out. I swear her shorts showed everything she has, and Michael was aroused. He's too young to get into that kind of trouble."

Tony's brown-eyed gaze settled on her. "Like us?"

"No, honey, I didn't mean it that way. Michael isn't even through high school. He has a bright future ahead of him. He might even be eligible for a sports scholarship if he plays as well here as he did in Massachusetts."

Tony rose and came over to her. "Sheena, I know your pregnancy prompted our marriage, but I can't imagine my life without you. I love you so much."

Sheena rested her head against his broad chest and inhaled the manly smell that was his alone. As his arms wrapped around her, a sigh escaped her. She loved him, but she couldn't help wondering about the young girl whose dreams of becoming a nurse had been shattered by the unexpected news of her pregnancy. She didn't want that to happen to either of her children.

Michael walked into the room and stopped. "It's a nice day for the beach. I suggest you two go on outside and enjoy the day," he said in a mocking tone.

Sheena pulled away from Tony and turned to her son. "Dad and I were just talking about you and the situation I found you in this afternoon. Michael, we know very well what it's like to lust after someone, but we want you to be careful."

"Well, you embarrassed me, Mom. Kaylee is going to think I'm a baby."

"I doubt that," Sheena said, unable to hide her sarcasm. "You need to be careful for her sake as well as your own."

"Aww, Mom ..."

Tony put a hand on Michael's shoulder and gave him a steady look. "We're serious, son. This is important stuff. Surely you know how to use protection, not that we're encouraging anything. You know how we feel."

A pink tinge of color brightened Michael's cheeks. "Gawd! We were just making out, okay?" He stormed out of the room.

Sheena and Tony exchanged worried looks.

"Methinks he doth protest too much," said Sheena, misquoting Shakespeare.

"I'll have a man-to-man talk with him later," said Tony, wiggling his eyebrows at her. "After I make sure I know what I'm talking about."

Sheena laughed. She and Tony had always had a good time in bed.

CHAPTER EIGHT

REGAN

Regan sat in front of her computer checking out the restaurant chain Arthur Weatherman owned. With an emphasis on fast-food, seafood meals, the chain had done well, mostly because of the good, fresh food that brought customers back time after time. The restaurants, themselves, were not very exciting—an overdone, fishing-boat theme.

Studying the pictures of them, Regan thought maybe she and Mo could approach their bid on a whole different level. She couldn't wait to talk to Mo about it. They planned to meet the next morning to discuss it.

In the meantime, she, like her sisters, was waiting for the arrival of Cyndi's brother, Kenton Stanislowski. Darcy had confirmed Nicole had agreed to join Tom, Cyndi, and her brother for dinner, and they were all dying to see him.

Regan was cleaning out the supply closet when the bell over the office door tinkled, signaling a new customer. She straightened and hurried to the registration desk. A man wearing sunglasses and a baseball cap pulled low stood in front of the desk.

"May I help you?" Regan asked.

"Registration for Ken Stanislowski," he said in a smooth, lilting voice that sounded a little foreign to Regan. She smiled at him. "We've been expecting you. Cyndi and Tom are out at the pool. I know they'll be glad to see you."

"Great," he said. "I'm looking forward to seeing them."

Regan handed him the key to his room. "I'll escort you there. Do you have any bags?"

He indicated the backpack he had slung over his shoulder. "Just this."

As Regan walked Ken to the Egret Building, she couldn't shake the feeling she knew him, but it didn't make sense. The name wasn't recognizable. She studied his blue jeans, his imported loafers, the expensive watch on his wrist.

He stood by as she opened the door to his room. "We hope you will be comfortable here."

"I'm sure I will be," Kenton said, following her inside.

"There are bottles of complimentary water in the small refrigerator, and I'll go get you some ice now."

She left the room with the ice bucket.

When she returned, she stopped and stared at their guest. He'd removed his hat, sunglasses, and shirt. "You ... you ... are Kenton Standish?"

He gave her a smile women had been swooning over for years. "Last time I checked, I was. They haven't fired me yet."

Kenton Standish was an actor featured on a cable program that people, women especially, loved. As he played the role of a swashbuckling, Scottish hero of an earlier time, his muscular chest had invoked a million sighs around the world. With blue eyes that offset sandy-colored hair, he was almost pretty.

"Wel ... welcome to the Salty Key Inn. We hope you enjoy your stay." Regan could hear the tremor in her voice and chided herself for being so foolish. "If you need anything, don't hesitate to call the desk."

Embarrassed by her silly behavior, Regan all but fled the room.

Later, as she told Darcy and Sheena what had happened, they laughed. "Wait until Alex finds out who Nicole's date is. She'll be all over him."

Darcy held up her hand. "Don't mention it to anyone. If Alex finds out, she'll ruin it for Nicole."

"And, as hotel owners, we must respect the privacy of others." Sheena's serious expression exploded into a smile. "But can you believe it? Maybe, if he likes his stay, it will help our business."

Darcy shook her head. "I don't mean to be cruel, but why would someone like him choose the Salty Key Inn over a glamorous hotel in, say, South Beach?"

Sheena straightened with indignation. "Because the Salty Key Inn is a family place, where we welcome every guest with the same care as everyone else."

"Right," said Regan. "That makes a world of difference to a lot of people. Even famous ones. Darcy, when you interview Cyndi tomorrow, find out what he thinks of the place."

The phone on the registration desk rang. Regan picked it up.

"I'm back," said Mo. "Can we meet for dinner tonight? My treat."

"Sounds good. Hold on. I'll check with my sisters." She turned to Darcy and Sheena. "Okay if I have dinner with Mo tonight? I'm technically off duty at six."

Darcy looked at Sheena. "I don't think it's fair, do you?"

"Not at all." Sheena tried to give her a severe look but ended up grinning at her. "We're teasing. Go. Have fun. We'll handle things here."

Regan laughed. "You two!" She went back to the call. "Okay, six o'clock."

"Since you'll be my only date of the weekend, why don't we say the Key Pelican? It'll be a treat for both of us."

"Sounds great."

"I'll pick you up. Thanks, sweetie."

He hung up before she could answer him. She paused. Mo had sounded so depressed. She guessed the dating scene was as hard for him as it was for her.

Regan took her time dressing. Mo always looked nice, and she knew he'd be pleased. The deep-purple sheath she'd recently purchased brought out the violet-blue in her eyes. When Darcy had seen her trying it on, she'd declared Regan had to buy it. Now, at herself, Regan was glad she'd splurged on the dress. A simple shell necklace added just the right touch. That, and the dangly earrings that matched it.

When Mo came to pick her up, Regan couldn't help the smile that spread across her face. She swore the two of them had some kind of mental telepathy going on. He was wearing a lavender dress shirt, yellow bow tie, and cream-colored slacks. He looked, well ... endearing. As usual.

His brown, fine-featured face lit up at the sight of her. "Love your dress," he said, beaming at her.

"You look very nice yourself," she responded. Though he was slight in stature, Mo was a good-looking man who had a large presence.

He held out his elbow, and Regan happily looped her arm through his, thinking he was the perfect person for her.

Mo led her to his old, white Nissan 300 ZX and, once settled inside, they drove in comfortable silence to the restaurant. The Key Pelican was the kind of restaurant their Uncle Gavin had wanted for the Salty Key Inn. In deference to him, they were naming the restaurant under construction after him. Gavin's would be different in appearance from the outside, but it would be as elegant inside as the Key Pelican.

Mo pulled his car up to the entrance of the restaurant. The turquoise building, trimmed in pink, had surprised Regan when she'd first seen it. But she'd grown to love the funky colors of the buildings in this area of the Gulf Coast of Florida.

A doorman helped Regan out of the car.

As she waited for Mo, Regan studied the colorful, carved-wooden statue of a pelican perched on a piece of wood beside the front entrance. Carvings like this were a decorative theme special to the area. Gracie's even had one of a pirate they called Davy.

Inside, the wood-paneled walls of the small restaurant gleamed a warm brown. The sand-colored tile entrance gave way to a richly carpeted room in blues and greens. Tables were covered in crisp pink linen and held sparkling crystal glasses and heavy silverware. In the center of each table, colorful hibiscus blossoms nestled inside a glass container shaped like the blossom itself.

A sigh of pleasure escaped Regan. She hoped the interior of Gavin's would be just as elegant.

"Nice, huh?" said Mo, after they'd been seated at a table in a corner, overlooking a small garden.

"Yes," Regan said. "I can't wait until Gavin's is done. We're still aiming for the middle of December."

"I think we'll be happy with what we've chosen for the interior decorating. Now, Regan, let's talk about Arthur Weatherman's proposal."

Their waitress came, and after ordering drinks, Regan told Mo everything she and Arthur had talked about. "I've done some research, and I think we ought to try a different approach from the other proposals that may be presented. I suspect everyone will be doing a boat, fish, or water theme. Let's try something unique."

Mo leaned forward. "Okay. What do you have in mind? His

restaurants are noted for their seafood items."

Regan drew a deep breath, suddenly unsure of herself. "Why don't we do different land themes? Places where the menu items come from? New England for the lobsters? The Northwest for Dungeness crabs or Maryland for soft-shell crabs?

A smile creased Mo's handsome, brown face. "I like it, Regan. We can work on it together and come up with definite ideas. But, it's good."

Regan felt her shoulders relax with relief. After being considered dumb for so many years, she treasured small triumphs like this. If she and her sisters never won Gavin's challenge and the money that followed, her time here in Florida would have been worth it.

She leaned forward and reached for his hand. "Okay, now, Mo, let's talk about your trip to the Keys. What happened?"

He shook his head with dismay. "Nothing. Absolutely nothing. I realized I wasn't interested in going through all the motions of meeting someone else. I guess I need time to heal from Juan's dumping me. And, like you, I wanted to be with someone who makes me happy. You know what I mean?"

"Yes, I finally dumped Chip. I deserve someone who respects my wishes. I can do better than him. And you know Darcy's old roommate, the girl I've told you about? Alex Townsend? She went out with Chip last night, and she's going out with him again tonight." A disturbance at the doorway caught her attention.

"What's going on?" Mo said, turning to see.

"It's Kenton Standish," Regan whispered. "He's staying at the hotel. And his date is Nicole Coleman, Darcy's other old roommate—the nice one."

Nicole, an attractive blonde, looked stunning in a white linen dress and strappy sandals. Watching the easy manner in which she conversed with Kenton, Regan knew how silly she'd acted with him. Kenton was a good-looking man—okay, a hunk—but he was human, after all.

Cyndi noticed her and came over to her table. "Oh, hi, Regan. I didn't expect to see you here. Thanks for taking care of my brother's reservation. We're having a wonderful time. I told Darcy the Salty Key Inn is the perfect place to hold a little family reunion. Next time, we'll try to bring the kids."

"Thanks. Cyndi, I want you to meet Moses Greene, the best interior designer I know. And Mo, this is Cyndi Jansen and her husband Tom, who are guests at the hotel."

Mo stood. "Nice to meet you."

Kenton came over to their table. "Aren't you the woman who helped me get checked in?" he said to Regan.

Regan felt her cheeks grow hot. "Yes. Cyndi tells me you're enjoying your stay." She indicated Mo. "Meet Moses Greene, a friend of mine and a talented interior designer."

Kenton held out his hand. "Hi, I'm Kenton Standish."

A smile lit Mo's face as he politely shook hands with him.

Cyndi tugged on Kenton's arm. "Unless you want people to recognize you, we'd better go to our table."

"Right-o," he said, winking at Regan. He nodded to Mo and left.

Regan and Mo both sighed as Kenton joined the others at a table not far away.

CHAPTER NINE

DARCY

Darcy was alone in the registration office when Alex stormed in. "Why didn't you tell me Nicole was going out with Kenton Standish? And why wasn't I included?"

Working to get her anger under control, Darcy drew a long breath. "First of all, we didn't know Cyndi Jansen's brother was Kenton. Secondly, you'd already planned to go out with Chip Carson."

"Yeah? Well, Chip canceled on me, and now I'm left on my own with no plans."

"Like you left Nicole the other night," Darcy couldn't help saying.

Alex plopped down into a chair and stared at her. "You've never liked me, Darcy. Don't think I don't know that."

Darcy gave Alex a steady stare. "What's to like? You've always made disparaging remarks about my family and me. You never even gave me a chance."

"Well, you have to admit your family isn't exactly high society," said Alex. "Like mine."

"And that makes you what? Besides a rich bitch?" Darcy knew she was being childish, but she couldn't prevent herself from playing this game. Alex had hurt her feelings so often in the past it felt good to say some of the things she'd kept bottled up inside.

Alex jumped to her feet. "You think you're so much better than me now that you are engaged to a handsome, well-to-do guy. But, Darcy, you're not. And I don't care if you make it with this hotel or not. I'm never coming back here."

Darcy made no move to stop Alex from leaving.

Alone in the office once more, Darcy sank down into a chair. Her heart pounded inside her chest. Typical of her, Alex had judged Austin by the size of the engagement ring he'd given her. She was well aware they'd have a wonderful life together with opportunities she'd never had growing up, but he wasn't wealthy except in spirit, love, and kindness.

Sheena came in, took one look at her, and said, "What's the matter?"

"It's Alex. She's furious I didn't inform her Nicole was going out with Kenton Standish. Chip backed out of his date with her, and she's been left on her own. Furthermore, she says she's never coming back here."

"Good. I fed my family an early supper. I can close up the office for you if you want to meet Austin."

Darcy smiled at her sister. "Thanks. That's sweet of you." She rose, gave Sheena a quick hug, and stepped away. "I'm sorry I resented you for so many years for leaving me to help take care of Regan with Mom's being so sick. I see now how selfish that was."

"We all had to assume responsibility for each other when Mom had one of her devastating headaches. But I'm glad you understand I had the right to leave home for college. Too bad it didn't work out as I'd planned."

"Yes, but what you have with your family is so much better than what we had growing up. What are you and Tony going to do when both the kids are gone?"

Sheena's eyes lit with mirth. "Have a good time. As they say, 'The best is yet to come.'"

Darcy laughed. "I hope Austin and I will still feel that way when we've been married as many years as you and Tony."

"Keeping a marriage together isn't always easy, but it's worth it if true love is there. You'll be fine. Don't worry."

"I told Regan my wedding plans. Want to hear them?"

"Of course," said Sheena. "Spill."

Darcy gave Sheena the details, adding a few ideas about the kind of music she wanted for her reception. "I want the first dance with Austin, and, Sheena, I want to do a father-daughter dance with Dad. We weren't that close as I was growing up, but it's important to me. Do you think he'll come and be part of my wedding?"

"I'm sure he wouldn't want to miss it," said Sheena. "He loves you."

"Yes, I know," Darcy said. "But it means he'll see all Gavin has done for us, and he won't like that."

Sheena searched Darcy's eyes and nodded. "Maybe it's time he settled those resentments. He's not getting any younger."

"Do you suppose Mom was really in love with Gavin like we think?"

"I'm not sure, but maybe so," said Sheena with a tone of finality Darcy couldn't ignore. She studied Sheena, wondering why she seemed so eager to end the conversation.

Darcy and Austin were sitting on the couch watching television when Regan returned from her date with Mo.

"Have fun?" Darcy asked.

"Yes, and you'll never guess who we saw. Nicole and Kenton were having dinner with Cyndi and Tom at the Key Pelican. She looked great, and they seemed comfortable together. Nice, huh?"

"Very nice," said Darcy. "Alex is furious she wasn't included, especially after Chip bowed out of their date."

Regan shook her head. "Serves her right. She dumped Nicole as quickly as she could to go out with Chip."

"Was Mo excited about your plans with Arthur Weatherman?"

"Very," said Regan. "We're going to try something new for decorative themes for his restaurants. And he thinks I'll be a great spokesperson for him."

"Sounds as if you're going to be busy," said Austin. "Good luck with everything."

"Thanks. Well, I'll leave you two lovebirds alone and head into my room. I want to make some notes while I'm thinking of them."

After Regan left the room, Austin turned to her. "Lovebirds, huh? Sounds good to me." His lips curved into a crooked smile she loved. "Better come here."

Darcy chuckled, scooted closer to him, and lay her head on his shoulder, loving this man who made her feel so good, so worthy of love.

The next morning, Darcy rose early for her usual morning walk on the beach, eager to see how the final two days of the holiday weekend would go. So far, things had remained pretty calm, except for the constant demands of her roommate.

As she made her way through the hotel grounds to the beach, she could smell delicious aromas emanating from Gracie's. She inhaled them and forced herself to keep moving. She'd found a brisk walk on the beach was a great way to start the day, allowing her to contemplate the novel she wanted to write.

She crossed Gulf Boulevard and walked down the boardwalk to the sand. Kicking off her sandals, she set them aside and stepped onto the soft surface. The chill of nighttime still clung to the grains of sand, and it felt good. As she usually did, Darcy headed for the water's edge, where the waves lapped the shore in open invitation. The wind was still, allowing the water to move forward and back in slow motion, making her wonder at the consistency of nature.

A few people roamed the beach in the distance, checking for shells. Darcy liked the feeling of being alone. For her, this magical setting was the perfect way to welcome a new day. Since Nick's death and with her engagement to Austin, Darcy tried to take a moment each morning to start the day with gratitude.

She turned at the sound of someone approaching.

"Good morning," said Nicole.

Darcy smiled. "I didn't expect to see you up so early after your date with Kenton Standish."

She laughed. "He's a very nice guy. We had a nice time, but there was no spark between us."

"Oh? Nothing to write in a diary?" teased Darcy.

Nicole grinned. "No, but don't let Alex know that. She's mad as hell because I didn't clue her in on the date."

"I'm sorry about all the turmoil with her," Darcy said seriously. "I hope it hasn't ruined your stay at the hotel."

Nicole shrugged. "I never realized how much of a buffer you were between us. I think it might be time for me to make a change. Do you and your sisters need a good marketing person?"

Darcy hid her surprise. "We might need someone like you in the future but, at the moment, we can't afford anything like that. In order to meet my uncle's challenge, we have very limited funds to pull it off." She placed a hand on Nicole's shoulder. "But thanks for the offer. It means more to me than I can say."

Nicole's smile was genuine. "I wish you and your sisters the best, Darcy. It's a funky place, but I like the Salty Key Inn, and others will too."

They walked down the beach together, and then Darcy said, "I've got to head back. It'll be another busy day."

"Okay, see you later," said Nicole. "I'm going to keep walking."

As Darcy walked back to the hotel, she thought of all the times Alex had belittled her and vowed never to let that happen again. With the advent of social media, bullies and people like Alex were allowed to get away with a lot.

Darcy hurried back to her suite to shower and change her clothes. She was meeting Cyndi for breakfast. Then they'd sit down for the interview and, perhaps, talk about Cyndi's book.

As Darcy entered Gracie's, she met up with Alex, who was leaving the restaurant with Brian.

"Hi," Darcy said, wondering if they were together.

Brian stopped. "Alex wants me to check their air-conditioning unit again. If it isn't working properly, we're going to have to think about getting some replacement units."

"I see. After you check it out, why don't we meet in the office? I'll text Sheena and Regan to let them know."

"Good idea," Brian said, unaware of the frown that had formed on Alex's face. Darcy had no doubt in her mind the air conditioner was fine, that this was another ploy of Alex's to be with him.

Cyndi waved at Darcy from a nearby table, and Darcy hurried over to it, eager to see what this meeting might produce.

Maggie O'Neill, a nurse and the youngest of Gavin's group, waited on their table. "What'll you ladies have? Eggs Benedict is the morning's special."

"Oh, I'll have that and a cup of coffee," said Cyndi. "How about you, Darcy?"

Darcy grinned. "Why not? They're delicious." She'd decided she wasn't going to be a bride who half-starved herself before her wedding. Besides, she had several months before the big day.

As Cyndi poured cream into her coffee and stirred it, Darcy studied her. Though Cyndi gave the impression of strength, Darcy knew from their earlier conversation she needed support.

"Are you okay with my starting the interview?" Darcy asked. "I write columns about various people in the community, telling their story, offering food for thought. I thought it might be a good way for you to express some of your concerns."

Cyndi gave her a firm nod of her head. "That would be great. I want other military spouses to know we can band together to get some help for our men and women. They return home from battle with injuries both visible and unseen. Living with someone with PTSD is not easy." She stopped talking when Maggie returned to their table with their meals.

Darcy observed the tears in Cyndi's eyes. "Let's enjoy our breakfast and then, perhaps, you'd like to walk down to the bay. We have some chairs and benches set up there, so it will be a good place to talk in private."

"Good idea," said Cyndi. "Sorry, I get so emotional about this."

"No apologies needed," Darcy said. "Tell me about your children. You say they're six and ten?"

A smile spread across Cyndi's face. "My daughter Kate is ten going on thirty, and my son TJ is six."

"What are their favorite things to do?" Darcy asked, trying to keep things light.

"Kate gave up on the idea of being a ballerina and is now determined to play baseball. TJ has become a demon on his bicycle. They're good kids. Active, competitive, and still able to be hugged."

"My fiancé and I are talking about having a family. Sometimes I want a houseful of kids, but then I worry I won't be a good mom and think maybe we shouldn't have any."

Cyndi waved her hand in dismissal. "Don't worry so. All mothers have moments when they're not at their best, but most of the time, we muddle through. As long as you try, you're doing all right." She pulled out her cell phone. "Want to see pictures of my two?"

Darcy nodded and waited for Cyndi to pull the photos up on her screen.

Studying the pictures, Darcy filled with excitement at the idea of starting a family. Cyndi's children were adorable. Kate had pigtails, and TJ was missing a couple of front teeth.

They finished their meal, and then Darcy led Cyndi across the hotel's lawn to the chairs by the bay. Their dock was being repaired, and if things went well with sales, they'd eventually have real waterfront activity combined with The Key Hole next door. At the moment, they could offer guests the use of two kayaks and seats in comfortable chairs beside the shore of the bay that formed the eastern edge of their property.

Cyndi sat down in an Adirondack chair facing the water. Darcy pulled a chair up next to hers and took a seat.

"Tell me what Tom was like before he went overseas," Darcy prompted.

Cyndi turned to her with a smile. "Tom and I had a magical relationship. He was fun and caring. Sensitive, even. But after his first deployment, he came home sullen, angry. We went to a counselor and got some help, so at least we had some good moments. But, of course, it wasn't the same."

"Was it hard to let him go back to war a second time?" said Darcy.

Cyndi dabbed at her eyes and nodded. "The worst thing ever because I knew even if he came home, things would be much more difficult."

"And when he came home this time?"

"Losing his leg was awful but not as bad as the silence between us. I never know who is going to appear—angry, bitter Tom, or the guy who tries to make light of things. It's trying to live with that pattern I want to share with other military spouses. I want to create a handbook of sorts for them."

"Obviously, you'll want to bring in experts to talk about it. But, Cyndi, maybe the thing to do is to have other military spouses share their experiences so everybody can benefit. You could call it 'Letters from the Heart" or something like it."

Cyndi scrambled out of her chair and gave Darcy a big hug. "Oh my God! I think that's perfect. Then it wouldn't be just me pretending I can or cannot handle a situation. We could all share how to live with someone who's injured in all kinds of ways. Will you help me do it?"

Knowing she had to be honest, Darcy drew a deep breath. "I can't. You need to talk to your counselor, the doctors, and others involved—people who are trained to help you go through all the materials you'll receive from other military spouses. I'm not an expert in the field and wouldn't have any way to judge what others have written. I can, however, ask someone at the newspaper to help me assist you in finding a publisher when the time comes."

Cyndi's eyes rounded. "Would you?"

"Yes," said Darcy. "I think it's important for you and the others to do this." She'd had great thoughts of writing a book with Cyndi, but Darcy knew she wasn't ready or able to take on a project like that and do it justice. In time, after learning more about the craft of writing, she would tackle something big, something everyone would love.

Cyndi sat back down and turned to Darcy. "I appreciate your honesty. Now, what can I tell you for your newspaper column?"

Back in her office, Darcy sat at her desk, her mind spinning with ideas. She wrote columns about ordinary people becoming angels to others.

Finally, Darcy began typing.

> Angels come in many shapes and sizes. Some make no bones about wanting to do good. Others live quietly, sometimes silently, concerned for others. How do I know this? Today I met a woman who is going to help others by shattering their silence—a silence that needs to be broken.

By the time Darcy finished her first draft of the column, she was in tears. Cyndi's story, so similar to others, was full of heartbreak everyone could understand. It was for this reason Darcy wanted Cyndi's story told. Because everyone—men and women—needed love and understanding.

CHAPTER TEN

SHEENA

Alone in her room, Sheena studied the gold coin her Uncle Gavin had given her as a child. Her sisters knew nothing about it. In fact, it had been a secret between her mother and her since the day it fell out of the stuffed monkey Gavin had given her. After showing her the gold coin, her mother had whispered, "Don't tell anyone about this. It's very valuable. Someday you might need it. Until then, I'll keep it safe for you. Your uncle loves you very much."

Sheena supposed she could use the coin to help them out if necessary, but something of more value would help her sisters and her meet Gavin's challenge—the loving bond that had formed between them. Besides, she had serious reasons to believe Gavin might be her father, not her uncle, as everyone believed. And if that were the case, her new relationship with her sisters might be destroyed, along with family memories, if she were ever to show the coin to anyone else. Besides, what did it matter if Gavin were her father? Patrick Sullivan had raised her as his own and had done the best job he could. And Gavin had given her and her sisters a chance to earn the sizeable reward he'd set aside for them.

Determined to keep its existence private, Sheena wrapped the gold coin in her mother's handkerchief and slid it under clothing in a bureau drawer. As she did so, she wondered as she often had, if her mother's unhappiness was because she was married to the brother of the man she really loved. At the thought, a sigh escaped her.

"Mom? Are you here?" Meaghan burst into the room. "Okay, if I go to the beach now? I finished my shift at Gracie's, and I'm meeting some kids there."

Sheena nodded and smiled. "Sounds good. Be back by five. We're going out to dinner."

"Okay. See you then."

Sheena walked into the living room and stood by the sliding glass door to the patio. They'd soon be celebrating Meaghan's fifteenth birthday. Watching her daughter cross the hotel grounds toward the beach, Sheena wondered where the time had gone. She and Tony were young parents, but seeing her children in their teens made her feel old.

Tony came into the suite. "Thought I'd take a break and come home for lunch."

"You're just in time," said Sheena. "How's the slab for the house coming along?"

He wrapped his arms around her. "I think you're going to be pleased with it. We should be able to do the pour sometime soon. With my doing so much work on it myself, the construction of the house will take longer than it should, but it gives us a way to afford it and the opportunity to make it exactly like we want. I've got updated plans to show you."

"As long as it has plenty of bathrooms, I'll like it," said Sheena laughing. "After sharing one old-fashioned bathroom with two sisters for a few months, I decided when the time comes, I want to have my own, private space."

Tony grinned. "Wait until you see what the master bedroom will be like. I intend for that to be a private playground for you and me."

At the sexy look he gave her, Sheena felt her cheeks grow warm. Maybe being young empty-nesters wouldn't be so bad after all.

###

After lunch, Sheena hurried back to the registration office, which had turned into the heartbeat of the hotel's operation. Guests came and went with questions, and from there, Sheena could watch activity at the pool and beyond it to the bocce ball court and waterfront.

Darcy was manning the desk when she arrived.

"Where's Regan?" Sheena asked. "I thought she was scheduled to be here."

"I'm exchanging places with her so Austin and I can go out tonight. She said she didn't care because she has no intention of dating anyone for some time."

"Yeah, right. What else is going on? Did you have your interview with Cyndi?"

"Yes. And after listening to the reality of her life, writing the story was emotional for me. With all the disruptions to family life military people go through, dealing with their spouses suffering PTSD seems to me to be the hardest. It affects not only the two of them but their children and even other, extended-family members." She paused. "Do you remember how difficult Dad was at times, growing up?"

"Very well. Do you think he suffered from something like that after being in Vietnam ? He would sometimes rant and rave about things and then have too many beers, which only made the situation worse. But he held a steady job as a firefighter."

"Yes, but, even so, he was difficult," said Darcy. "Looking back at the situation now, I remember he seemed to thrive on the excitement of working a fire, which caused Mom distress."

"Funny, isn't it? How we, as children, never see parents as real people with real problems."

Darcy gave her a knowing look. "As I write my newspaper

columns, I'm learning a lot about people and how they have handled the issues they have had to face."

"You're doing a good job, Darcy," said Sheena. "I'm sure Mom would be pleased by it. Uncle Gavin too. He left you that note, remember?"

"Yeah, I didn't understand what it meant at the time. 'Darcy, you are not who we think you are.' Are you any closer to figuring out what his message to you means?"

Sheena shook her head, not about to tell Darcy she was becoming more and more certain Uncle Gavin was her father. But, as she'd decided earlier, what difference did it make? Both he and her mother were dead, and she would do nothing to destroy her father or the family she knew as hers.

"I'm going to check the towel situation at the pool," said Sheena. "Bernice and her housekeeping crew are trying to keep up with the demand for clean pool and beach towels, but we underestimated the use of them."

Darcy frowned at her. "Are we going to make it? Every time we get some income, there's more reason to spend money."

"We're going to do our best by making sure people have a comfortable stay," Sheena said more sharply than she'd intended because she was as worried as Darcy. "The opening of the restaurant will add a needed dimension to the property and bring in more money," she said in a softer tone. "Graham Howard is stopping by sometime this weekend to check out the progress on construction. I'm happy he's agreed to be our chef. And after the first of the year, if we bring on Casey Cochran, he can assist in training someone to staff the restaurant and supervise them."

At the idea, Darcy smiled. "Nick would be so pleased his nephew will be working for us. At one time, Nick thought Graham and I should get together."

"Seems to me Graham and Regan are more suited than you

and Graham." Sheena's spirits lifted. "Maybe we can push that along."

Darcy laughed. "Playing matchmaker, are we?"

"Perhaps," said Sheena, liking the thought more and more.

CHAPTER ELEVEN

REGAN

Regan didn't mind working the late shift in the office. In a small operation like theirs, things usually settled down right after six, making it easy to close the office by keeping an emergency line open.

As she locked the door, Regan noticed some of their guests returning to the property from the beach. Two other couples were making their way to The Key Hole. Still others could be seen lounging on their patios.

Regan observed the activity with satisfaction. A visit to the beach and the Salty Key Inn seemed to be working for their guests.

As she headed across the lawn toward her suite, Regan decided to check on the progress at Gavin's. She and Mo had given a lot of input on the design of the restaurant, and now, as she drew closer, a sense of pride filled her. The walls and roof of the building were up. Even at this early stage, she could envision how plantings and small gardens would enhance the dining experience and views for those sitting by the numerous windows inside.

"It's going to be nice, huh?" said a voice behind her.

Regan whirled around. "Oh, Graham, I didn't see you!"

His green eyes filled with laughter. "Sorry. I'm usually pretty hard to miss." At well over six feet, he was someone who had a natural, large presence. That, and his deep, rich voice.

Her lips curved. "Guess I was too busy thinking of what the

place will look like when it's done. Mo and I have already chosen the interior finishes."

"It's the kitchen I'm concerned with. I need to make sure I will have everything I need there if we're going to make it the success we all think it can be."

"My sisters and I are so happy you've decided to come to Gavin's," said Regan sincerely. "It should give you a great opportunity to showcase your work."

"I hope so. I've been creating special recipes already, just for Gavin's. Do you want to join me for dinner sometime? You can check out a couple of new dishes."

Regan hesitated and then nodded. "Thanks. That sounds good. If you don't mind, I'll ask my sisters to join us. I'm sure they'd like to do a tasting too."

"Not a problem. I'm renting a house just down the beach. Let me know how many and when, and I'll have things ready for you."

Regan gave him a thumbs-up. "Sounds good. Want to look around here with me?"

"Sure. Like I said, I want to check out the kitchen too."

Inside, the wall studs were up, and most of the electrical wiring had been installed, giving them an initial idea of how the spaces would appear.

Regan walked over to one of the windows and looked out, imagining the gardens that would enhance the view.

"I like the way this lays out," commented Graham, indicated the space. "A plain rectangular room can be so boring, but with all these nooks and crannies, this space is intriguing."

"Mo Greene and I designed it this way," said Regan, smiling at Graham with a sense of accomplishment.

They toured the kitchen, the various hallways, and smaller rooms, and then they climbed the stairs to the second story.

"What are you going to do up here?" Graham asked. "The plans don't show anything."

Regan shook her head. "I don't know. We probably can't do anything with it now. Not with the funds we have."

"Guess you'll figure it out. Thanks for showing me around."

When Regan turned to leave, Graham stopped her. "I was about to go to The Key Hole: Care to join me?"

"No date?" Regan asked, wondering why anyone as hot as Graham would be alone on a holiday weekend.

"Naw, I'm single. It's hard to find someone who's willing to put up with a chef's normal hours, and after breaking up with my girlfriend, I decided to just cool it for a while."

"Yeah, me too," said Regan. "Okay, let's go have some regular food and a drink or two. Dutch treat."

"Sounds good." Graham playfully offered her an arm, and Regan took it, happy for the chance to socialize with no obligation beyond having a nice meal with a good guy.

As Regan and Graham were sharing a laugh at the bar, Alex and Nicole entered the restaurant. They noticed Regan and came right over to her.

Alex frowned at Regan. "I thought you weren't dating."

Regan shrugged. "I'm not. This is Graham Howard. He's going to be our chef at Gavin's when it opens. Graham, this is Alex Townsend and Nicole Coleman, Darcy's old roommates from Boston."

A smile slid onto Alex's face. She turned to Graham. "A chef? Sort of like Gordon Ramsay or some of the other famous chefs?"

"Not exactly," he said, smiling.

"How about me buying you a drink to celebrate, and then maybe we could do something together?"

Graham studied Alex for an uncomfortably long few seconds. "Hmmm, don't think so."

Alex tossed her hair behind her. "Oh, well, I wanted to check out a few other places for drinks, anyway." She turned to Nicole. "You coming?"

Nicole shook her head. "You go ahead. I'm going to stay here."

"Really?" Alex glared at Nicole. "Okay then. See you later." She left without looking back.

"You can sit with us," Regan offered, as Nicole stood by alone.

"I'm sorry about Alex," Nicole said to Graham, sliding onto a bar stool next to him.

"Don't worry about it," said Graham. "How are you finding the Salty Key Inn?"

"Our room is great, and having the pool close and the beach right across the street is super nice. And, of course, who doesn't like Gracie's?" said Nicole with a smile.

"Glad you like it," said Graham.

"Yes. It's a nice place to come for a rest. I've met some interesting people, and I'm really happy Darcy and Regan and their sister have this kind of opportunity," Nicole said.

Graham smiled at Nicole. "I'm glad you're here. What can I get you to drink?"

As the three of them chatted, Regan realized Nicole was becoming interested in Graham. She stood. "Another busy day for me tomorrow. Hope you don't mind, but I'm going to leave the two of you alone."

Nicole beamed at Regan, giving her a smile that told Regan she'd made the right decision.

Later, in her suite, Regan sat on the couch watching a

movie when Darcy appeared.

"I just saw Nicole and Graham get into his car and drive away. What's going on? How did they meet?"

"I introduced them. Why?" said Regan, wondering at the frown that creased Darcy's brow.

"Because Sheena and I think you and Graham would be great together."

Regan gave her sister a withering look. "Darcy, I'm not interested in anybody right now. I have the chance to work for Arthur Weatherman, and between that and the work at the hotel, I'm too busy to even think of dating."

"Okay," said Darcy, "but Sheena is going to be disappointed."

Regan shook her head. "Big sisters. Are they always this pushy?"

Darcy laughed. "Now that we're all living together, you have to put up with us."

"Love you, but I can find someone on my own. Just so you know, Graham is really a good guy. If he asks me out, I'll go, because he's not interested in getting serious with anyone either."

"Hmmm, we'll see," said Darcy, ducking when Regan threw a pillow at her.

Later, lying in bed, Regan thought of Graham. It would be nice to date someone like him—someone she didn't have to worry about wanting to take her to bed. He'd be another male friend. Like Mo. She wondered why Mo hadn't called her as he said he would. Maybe, he's found a new friend, she thought. Someone he wouldn't have to worry about hurting him. She hoped so. He was such a sweet guy.

The next morning, Regan sat in Gracie's sipping her coffee

peacefully, gazing at the guests from the hotel who were obviously enjoying their meals. All but one couple would be leaving today, going home, no doubt, to their regular routines now that Labor Day Weekend was ending. She couldn't wait to hear how the hotel had done financially. The opening of it was just the beginning of what they all hoped would be a successful fall campaign.

Darcy entered the restaurant and walked right over to the "family" table in the corner of the room where Regan was sitting. "Lots of checkouts today. Are you sure Bernice is going to be able to handle all of them?" Darcy said.

"Guess we'll find out. Some rooms can wait, if necessary. But I'm not worried. Bernice has been terrific so far."

They looked up as Nicole approached their table.

"May I sit down?" she asked.

Regan and Darcy nodded together.

"I've been doing a lot of thinking while I've been here, and I've decided to move to Florida. After talking to Graham last night and Brian Harwood the other day, I think I can find a good marketing job in the area." She turned to Darcy. "As a thank you for a lovely stay, I want to offer my services to help you win the challenge you told me about. It's also a way to say I'm sorry for not speaking up when Alex was mean to you. I see now what a mistake it was to let her sway me into thinking her behavior was all right."

Regan felt as surprised as Darcy looked.

"Wow," said Darcy. "That means a lot to me."

"It isn't entirely selfless on my part," said Nicole. "I'll add your portfolio to my others to present to companies down here."

"A marketing campaign? That would be terrific," said Regan.

Nicole shrugged. "You've made a lot of friends here.

Everyone has told me how hard you all have worked to try and meet your uncle's challenge. I figured I could help."

Darcy's eyes shone. "Let's go see Sheena. The three of us have to agree on something like this, but I'm pretty sure she's going to be as excited as I am."

As Nicole pulled to her feet, Darcy threw her arms around her. "Thanks, Nic."

Nicole returned to her smile. "You're welcome. Don't say anything to Alex about this. I need the chance to explain everything to her first."

The three of them trooped over to the registration office. Two couples were checking out.

"Sheena, I'll take over here," said Regan, sliding behind the desk. "Darcy and Nicole want to talk with you."

Sheena gave her a puzzled look, but she stepped aside and followed Darcy and Nicole into the back office.

As she prepared final bills for them, Regan chatted with the guests, making sure they knew more renovations and changes would come to the property.

An older couple from Tennessee glanced at the brochure she handed them. "Are you going to offer long-term rentals for retirees like us?" the woman asked.

"We certainly hope to," Regan responded, wondering if that was even possible. "Please keep in touch, and I'm sure we can work something out."

"People think Tennessee is the south, but our winters can be brutal," the woman said.

"Not the south at all," said her husband. "Thanks for a very nice stay. And good luck to all you women. It's a good story."

Regan had just finished checking out the second couple when Alex appeared. "Have you seen Nicole? It's almost time for us to leave, but I can't find her."

As Alex spoke, Nicole, Darcy, and Sheena walked into the

office together.

"What's going on?" Alex asked, looking puzzled.

"Just making some plans," said Nicole. "I'll tell you about it later. Right now, we'd better check out. I didn't realize it was so late."

"I'll take care of you," said Regan, pulling up their account on the computer. Within minutes, each had paid her share.

"Thanks again," said Nicole.

Alex nodded. "Hope you guys make it. There's a whole lot to be done here."

Regan avoided looking at Darcy. Alex could make even something nice sound nasty.

After they left, Sheena turned to Darcy and Regan. "It's been a very surprising weekend in many ways, but none more surprising than the visit from Nicole and Alex."

"You're okay with Nicole's offer to help us?" Regan asked.

Sheena nodded. "Oh yes. Now that the weekend is over, we, dear sisters, are going to need all the help we can get."

CHAPTER TWELVE

DARCY

Darcy was alone in the office when Cyndi came inside to check out.

She came right over to Darcy and hugged her. "How can I ever thank you for such a delightful stay? Being able to talk to you about the book of my heart has made all the difference. Now, I have a worthy project to work on. Not only will it keep me busy, but it will be a great source to help others."

"It's going to be great. I'll send you a copy of the column in the newspaper I wrote about you and your cause, and I want you to keep in touch. When the time comes, we'll get someone to help you approach publishers."

"Thank you. How about giving me a lot of brochures? I'm going to spread the news about the hotel among the other spouses I know. It's marvelous you allow military couples to stay here at such a special rate."

"We're happy to do it," said Darcy sincerely. She'd interviewed several people who'd served in the military at one time or another and had come to realize the sacrifices they'd made to serve the country.

Another couple entered the office. Cyndi signed for the bill, took the brochures, and left.

Darcy worked steadily to take care of checkouts. By the noon deadline, all who were scheduled to do so had either left or made arrangements to stay late.

While Bernice and her crew were kept busy cleaning the

rooms, Sheena worked on financials, and Regan oversaw Michael's cleaning of the pool and the straightening of the furniture on the deck. They'd agreed to give Michael the job of pool boy to pay for gas and other expenses as long as he did good, competent work.

Darcy looked through the upcoming reservations. Her mouth grew dry at the number of empty rooms.

A week later, Darcy was just finishing checking out their weekend guests when Austin walked into the office.

He waited until the guests left and then asked, "How's it going?"

"Pretty well. The system Chip and I worked on is a good one. But, Austin, we need to be able to fill the rooms or we're not going to make it."

"I hand a brochure out to every patient of mine," he said seriously. "But give me more, and I'll take them to all the other offices in the building."

Darcy smiled at his eagerness. Though they'd talked of travel and her writing in the future, he knew how important the hotel was to her.

"How are things going at the condo?" she asked him. He'd bought a good-sized condo in St. Petersburg in an established subdivision rich with trees and lush landscaping, providing shade and privacy. He was building bookcases in the den and updating the kitchen cabinetry.

"It's going well, but, Darcy, I can't wait for you to move in with me permanently. Having you remain at the hotel is one of Uncle Gavin's challenges I don't like at all."

She laughed. "It's weird, but I guess there was a reason he wanted all of the Sullivan sisters together. Just a few more months and the challenge will be over, and then you won't be able to get me to leave you and the condo."

He drew her to him and lowered his lips to hers.

"Am I interrupting anything?"

Darcy whirled around to find Brian Harwood smiling at them.

"Sorry, I thought we were alone," Darcy said, unable to stop the heat that rose to her cheeks. "What can I help you with?"

"Actually, I'm here to talk to Austin. I'm looking at motorcycles. Want to join me?"

Austin's eyes lit with excitement. "Yeah, thanks. That would be cool."

Darcy shook her head. "Austin, promise me you won't buy one. They're dangerous."

Austin laughed. "I'm just looking, okay?"

She nodded. "Okay. See you later."

Darcy checked her watch, made sure everything was in order, and closed the office early. But at four o'clock and with just one couple registered, there was no need to stay open.

As she headed to the Sandpiper Suites Building, Meaghan joined her.

Darcy threw an arm across Meaghan's shoulder. "Where have you been? The beach?"

Meaghan grinned. "Yeah, a whole bunch of us got together."

"Have you decided which boy you like the best?"

Meaghan's eyes rounded. "How did you know?"

"Certain aunts have special powers to know these things," Darcy teased. "So, is it the cute guy with the dark curls or the redhead like me?"

Meaghan looked away and then gave Darcy a shy smile. "The redhead. His name is Rob Wickham, and he's captain of the Junior Varsity football team."

"Sounds good to me," said Darcy.

Meaghan held up a hand. "Don't tell Mom or Dad, or especially Michael. I don't want them to ask me about him. Okay?"

Darcy gave her a steady look. "Okay, but it's not a good idea to keep things from your parents. It shouldn't be a problem unless you're doing something they wouldn't like. Right?"

Meaghan nodded. "Nothing bad is happening. I just like him. That's all."

"Darcy! Wait up!" Regan called to her.

As Darcy stopped and waited for Regan, Meaghan skipped ahead. Watching Meaghan go, Darcy wondered what it would be like to have children of her own. Would she worry about them like Sheena?

"What's up?" Regan asked. "It looked like you and Meaghan were having a serious conversation."

Darcy shrugged. "We were just chatting. That's all. What are you up to?"

"Just finished doing a towel inventory. I'm not sure what's happening, but we're missing several towels. We're definitely going to have to order some new ones. I also did a check on rooms to make sure everything is in order."

"We'll discuss purchasing towels with Sheena," Darcy said and stopped when she heard the roar of a motorcycle. She turned as Brian pulled into the parking lot behind the Sandpiper Suites Building on a big, black motorcycle. Austin rode behind him.

She and Regan hurried over to them.

"You did it," said Darcy to Brian. She placed her hands on her hips and turned to Austin. "You didn't, did you?"

He shook his head. "I wanted to talk it over with you before I made the move. But, Darcy, they're cool, and it's a lot of fun."

"I don't like them," Darcy said firmly.

"How about you, Regan?" said Brian. "Dare to take a spin with me?"

Regan studied the bike, studied him, and nodded. "Okay, I'll try it. But you won't go very fast, will you?"

"I promise," he said.

Austin handed Regan his helmet. "Have a good ride."

CHAPTER THIRTEEN

REGAN

As Regan slipped on the helmet that was too big for her, she chided herself for meeting the challenge in Brian's eyes. She, like Darcy, didn't like motorcycles. They were noisy and not that comfortable.

She bravely slid onto the seat behind Brian and wrapped her arms around his waist. "Remember, not too fast," she warned him.

He nodded, gave her a thumbs-up sign, and started the engine.

The roar of it filled Regan's ears. And when he revved the motor, a shiver traveled across her shoulders. She hadn't done anything as dangerous as this in a long time, not since she rode in a car with Johnny Pizzolo in a pseudo drag race her freshman year in high school. She'd been scared to pieces then. And she was now.

As they pulled out of the parking lot, she waved goodbye to Darcy and Austin. She caught sight of Sheena and Tony and waved to them too. Then she settled against Brian's back and let the rush of the wind take over.

Brian set the bike at a steady, reasonable pace. Soon, Regan felt brave enough to open her eyes to look out at the beach. It was a beautiful day. In the late-afternoon peacefulness of the day, people were lazing on the beach, swimming, or walking along the shore. She closed her eyes and let out a sigh of contentment. Riding the motorcycle was kind of fun.

She drew a deep breath and stared out at the beach again. *Beautiful.* Her interest swung to a delivery truck pulling out of the driveway of a restaurant in front of them.

"Look out!" she screamed and tugged on Brian's arm.

He glanced back at her.

She watched helplessly as they continued to race forward into the sound of screeching tires.

Brian squeezed the right-hand brake lever on the handlebar, stepped on the right foot pedal, and swerved the bike trying to avoid the truck, but, ironically, as the truck moved to avoid them, it blocked their way.

Regan watched in horror as Brian skidded into the truck, and then she was thrown off the bike. Her helmet snapped off her head, and the world turned black.

Several hours later, Regan could hear sounds around her and could smell an odor she'd never liked. She tried to open her eyes, but they felt as if heavy weights lay atop them.

She stirred restlessly.

"Where am I?" she asked, groaning at the pain speech caused.

"Regan? Oh my God, Regan? It's Sheena, darling. You're going to be all right."

"You're in the hospital," came Darcy's voice. "You've been sleeping from the anesthesia, but you're going to be okay."

"Bri ... n?" she asked through lips so swollen she wasn't sure her sisters could hear her garbled speech.

"Brian's in surgery now," Sheena said in a calm manner, though Regan could hear a tremor in her voice.

A nurse hurried into the room. "Is our patient awake?"

Regan forced her eyes to open and then fought to keep them from closing. A woman in some kind of uniform stared down at her, checked what was an IV in Regan's hand, and studied the monitor hooked up to her.

"Do you know where you are? And can you tell me your name?" asked the woman, whom Regan now recognized as a nurse.

Regan nodded and moaned. "Hos ... pit ...al. Regan." She stared at the beeping green flashes and moving lines on the monitor's screen. She hurt like hell, but, thank God, she was alive. Her gaze swung to Sheena and Darcy standing by.

"Bri?" she managed to get out.

"We'll let you know about Brian as soon as we get any news," Sheena assured her. "Do you remember what happened to you?"

"Bike ... truck ..." At the memory of Brian flying through the air, she wondered how he could be alive. She tried to sit up but was forced to fall back against the pillow. Carefully, so as not to disturb anything, Regan moved her arms, flexed her fingers. *Good.* She tried her legs and wiggled her toes. *Good. Then why,* she wondered, *do I have so much pain?*

Sheena seemed to sense her question. "You have no broken bones, probably because you landed on the far, grassy side of the road. But you have several bad scrapes on your arms and legs. And ..."

She paused, looking uncomfortable.

Regan lifted a hand to her face. A huge bandage covered her chin. Her fingers found smaller bandages placed on her cheeks and a long one on her forehead. At what it meant, she felt woozy.

"Face?" she asked, forcing the word out.

Sheena and Darcy each took hold of a hand.

"There's been damage," said Darcy, "but plastic surgery can do wonders with injuries like yours. Fortunately, you kept your insurance, which should cover it."

"Yes, in time, no one will know you've been in an accident like this," Sheena said.

Stunned, Regan studied the tears on her sisters' faces and wondered if anyone would ever call her beautiful again.

Sometime later, a doctor came into her room. Sheena rose from the chair in which she'd been resting and stood by Regan's bed.

"How are you doing?" the doctor asked Regan, taking her pulse and gazing into her eyes. "I'm Dr. Milford, your plastic surgeon." He smiled. "Trying to give me a challenge, are you?" He squeezed her hand. "No need to worry. You're a very lucky young woman. Apparently, you landed on a softer surface than your friend, and what cuts and scrapes you have should heal easily. You'll be your beautiful self in no time."

Regan studied him. Short dark hair edged in gray surrounded a face that held intelligent eyes. He exuded a confidence that calmed her racing thoughts. Still, her fingers turned cold as she imagined the damage done to her face.

"Scarred?" she asked.

"Nothing that will be really noticeable. The facial nerve wasn't cut but it was severely injured. Time will tell how quickly it will heal."

"What does that mean, doctor?" Sheena said.

"We won't know the effects of the injury until the swelling goes down. Then we'll have a better idea," he said calmly.

"And when will that be?" Sheena persisted as a nurse joined them.

"In a week or so, we'll look at what has been corrected surgically and see what nature has begun to heal on her own."

"Don't worry," said the nurse. "Dr. Milford is the best plastic surgeon in the state. He always does a great job."

Regan lay in bed listening to the conversation as if they were talking about some stranger. She didn't like what they were saying, and she didn't like the idea of staying in the hospital any longer than she had to. "Home?" she murmured, giving the doctor a pleading look.

"We're going to keep you a day or two to make sure something unexpected doesn't surprise us; then we're going to send you home. These days, we don't keep patients in the hospital any longer than we have to because of the risk of infection. Besides, patients do a better job of healing at home."

"We'll make sure she gets excellent care," Sheena assured him, giving Regan a smile she appreciated.

Dr. Milford smiled. "Dr. Hollister, who's treating your friend, will check on you in the morning, and I'll see you later in the day. Rest and begin to heal. Your body has been through a lot of trauma."

After the doctor left, the nurse checked Regan's vitals. "Try to get some rest. And let us know if you want anything to eat or drink. Though we don't want to force it, you're allowed to have some soft, easily swallowed items—things that won't disturb the sutures."

When Sheena and Regan were alone in the room again, Regan said, "Thanks for being here, Sheena. Where's Darcy?"

"At the hotel, covering for the two of us. Why don't you rest now? I'm going to the cafeteria for a cup of coffee, but I'll be here when you wake up."

Regan's eyes closed of their own volition, and she was soon caught up in weird dreams.

Morning light shone into the room when she finally woke. Regan glanced over at the chair next to her bed. Sheena was sound asleep, her head thrown back, soft snores coming from her open mouth. Love for her sister surged through her.

Afraid to disturb her, Regan rang for the nurse.

"Yes? What can I do for you?"

"Bathroom," said Regan, waking Sheena.

"I can take her," said Sheena, rising to her feet.

The nurse nodded. "Ring if you need me."

Sheena helped Regan roll the IV pole into the bathroom and stood by as Regan painfully lowered herself to the toilet seat.

When she was through with her task, Regan stood and went to the sink to wash her hands.

When she saw her battered face in the mirror, she let out a small cry. Bruises circled her swollen eyes. Dark lines where her skin had been stitched here and there gave her a scary, Halloween look. But the thick bandage covering her chin and the lower part of her face made Regan grab the edge of the sink and hold on.

Sheena took her elbow and steadied her. "Come, let me help you back to bed. I'll bring a washcloth for your hands."

On wobbly legs, Regan allowed Sheena to lead her back to bed. Lying down, Regan stared up at the ceiling, wondering what the future held for her.

Sheena returned with a warm, soapy washcloth for her hands and gently washed her fingers.

Regan studied her. "What happened to me? Give me all the details."

Sheena frowned and shook her head. "I'm not sure it's a good idea. I don't want you to get upset."

"Please, Sheena."

Sheena drew a deep breath. "All right. When you were found, which was right after the accident, your helmet was off, and you were unconscious. At the hospital, they checked for brain injury, of course, but there is none. Your chin took the brunt of the fall, even as you slid onto the grassy verge, which was fortunate. It could have been so much worse. Darcy and I got to the hospital as they were taking you into surgery. Do you remember being awake and talking to us?"

Regan searched her mind and shook her head. “Not really. It’s all pretty foggy.”

“Dr. Milford stitched you up where he could.”

“What about the facial nerve he talked about?” Regan asked.

“We’ll find out more about that in the next day or two,” said Sheena. “We want to get you home and healing as soon as we can. Then, we’ll all have a better idea.”

Regan grabbed Sheena’s hand. “I need to see Brian, Sheena. You’ve got to help me. I have to know he’s okay. The accident was my fault.”

“No, honey, it wasn’t your fault. It was just an accident.”

Regan lay back against her pillow. As she recalled the moments before the accident, tears burned a trail down her bruised, sore cheeks. If she hadn’t tugged on Brian’s arm, the accident might never have happened.

Seeing her distress, Sheena said, “Let me talk to the nurse, and I’ll see what I can do to help you get to Brian’s room.”

Regan nodded numbly.

A few moments later, Sheena returned with a wheelchair. “Okay, I can take you to his floor, but you have to ride in this, and we have to keep your IV hooked up.”

“Thanks,” Regan said, too emotional to say much more than that. She climbed off the bed, sat in the wheelchair, and waited for her sister to hang the IV bag from the hook on the pole attached to the chair. The need to say, “I’m sorry” wasn’t the only driving force behind her eagerness to see Brian. She needed to make sure he was all right.

They left the room, got on an elevator, and rode two floors down to the surgical ward. As Sheena rolled Regan off the elevator, they caught sight of Holly Harwood in the nearby waiting area.

“Holly, so glad we found you,” said Sheena, pushing

Regan's wheelchair over to her.

When Sheena gave Holly a hug, Regan observed the tears that spilled from Holly's eyes. Her heart skipped a beat and then sprinted ahead.

"Is Brian ..." She stopped, realizing with the bandages and her swollen lips they couldn't hear or understand her.

Holly turned to Regan. "Oh, honey. I'm so sorry. Are you going to be okay?"

Regan glanced at Sheena and nodded to Holly. "Guess so."

Sheena gave her a bright smile. "Yes, she's going to recover nicely. She has a great plastic surgeon."

Holly studied her and let out a long breath. "I told Brian I didn't want him to get a motorcycle, but he's not a kid anymore and has to make his own decisions. I'm so, so sorry this happened to you, Regan."

"How ... is ...?"

"How is Brian?" Sheena said, speaking for her. "Regan says she needs to see him."

"The surgeries on both his arms and his right hip went well, they tell me. But it's going to take several weeks, even months for him to heal. I don't know what he's going to do. He won't be able to work for a while." Tears flooded her eyes. "And for the next few weeks, I don't see how he'll even be able to feed himself or do many other normal things we take for granted."

Regan made a motion with her arm to move forward.

Sheena said, "Can Regan see him?"

Holly nodded. "He's in and out of a deep sleep with the medication following surgery, but, sure, go ahead. While you're with him, I'll run down to the cafeteria for a bite to eat. Thank goodness, it's open 24/7."

Regan drew a deep breath, bracing herself for the meeting with Brian. How do you tell someone you're sorry for something like this?

CHAPTER FOURTEEN

SHEENA

Sheena pushed Regan's wheelchair to the door to Brian's room and stopped to peek in. Brian was lying on the bed looking more like a little boy than the strapping, handsome man with whom they'd all fallen a little in love. Tubes, monitors, and casts—both hard and soft—made him seem so vulnerable her breath caught.

When he noticed her, his lips curved enough for her to understand he was trying to smile.

"Okay if we come in?" she asked softly. "Regan wants to see you, and I want to make sure you're all right too."

At his nod, Sheena returned to the wheelchair, opened the door wide, and pushed her sister into the room.

At the sight of Brian, Regan let out a soft cry and lowered her head into her hands.

Sheena wheeled the chair to Brian's bedside and turned to Regan. "Should I give you two some privacy?"

"No," said Regan, lifting a tear-streaked face. "I want you to hear this. Get closer."

Sheena maneuvered the chair closer to Brian, turning it so Regan could talk directly to him.

"Bri ... n. So sorry. My fault. Your arm ... I pulled ..."

Brian shook his head. "No, it was my fault. Your face?"

"She has a good plastic surgeon," said Sheena, eager to give them both comfort.

Brian blinked at them sleepily. "Always beautiful," he

murmured and closed his eyes.

Sheena was wondering if she should spend the rest of the morning at the hospital when Darcy appeared. At the sight of her, relief filled Sheena. This was a big day for both of her children—football team selection for Michael and cheerleader tryouts for Meaghan—and she needed to talk to Tony about Brian's injuries. Tony had been working full-time for Brian, but if his business had to slow or temporarily end, she and Tony would be hurting for money.

"How's the patient?" Darcy said to her, nodding in Regan's direction.

"She's asleep and doing better. She had some soup and soft crackers. Her jaw isn't broken, but it's sore, and it's difficult for her to chew."

"Is she really going to be okay?" Darcy asked quietly, giving Regan a worried look.

"Yes," said Sheena, "except she's blaming herself for the accident and Brian's injuries."

"I mean her face. Is that going to be all right? She might not be able to work as Arthur Weatherman's spokesperson. How is that going to affect her?"

Sheena sighed and shook her head. "I don't know."

At home, the kids were just preparing to leave for school when Sheena walked in.

Meaghan jumped up. "How's Auntie Regan? Is she going to be all right? Darcy said she hurt her face."

"She's going to need some plastic surgery, but the doctor is optimistic she's going to be fine."

"How's Brian?" said Michael.

"He's broken some bones in both of his arms, and he has a broken hip. I would say considering what happened, he's a very lucky young man to have avoided something worse."

"Were you able to talk to him?" asked Tony, looking worried.

"For only a few minutes. He was still drifting in and out of consciousness following the surgeries to repair the bones. We saw Holly briefly, but got no real medical information beyond the broken bones."

She and Tony exchanged glances of alarm.

"How's he going to work?" Michael said, voicing their concern.

"I've been wondering that myself," Sheena answered honestly. "I'm sure he's going to want to talk to his staff, including you, Tony, when the time comes to assess things."

He nodded. "I'll try to go see him later today, just to make sure he's okay. I'll ask him if there's anything I can do for him beyond overseeing the crews like I'm already doing."

"Okay, thanks. Mike, do you need me to do anything for you today? It's final tryouts for the football team. Right?"

"I'm all set."

"And what about you, Meaghan?" said Sheena. "Do you want me to come see the tryouts for cheerleading this afternoon?"

"No, Mom. Thanks anyway, but that would make me more nervous than I already am."

"Okay, you two. I'm going to bed. It's been a very long, upsetting night."

"I'll see them off," Tony offered, "and then I'll come join you."

Alone in her room, Sheena peeled off the sundress she'd worn to work yesterday. After feeling enslaved by her family, the fact that no one seemed to need her anymore stung a little. Was that what her future held? Someone people needed less and less?

Feeling conflicted, Sheena went into the bathroom and took a quick shower. Her muscles ached from the tension she'd felt most of the evening and night. She was brushing her teeth when she felt Tony's hands on her back. He automatically began kneading her skin.

"Ah, that feels good," she murmured. She rinsed out her mouth and turned to face him.

He smiled at her. "Thought it might. Now, come lie down and rest, and let's talk about Brian. What do you think I should do about him? About the business?"

She grinned. "What do I think? I think we need to talk about that later. Right now, you'd better kiss me."

His dark eyes lit with pleasure. "Well, now, I can do that and more."

"How about just the 'that' for now?" she said, chuckling.

"Okay," he said and pulled her to him.

Their lips met, and a surge of energy swept through her. It was good to feel so alive after being among the sick and injured.

When they pulled apart, a sigh of satisfaction escaped her. This is what she'd needed.

That afternoon, Sheena waited anxiously for the school bus to drop off Meaghan. She'd offered to pick her up at school, but once more, Meaghan had put her off, saying she'd ride the bus as usual.

Sitting on the patio of Gracie's, Sheena surreptitiously waited for her daughter to arrive, hoping to receive good news.

When the bus finally arrived, Sheena hunkered down into her chair, hoping Meaghan wouldn't see her and accuse her of being an overly zealous mom.

From a distance, she watched Meaghan descend the stairs of the bus, followed by a red-haired boy. The two of them stood talking as the bus pulled away. Meaghan laughed at something the boy said and then leaned forward and gave him a quick kiss on the cheek.

"See you later, Rob!" she said, shifting her backpack on her shoulder. Then she turned and ran past Gracie's, heading for the Sandpiper Suites Building.

Sheena quickly rose, deposited her iced tea glass on the front counter, and left the restaurant, eager to see how Meaghan's day went. From where she'd been sitting, Sheena thought it must have been a good one. As she walked into the kitchen, Sheena found Meaghan on her cell.

Meaghan waved to her and spoke into her phone. "My mom's here. I'll talk to you later."

When the call ended, Sheena said, "How did you do with the tryouts?"

Meaghan beamed at her. "I made it, just like you told me I would. Mom, it's the greatest because we sometimes get to travel with the football team."

"Oh, do you know a lot of boys on the team?" Sheena asked, hoping for some information on the redhead her daughter had kissed earlier. From past experience, she knew if she probed too deeply, Meaghan would shut her out.

Meaghan shrugged. "A few. I'm going to change into my bathing suit and meet Tara at the beach. She made the team too."

"All right. Be back by five."

"Okay."

Looking as if she was about to do a cartwheel, Meaghan sprinted out of the kitchen and then quickly returned. "Oh, I forgot. Can you wash my cheerleading outfit? I need it tomorrow."

Sheena stared at her daughter.

Meaghan gave her a sheepish look. “Please? Next time, I’ll do it myself. I promise.”

Sheena shot Meaghan a smile. “That’s more like it.”

As Meaghan left, Michael arrived.

“How’d it go?” Sheena asked, suspecting from his grim expression there were problems. “Did you make the team?”

He nodded. “No problem. But, Mom, I’m the second-string quarterback. Jésus Sanchez is the number one guy. It pisses me off. I’m as good as he is.”

“You don’t get to play much?” She understood how heartbreaking that would be to him.

“I’ll be a wide receiver most games, but it isn’t fair. I wanted to be quarterback.”

“Michael, I know enough about football to understand being a wide receiver is a great position for you, and it’s going to take cooperation between you and Jésus to make good plays. Seems to me, you did very well.”

“Aw, Mom, you don’t get it. I want to be the star.”

“Some stars don’t shine as brightly as others, but they’re stars all the same. Think about it, son. Now, how about one of your favorite snacks?”

“Oatmeal cookies?” he said, looking like the hopeful little boy he once was. Michael might think he was all grown up, but she knew better.

As she told Tony later, living with teenagers was like riding the bumper cars at a carnival. Exhilaration, fear, and joy were mixed in a tumultuous blend as one looked both ahead and behind.

CHAPTER FIFTEEN

REGAN

Two days later, Regan sat in a chair in her hospital room, trying to hide her impatience as Darcy talked about what was happening at the hotel. She loved her sister and was grateful for the attention, but all she could think about was getting to Brian. That morning, a nurse told her he had been moved to her floor. She hoped he'd be more fully awake now and she could learn more about his injuries and what it would mean for him. It had been a huge shock to see him so injured.

"Thanks for coming," Regan said during a lull in the conversation. "I think I'll nap, so you're free to go. Sheena is going to pick me up when the doctor releases me."

"You sure?" said Darcy. "I'm willing to stay as long as you need me."

Regan tried to smile and, unable to feel that part of her face, lifted a hand to her bandage before letting it drop. "It's all right. You and Sheena can't be with me all the time. You have your own lives to lead. I might as well get on with mine, such as it is." She heard the note of bitterness in her voice and reminded herself she was lucky to be alive.

Darcy rose, came over to her, and gave her a gentle kiss on the cheek. "Okay. Call me if you need me. Anything I can get for you before I go?"

Regan shook her head. "No, but thanks."

As soon as Darcy left, Regan struggled out of the chair in which she'd been sitting and buzzed the nurse.

Moments later, one of the nurses stuck her head inside the room. "Yes?"

"Any chance I can get the IV set up so I can take a walk? The doctor mentioned it would be good for me."

The nurse entered, checked her chart, and said, "I don't see why not."

Once the IV was arranged on a moveable pole, Regan tightened her robe around her. "Okay if I go see my friend? It's really important to me."

The nurse checked her pulse, studied her face, and nodded. "Okay, but when you come back, I'll have to hook you up to the monitor again. We need to keep checking you until the doctor signs your release. Deal?"

Regan nodded, "Deal." She'd do anything to get to Brian.

Regan stood outside Brian's hospital room swallowing nervously. She'd tried earlier to tell him she was sorry, but he'd been too drugged to respond, leaving her with a deep need to make sure he understood.

She tapped on the door to the private room and stuck her head inside.

A white-coated man was standing next to Brian's bed. She started to close the door and heard a voice saying, "It's okay. Come on in."

She drew a deep breath and managed to wheel the IV pole through the doorway.

The doctor helped her come closer to Brian's bed. "Who do we have here?" he asked Brian.

"That's the girl I'm going to marry," said Brian in sleepy tones that indicated he wasn't fully awake.

The doctor smiled at her. "I see you fared a little better than this tough guy here." He indicated Brian with a nod in his direction. "But don't worry, both of you will be able to celebrate in style in a few months. When is the wedding?"

Regan stared at the doctor wide-eyed. "Brian must be drugged. There's no wedding." She turned to Brian. His eyes had closed, and he was breathing deeply.

"Can I help you back to your room?" the doctor asked her kindly.

Regan shook her head, not knowing whether to laugh or cry. *She and Brian married? No way!*

When she got back to her room, Regan stared in surprise at the huge bouquet of pink roses in a crystal vase on top of her bedside table. She made her way over to it and picked out the gift card. She opened the envelope, pulled out the card, and read: "Regan, sweetie, so sorry to hear about the accident. I'm away but will see you as soon as I get back. Be better soon! Love, Mo"

Regan set the card down and sank down onto the bed, her thoughts whirling. How was she going to tell Mo they might lose the job with Arthur Weatherman? Arthur surely wouldn't be interested in having a woman like her represent his company. He might not even want them to enter the bid they were working on to redecorate his restaurants.

Tears rolled down her cheeks. She was in such a mess, all because she couldn't let Brian Harwood think she was too scared to ride a motorcycle. Anger at him, at herself, at fate boiled out of her. She often saw motorcyclists race dangerously down highways, dashing in and out of traffic, causing others to worry. She and Brian had simply been traveling down the road along the beach in a very careful manner. Why were they the ones who got hurt? Why Brian? Why her?

A nurse came into her room. "The doctor has signed your release. You can get ready to go home. Do you have some clean clothes?"

"Yes, my sister brought them. I'll call her now."

The nurse unhooked Regan's IV, filled out her chart, and helped Regan get her bag of clean clothes out of the closet. "Guess your sister took your other clothes home."

Regan nodded. She never wanted to see them again.

The nurse handed Regan a bunch of papers. "Here are instructions for at-home care. You're to see Dr. Milford in a couple of days. Everything is written down for you. I just need your signature on a couple of these forms."

She studied Regan. "How are you feeling? Are you ready to go home and deal with the healing process? It may take several weeks."

Regan decided not to hold back. "How do I feel? I'm pretty pissed. We were just riding along when a truck pulled out in front of us. And then I ..."

The nurse placed a hand on her shoulder. "It's normal to go through a period of anger. Life isn't fair, and accidents happen. But you have the best plastic surgeon I know. He'll make you as perfect as you were. Some patients say he makes them even better."

Regan let out a long sigh. Like the nurse said, life wasn't always fair. At least, she and Brian were alive and, according to him, about to get married. She hoped he wouldn't remember saying something like that because she couldn't imagine their marrying ever, especially after all of this.

Regan had just finished dressing when Sheena walked into the room.

"Ready to go home?" Sheena asked, giving her a bright smile.

Regan nodded. "As ready as I ever will be."

The nurse rolled a wheelchair into the room. “Can’t let you leave the hospital without feeling like royalty,” she joked.

Feeling broken, Regan reluctantly sat down in it.

Sheena handed the packet of paperwork to her and picked up the bouquet. “Who are these from?”

Regan tried to smile and stopped. “Mo.”

“I left a message for him. Did he come to see you?”

Regan shook her head. “He’s away.”

Sheena gave her a sympathetic look. “Well, I’m sure he’ll come see you as soon as he can. I knew he’d want to know about the accident.”

“Thanks.” Regan wished she could feel her mouth moving and form her words better. There was so much more she wanted to discuss with her sister.

Regan’s spirits drooped when they pulled into the parking lot behind the Sandpiper Suites Building. She didn’t want anyone to see her like this. The bandage and bruises on her face were scary. What lay beneath the bandage scarier still.

Sheena came around to the passenger side of her car and stood by as Regan climbed out.

“Hurry,” said Regan, walking as quickly as she could with her sore body.

Meaghan saw them and came running down the walk to greet them.

“Auntie Regan? Are you all right?”

Regan stopped herself from saying a sarcastic, “Sure.”

“She’s sore and bruised, but she’s going to be fine,” Sheena answered for her with a firmness Regan recognized from childhood.

Tony stood by the entrance to the building. “Saw you coming.” His gaze settled on Regan. “Glad to have you home.”

Tears filled Regan's eyes. Home, such as it was, felt so much better than the hospital. Her thoughts turned to Brian. When would he be able to come home? Darcy had told her with his hip injury, he'd be forced to go to rehab for a while.

Sheena walked Regan into the suite she was sharing with Darcy.

"Surprise!" shouted Darcy and Mo together.

The tears that had threatened earlier spilled out of Regan's eyes. Her knees felt wobbly.

Sheena gripped her arm and led her over to the couch. "Have a seat. Now, what can I get you? Water? Snacks? Whatever you want. I've made Jello, a mashed potato and cheese casserole you liked as a kid, and I bought you some ice cream. Anything that's soft."

"Thanks. How about some water?" Regan said, too unsettled to think of food at that moment.

Mo came and sat beside her. "I decided to come right home. I had to see you and make sure you were all right."

Regan nodded. "I'll know more in a couple of days. Where were you?"

Mo glanced around at the others and hesitated.

Sheena said, "Okay, family, let's go next door to my suite to give Regan and Mo some privacy."

When the two of them were alone, Mo clasped Regan's hand. "Oh, sweetie, I've been so worried about you."

"I look awful, huh?" Regan said, knowing he'd tell her the truth.

"A little scary right now, but Darcy said you've got a great doctor."

"Where were you?" Regan said.

"Kenton asked me to come to California. So, I went."

"Kenton?"

"You know, Kenton Standish. Since Labor Day Weekend,

we've spent a lot of time talking on the phone, getting to know each other."

Though Regan's jaw was without feeling, it loosened. "You and Kenton are an item?" Cyndi Jansen's brother was an extremely handsome and nice guy. No wonder Kenton and Nicole hadn't shared any sparks of real interest. He was gay.

"Shhh, our getting together is a secret for now," said Mo. His brown eyes gleamed with happiness. "Kenton called me a couple of days ago and asked me to come to California, so we could spend some time together as friends. Neither of us wants to rush anything, but after spending a couple of days with him and seeing what a nice person he is, I think this might become the real thing. We're so compatible. He loves to cook, and he took me to an art exhibit where I helped him pick out a painting for the house he's redoing on the beach."

Regan placed a hand on Mo's arm. "Be careful, Mo. Juan broke your heart. I don't want to see it get broken again. Kenton lives a very different kind of life."

"I know," said Mo. "I've been telling myself that on the flight back home. And, Regan, he might be as kind and sincere as I think, but then what do I do? I can't leave Florida, my family, and you."

Regan lowered her head and gripped her hands together. She had to be truthful, and the truth hurt. She forced the words out through lips she couldn't feel. "I can't imagine Arthur Weatherman will want me to be his spokesperson after this. And maybe he won't want us even to submit a bid. So, you might be free to leave."

Mo's look of surprise changed to one of determination. "Regan, look at me. Your talent isn't in your face; it's in your head. Stop this kind of talk. We're going to go ahead with our bid, and we'll push for you to be the spokesperson like he wanted. The campaign isn't going to start until after the first of the year, and four months is a good, long time for healing."

Regan remained quiet, wondering if she could believe the optimism in Mo's voice.

"How's Brian?" he asked into the silence.

"He has to go to rehab for a broken hip, and both of his arms are in casts. I don't have all the recovery details yet." She leaned back against the cushions, exhausted by her worries.

"You okay?" Mo asked softly.

She sat up and stared at him. "The accident was my fault. I tugged on Brian's arm, and then we went out of control."

Mo shook his head. "Sweetie, it was an accident. I doubt you caused it. I was told Brian swerved to get out of the way of a truck and couldn't avoid hitting it. Don't take on any guilt for it. Neither should Brian. It was an accident. Understand?"

Regan nodded. "Thanks. I needed to hear that from someone other than my sisters."

"Believe them. Believe me," said Mo.

"I love you, Mo," Regan said, touched by his obvious concern. "You're my best friend. Thanks for coming to see me. Did Kenton understand?"

Mo's smile was filled with satisfaction. "I told you, he's the best guy I've ever met."

"Well, then, I hope it works out for you. What about the show Kenton is on?"

"This is the last season. After that, he's not sure what he's going to do."

Sheena knocked on the door. "Here's your water, Regan. Mo, can I get you anything?"

Mo stood. "No, thanks. I'd better be going. Regan needs her rest, and I have some calls to make."

"Thanks," said Regan, so tired she could hardly get the word out.

CHAPTER SIXTEEN

SHEENA

After Mo left, and her children were settled, Sheena helped Regan get comfortable in bed. Following the suggestion on the home-care sheet the nurse had given Regan, she packed soft towels around Regan's head to help prevent Regan from rolling over on her side and disturbing the wounds on her face. She placed ice packs on her chin and along each side of her face.

"When can the bandage come off?" said Regan in a garbled voice.

"It was suggested you leave bandages on until you see the doctor."

Regan's beautiful violet-blue eyes were troubled as she took hold of Sheena's hand. "What if the doctor can't fix me up the way I was? What will happen to me?"

Sheena squeezed Regan's hand, taking a moment to think of a good reply. "You will always be who you are. Your face may completely recover or not, but that won't change you and all you can do with your life."

"But I want ..."

Sheena stopped her. "You've always complained people judged you by your looks, not by who you are. This is an opportunity to prove otherwise. An opportunity I would never have wished for you, but one just the same. It's the beauty inside you that's important. And, Regan, you are truly beautiful that way."

Reagan closed her eyes.

Sheena planted a soft kiss on Regan's cheek. "Goodnight, little sister. Darcy and I will be here in the morning to help you."

"Where's Darcy?"

"With Austin. They're taking his grandfather out to dinner for his birthday. I'm staying here with you until she gets back."

"Thanks," said Regan.

"That's what sisters are for," said Sheena, hearing her mother's voice in her head. Their mother had always wanted them to get along, but it had taken Uncle Gavin's challenge to make it happen. Now, she couldn't imagine her life without her sisters' playing an active part in it.

When Darcy returned to the suite, Sheena went next door to the suite she shared with her family.

As Sheena walked into the living room, Tony looked up from the couch and turned the volume down on the television. "How's she doing?"

Sheena sank down beside him. "I think the most difficult thing she'll have to deal with will be the changes in her appearance. The scar under her chin extends beyond her chin a bit on either side. And though Dr. Milford did a great job of making it look like a fold in the chin and neck, it's apparent."

"What caused a cut like that? I wasn't about to say anything, but it looks like someone took a swipe at her with a sword."

"They think it was a broken shell lying next to the road. One of those weird situations of being in the wrong place at the wrong time. The good thing is the rest of her face and her body are expected to heal naturally, and those beautiful eyes of hers are okay."

"It makes you wonder what might have happened if they'd been going faster," said Tony.

Sheena shook her head. "I don't want to think of it, and I don't want either of our kids riding motorcycles."

"I agree," Tony said with surprising quickness. "Too dangerous. Almost losing them to a fire scared the hell out of me. I don't want anything else to happen to them."

"Meaghan has a boyfriend she's not willing to talk about. And Michael and that girlfriend of his will give us enough to worry about." Sheena rose and offered him her hand. "C'mon, old man. Let's go to bed. Tomorrow's another busy day."

He grinned at her. "Best suggestion of the day."

The next morning, Sheena checked on Regan and Darcy and then hurried over to the registration office. Two guest rooms were occupied. Though Holly had assured her it wasn't normally a busy time at the beach immediately following Labor Day, Sheena was worried. The excitement of their opening was over, and the long haul was before them. She hoped Nicole Coleman was sincere about moving to Florida and doing an advertising campaign for them. They needed it desperately.

She was checking data on the computer when one of the guests entered the office.

Smiling, she asked, "Can I help you?"

The man, half of a couple from Connecticut, gave her a grim look. "I want my money back. This hotel isn't even completed."

"Yes," said Sheena slowly, "I thought we explained that to you yesterday when you checked in. That's why the rate for staying here is low. We also offered you a discount at the bar next door."

"Well, my wife and I decided we don't like it. We want our money back. We're leaving." He stared at her with a defiant expression.

Sheena had dealt with difficult plumbing customers in the past and drew a deep breath, ready to politely do battle. Most of the time people like this were trying to get out of paying. "I'm sorry you feel this way. I can't give you your money back, but I certainly won't charge you for canceling your reservation within our twenty-four-hour window. Let's settle your account, and you can be on your way."

His look of surprise was telling. "Well, maybe I can talk my wife into staying one more night."

"I hope so," Sheena said. "It should be a beautiful beach day. And if you're interested in fishing, it looks like a good day for that too." She handed him a brochure for a fishing company located at St. John's Pass.

His eyes lit up. "I'm going to try and talk my wife into staying. Sorry for all the confusion."

As she watched him leave the office, Sheena frowned thoughtfully. She'd checked the couple into the hotel herself and knew very well she'd told them about the hotel's current condition and plans for future renovations. She posted a note by the computer to remind everyone to explain the situation to any guests when they called in.

She checked her watch, wishing she could go back to the suite to talk to her sisters. It made the reality of having the office open during business hours a problem.

Later, when Darcy arrived to relieve her, Sheena brought up the idea of asking one of Gavin's people to help them out.

"Who could it be?" Darcy said. "The only person I haven't interviewed for my new book is Sally Neal. She seems so timid I thought I'd wait to ask, but maybe it's time. I'll try to get in touch with her this afternoon."

"Great. I promised Regan I'd drive her to the hospital to see Brian. She's anxious to talk to him."

Darcy shook her head. "Good idea. I think she wants Brian's forgiveness. She's still blaming herself for the accident." She sighed. "Sheena, do you think Regan's face is ever going to be right again? It looks awful."

"I know," said Sheena, "but maybe the doctor is as good as he says. I hope so."

CHAPTER SEVENTEEN

REGAN

A couple of days later, Sheena helped Regan into her car for their trip to see Brian. "Comfortable?"

Regan shrugged. "As comfortable as I can be. Thanks." She knew she wasn't going to be comfortable for some time to come—with Brian, with others, with herself.

As they traveled along the highway into Tampa, Regan wondered how to handle Arthur Weatherman.

As if she'd read her thoughts, Sheena patted her knee. "No need to approach Arthur Weatherman yet about the accident. You and Mo should just go ahead and submit your bid for the restaurant designs. In a few weeks or so, you'll know more about what the future with him will look like. It may be after this time of healing, everything will be just fine."

"And if it isn't?" Regan blinked back tears.

"I'm sure you and Mo will get other chances to bid on projects," Sheena said, giving her an encouraging smile.

"I mean with my face," said Regan.

"You'll go on as you've always planned—working with Mo."

Regan wanted to tell her sister about Mo and Kenton Standish, but she couldn't betray Mo by sharing his news. "What if Mo decides for some reason not to work with me? What then?"

"Then you'll find someone else to work with until you can build your own business," said Sheena with unmistakable firmness. "We will not let this accident ruin your future."

Regan stared out the window. A counselor from high school had reminded her students only they could shape their own futures. It had sounded so easy then. Now, it seemed like an enormous task.

"Regan, you're much smarter and more put together than you realize. Don't slide into the self-doubt that's held you back in the past." Sheena's words, spoken kindly, felt like knife points poking at her.

Regan drew in a deep breath, wincing a little at the pain, and nodded. She would pull herself together ... after she talked to Brian.

Sheena dropped off Regan at the main entrance to the hospital. "I'll park the car and meet you upstairs in Brian's room."

"Give me some time alone with him, okay? Then, come on up."

Sheena gave her a steady look and nodded. "Okay. See you in a while."

Regan made her way into the lobby and walked over to the elevators. As she waited for one, she studied herself in the shiny surface of the elevator doors. The outer edges of her long scar were very visible, extending beyond the bandage. The scrapes on her face had scabbed and darkened, giving her countenance the weird look of someone who'd been mauled by a long-clawed monster. The black circles under her eyes already held a trace of green and yellow.

The elevator opened, and Holly Harwood emerged. She smiled when she saw Regan.

"Hi, there! How are you doing?"

"A little better, thank you," Regan said. "How's Brian?"

"He's pretty sore," Holly admitted. "Say, maybe you can do me a favor. It's almost lunchtime here. Can you help him with his meal? I need to get back to the bar."

"Sure, I'd be happy to," Regan said. She was relieved to know there was something she could do for him to take away some of her guilt.

She took the elevator to Brian's floor and got off, practicing her apology in her mind.

When she reached the door to his room, she knocked softly and opened it.

A sports event of some kind was playing on the television. Brian, lying in bed, turned to her and smiled. "Hello, beautiful."

Swallowing her nervousness, Regan stepped forward. "While we're alone and you're alert, I need to tell you how sorry I am about the accident. I know it was my fault, and I want to make it up to you."

Brian frowned at her. "What do you mean your fault? I should be the one apologizing to you. I couldn't stop us from ramming into the truck. I tried, but I couldn't get the bike out of its way."

"But ..."

Brian waved away her concern and winced. "Ow! Dammit!" His right arm was in a cast from upper arm to wrist, securing the elbow. The other arm was in a cast from elbow to wrist and rested in a sling. "It wasn't anyone's fault. Shit happens, and it happened to us. Got it?"

Regan nodded. "Your mother asked if I would help you with your lunch. I told her I would. Okay?"

A grin lit his face. "You're going to feed me?"

Regan felt the upper part of her cheeks grow hot. "Guess you're not so doped up with medication, after all. You're acting more like yourself."

He grew serious. "I'm taking something for the pain, but not the real heavy stuff. They only let you stay on that for a couple of days."

"How long are you going to remain in the hospital?" she asked.

"They're transferring me over to the rehab center tomorrow. They'll help me with both my arm and hip injuries."

"What exactly happened to them?"

"Want all the technical jargon?" At her nod, he continued. "Okay, in 'doctor speak,' the right elbow was fractured. The ulna and radius bones in my left forearm were also fractured. In both arms, the displaced bones were reduced and are held into place with wires and screws. The same thing with the hip. With a hip injury, I'm on blood thinners. Hopefully, I get the catheter taken out tomorrow."

Regan's attention automatically centered on his body.

He grinned at her. "Sorry, you can't see anything."

Regan felt more heat rise to her cheeks. *God, he was such a tease!*

At the sound of a knock at the door followed by Sheena's appearance, Regan stepped away from Brian's bed, glad for the reprieve.

"How's this patient doing?" Sheena asked cheerfully.

"I hurt like hell, but I'm going to survive," Brian said. "And, Regan has offered to help me with my meals. That's going to make me feel a lot better."

Sheena gave her a questioning look.

"I met Holly downstairs. She asked me to help him with his lunch today."

"And if she's good, I'll keep her on," said Brian, winking at them both.

Sheena smiled and nodded. "Good idea. For both of you."

"No broken bones?" he asked.

Regan shook her head. "Cuts and scrapes and this." She pointed to the bandage under her neck. Tears stung her eyes.

Though she tried to blink them away, her vision remained blurred. Embarrassed, she turned away.

In the silence that followed, Sheena said, “Dr. Milford is a wonderful plastic surgeon. I’m sure Regan will be back to normal soon.”

A tap on the door stopped their conversation.

Dr. Hollister, the orthopedic surgeon handling Brian’s case entered the room. “Ah, sorry to disturb you, but I wanted to make sure you understood about the rehab program. I just signed the orders for you.” He smiled at Sheena and turned to Regan. “How’s Brian’s fiancée today?”

“Fiancée?” said Sheena. She gave Regan a wide-eyed look and turned to Brian. “What’s this all about?”

Brian looked as surprised as Sheena. “I ... I’m not sure.”

They turned to Regan. Swallowing nervously, she said, “Under medication, Brian told Dr. Hollister he was going to marry me. I tried to explain to his doctor Brian was just dopey on the meds.”

At the grin that spread across Brian’s face, Regan wished the floor would open up and swallow her. She turned to Sheena for moral support, but Sheena was smiling as broadly as Brian.

Regan drew herself up. “Brian knows it’s not going to happen. Right, Brian?”

“We’ll see,” he said, chuckling.

“I’ll be back in a minute,” Regan said. “Time for a restroom run.”

“Remember, you’re feeding me my lunch,” said Brian.

His soft laughter followed her out of the room.

Moments later, standing in front of the mirror in the ladies’ room, Regan stared at the bruised, cut face staring back at her and knew Brian, in his usual way, was just teasing. They were not good together—never had been, never would be. And with women falling all over him, she couldn't compete anyway.

Having made that determination, Regan returned to Brian's room much calmer. She would not fall for such nonsense.

CHAPTER EIGHTEEN

DARCY

As Sheena walked into the registration office, Darcy looked up and smiled. "Regan get to see Brian?"

"Yes, and she's still with him. Holly asked her to help Brian with his lunch. Poor guy isn't able to feed himself." A smile crossed her face. "You won't believe it! While Brian was under the influence of his medication, he told his doctor he was going to marry Regan. I was as shocked as Brian when he realized what he'd said. But, together, they would be terrific."

"I think so too, but Regan has vowed more than once she won't get involved with him, that he's too much of a player. And what about Jill? He's back with her, isn't he?"

Sheena gave her a thoughtful look. "I wonder how real that is. But, you're right, we shouldn't push something like that. They really are very different people."

"Good news, I hope," said Darcy. "Sally Neal confirmed to me she has office experience, and she has agreed to give me an interview."

"Great," said Sheena. "We've got to get help here in this office. And on a similar note, have you heard anything more from Nicole?"

"I sent her an email, but haven't heard back yet. Maybe moving to Florida was a fleeting thought."

"Even so, I hope she hasn't given up on doing a real ad campaign for us. I'm worried about 'putting heads in beds.'"

Darcy nodded. "Me too."

###

Darcy sat in a chair opposite Sally Neal in her small apartment on the second story of the building that housed Gracie's restaurant, the administrative office for the hotel, and other hotel support facilities. The apartment was surprisingly cozy and nicely decorated with pieces of artwork hanging on the wall or resting on a bureau and small coffee table. As she studied a watercolor of a serene lake scene, Darcy's curiosity grew.

"I know you're a friend of Uncle Gavin's, or you wouldn't be here," said Darcy, hoping to give Sally a chance to begin the conversation. Sally was a small, quiet woman with gray-blue eyes and short, brown hair that at first glance made her seem a little mousy. But that changed when she spoke to people—her eyes shone with intelligence and wit. While most of the other women in the group were dedicated to working in Gracie's, Sally's role at the hotel was to be the housekeeper for Gavin's people and to assist in other ways at any given time.

"Anything I say will remain between us, right?" Sally said softly.

"Yes, unless you agree to have some of the general information included in the newspaper column I write without mentioning any names," Darcy added. She'd learned though some people didn't want their names mentioned, they were glad for their stories to get out.

Sally nodded. "Okay, that's fair. You wanted to know if I had any office experience. I do, or, I should say, I did. That's how I met your uncle."

"Did you work for him?" Darcy asked.

Sally chuckled. "Wish I had. He would've believed me."

"What happened?"

"I worked at a well-known investment company in Tampa

for several years. During that time, my boss and I became involved."

"As in an affair?" Darcy asked gently.

"Yes, it was quite something. He was so good in so many ways." Sally stopped talking and waved her hand in dismissal. "I didn't mean ... he was ... a smooth-talker. Gavin even called him a smooth-talking, lying, son-of-a-bitch to his face, but I'm getting ahead of my story."

She took a sip of water. "I'll start at the beginning. My husband left me with two teenage children, forcing me to go to work. I was lonely when I interviewed for the job at the investment company, and, Bob, the made-up name I'm giving him, and I clicked from the beginning. Several years later, I saw him for the manipulative, greedy man he was, but, at first, I was totally smitten by his interest in me and the kindness he showed his clients."

"But that didn't last?"

"No. After a few years of working with him, I began to suspect something was wrong with some of the accounts. Money was being withdrawn and reinvested in ways that didn't seem to suit the client. I asked about it, of course, but Bob told me to mind my own business, he was the investor, not I. And I couldn't deny everyone was happy with the way things were going. Clients sent Bob and me gifts on a regular basis, thanking us for our work."

"And then?"

"All good things come to an end. Right?" Sally said, giving Darcy a wry look.

Darcy nodded and waited for Sally to continue.

"And bad things can seem to last forever." Sally sighed. "I didn't know how bad it was or how bad it would become."

"Are you talking about a Ponzi scheme?" Darcy asked, anxious to hear the rest of the story.

Sally gave her a grim look and nodded. "We've all heard and read stories about the big guys in New York and on Wall Street. But little guys like ... Bob ... can ruin lives too. And several people lost their savings. Gavin was almost among them."

"He was?"

"Just before everything went down, Gavin pulled his money out of our company. He'd met Blackie Gatto and decided to help him start his business. But Gavin and I had already become friends, so he knew me well enough to know I wasn't out to get money that way."

"But, then, what happened?"

Sally drew a deep breath and stared out the window at a nearby palm tree before turning back to Darcy.

"Bob had me sign several letters for him, indicating I was suggesting our clients invest in a certain so-called company. Later, when I tried to explain to a jury I didn't know what signing those letters meant, I was almost laughed out of the courtroom. That's when Gavin hired a lawyer to help me. Even then, it was a struggle. But the lawyer was good enough I had to serve only five years in prison."

Darcy felt her breath leave her in a rush. "Five years? But you weren't involved, were you?"

"Not really, but it was hard to convince others of that when I had a lovely home, a new car, nice jewelry and other costly things. Given to me by Bob, of course. They thought it was payback for keeping my mouth shut." Sally sighed. "It was a mess."

"What about your kids?"

Tears filled Sally's eyes. "When it happened, they went to live with their father and his new wife. You can imagine how much sympathy I got from them and how they influenced my children. They're grown and entirely on their own now, but

I'm not sure they'll ever forgive me."

"What happened to the people who lost their money?"

"A lot of them got some of their money back. The sale of my house, my possessions, and Bob's was enough to repay something. Bob had bought a number of cars, a huge yacht, all kinds of crazy things."

"When you got out of prison, what did you do?"

Tears, silvery streaks of pain, rolled down Sally's cheeks. "Gavin met me on the day I got released and gave me a job. That's how I've come to be one of his people."

"What did you do for him?" Darcy asked, wondering at the generosity of her uncle.

Sally's lips curved. "I did bookkeeping for him. That's how great a person he was."

Darcy sat back in the chair, her mind spinning. Maybe she'd do a column on believing in others. For the moment, though, she had to convince Sally to work for them.

"Sheena, Regan, and I need help at the registration desk answering the phone, checking in people, and handling any problems that come up. Are you willing and able to give us several hours per week?"

"I'd love to," said Sally with such eagerness a lump formed in Darcy's throat.

"Great," said Darcy. "As soon as you get the chance, come over to the office, and one of us will show you what needs to be done."

Sally rose and gave Darcy a quick hug. "It means so much to me you'd trust me to do this."

Darcy beamed at her. "Of course. You're not only one of Gavin's people, but a member of our family now."

Darcy left Sally and went downstairs to Gracie's. Maggie O'Neill was wiping down empty tables. Darcy had always been intrigued by the mystery behind her eyes.

Maggie saw her and hurried over to her. "How's Regan? I've been so worried about her."

"She's a little better every day, but it's going to take time for her face to heal."

"If there's any way I can help, please let me know," said Maggie. "I've already offered to help Brian with his meals and exercises from time to time."

Darcy smiled. "That's nice of you. Regan is helping him with his lunch today."

Maggie's eyebrows shot up. "Oh? Well, maybe I should leave feeding him to her."

"Maybe not," said Darcy bluntly. "Their relationship is a little complicated."

Maggie nodded. "Yes, I know."

They said goodbye, and as Darcy left the restaurant, she hoped she'd just saved her sister a lot of heartbreak.

CHAPTER NINETEEN

REGAN

Regan sat in a chair in Brian's room watching the rise and fall of Brian's chest as he slept. Feeding him lunch had been a surprisingly intimate thing, and she was still reeling emotionally from the effect. The way his eyes had remained on her as he took bites of food had been unsettling, especially with her face in such bad shape.

As she waited for Sheena to pick her up, her thoughts continued to whirl. She'd always believed Brian was dangerous for her, that he could break her heart. Now, she knew it was true. His girlfriend, Jill, was on her way to relieve Regan from her duties.

Regan stood and looked out the window. Palm trees gave the urban setting a tropical look she'd come to love. No matter how confused she felt about Brian, she was determined to keep Florida and the Salty Key Inn her home.

Jill entered the room, a bundle of energy. "Oh my God! How is he? I'm so sorry I was away when this happened. And when I tried, I couldn't get an earlier flight from London." Her eyes widened as she studied Regan. "Your face! How awful!" As she realized what she'd just said, Jill's cheeks grew pink. "Oh, I'm sorry. I didn't mean that like it sounded. You'll be fine, of course."

"Hey, Jill," said Brian, awakening and giving her a wide grin. "You're here."

Jill rushed to his bedside. "Of course, darling. I came to the hospital right from the airport. My luggage is outside the room." She leaned over and gave him a long kiss.

"Guess I'll wait for Sheena downstairs," Regan said, but quickly realized they didn't even hear her. And Regan could understand why.

Brian and Jill together looked like an advertisement for beautiful people. Brian's tall, buff, tanned body was offset by a handsome face surrounded by sun-bleached brown hair. His dark eyes shone with ... well, sexiness. Jill was equally attractive. Tall and thin but with nice feminine curves, she had blond-streaked hair, sparkling blue eyes and stunning facial features—the kind you found on front covers of magazines. They were a match made in heaven, she'd heard some of Holly's customers say.

As Regan stepped outside Brian's hospital room, she saw Sheena emerge from the elevator and hurried to greet her.

Sheena greeted her with a look of surprise. "Hi, what's up?"

"Jill's here, and I wanted to give Brian and her privacy. Not that they cared," Regan said, unable to hold back the emotional turmoil she was feeling.

"Okay. You're ready to go?"

Regan sighed. "I forgot my purse. Will you get it for me? I'm exhausted."

Sheena gave her a steady look and nodded. "I'll be right back."

Regan sank onto a wooden bench opposite the elevators relieved Sheena hadn't pressed her for more information. She didn't want to have to try to explain her emotions.

Sheena returned with her purse and helped Regan to her feet. "C'mon, honey, let's get you home. It's been a long day for you, and it's far from over." She put an arm across Regan's shoulder. "Brian says thank you, and he'll see you tomorrow."

"Tomorrow?"

Sheena nodded. "Guess you told him you'd help him with lunches."

"Oh, but I didn't mean every day!" Regan exclaimed.

"Well, you'll have to work it out with him. In the meantime, he's expecting you tomorrow."

"Okay," Regan said reluctantly. "I'll see how it goes."

After a long nap, Regan awoke feeling more optimistic about her life. She would heal, go into business with Mo, and help her sisters win the challenge at the hotel. Rising, she went into the bathroom and went about her business without once looking into the mirror. That image, she knew, would bring her down.

In the kitchen, she fixed herself a glass of iced tea and took a seat at the kitchen table. She and Mo had done the bulk of the work on the designs for Arthur Weatherman. They just needed to go over them again before submitting them. She called Mo, determined to move forward.

He answered right away. "Hey, sweetie! How are you doing? I called earlier, but you didn't pick up."

"Sorry. I was at the hospital with Brian and must not have heard the phone ring."

"I can understand why," teased Mo.

"No, it's not that way at all. Jill showed up, and it was a little confusing."

He chuckled. "I imagine. I met her once. She's a bit of a whirlwind. How's he doing, by the way?"

"They're moving him into the rehab section of the hospital to work on strengthening his arms and his hip."

"Bet he won't like that. Listen, Regan, I want to be certain you're willing to go ahead with the Weatherman project. I've thought if you're not, I might spend some time in California."

Regan's stomach felt as if it had sunk to the floor. "No, no! I want to go ahead with it. We need at least to submit our designs to him, don't you think? We need to review them one more time, and then you'll have to present them. I can't. Not when I look like this."

"Okay, I just needed to make sure. Kenton is due for some time off, and he can come here. He's thinking of renting a house on the beach or buying one."

"Nice," said Regan. She paused. "Mo, you're not rushing into anything with him, are you? Things seem to be happening awfully fast."

"Thanks for your concern, Regan, but I can handle this," Mo responded in a quiet, firm voice.

Regan blinked in surprise, stung by his underlying irritation. "Sorry. I just don't want you to get hurt. Shall we meet sometime tomorrow?"

"How about four P.M. I have a client meeting in the morning."

"Sure, that'll be fine," Regan hung up and stared out the window at the fronds of a nearby palm tree rustling in the wind, feeling as unsettled as they.

The next morning, Darcy drove Regan to her doctor's appointment. "You're very quiet, Regan. Are you nervous?"

Regan nodded, still upset by the image of her face in her mirror this morning. "The scar is worse than I thought, and my lip is drooping on one side."

"I'm sure Dr. Milford will do the best he can," said Darcy sympathetically.

"If he doesn't, my plan will be ruined. The only reason I want to be the spokesperson for Arthur Weatherman is to earn some money after the New Year, so if we don't meet Uncle

Gavin's challenge , we could still keep the hotel going."

"Whoa! That's really nice of you." At her sister's sweet gesture, Darcy's blue eyes filled with tears.

"Until now, this has been the best time of my life." Regan gave her a pleading look. "We've gotta make it work."

Darcy patted Regan's shoulder. "We're going to give it a good try."

Dr. Milford's luxurious office indicated his success. A large Oriental rug in shades of grays and blues lay in the main waiting room. Beautiful artwork hung on the walls. Office staff quickly ushered her down a side hallway to an exam room for privacy as they did for other patients who'd already had surgery and were in various stages of healing.

In her private exam room, Regan sat in a chair pretending to read a magazine as she watched a number of people pass by the door she'd left cracked open.

One little girl walking down the corridor with her mother stopped and pointed at Regan. "You have a star too!"

Confused, Regan looked to the mother.

"Emily refers to her scars as stars. And that's how we like it, with a little bit of magic thrown in."

Regan turned to the little girl she guessed to be about four or five. One of her cheeks bore several small, jagged scars.

Trying her best to make her lip form a smile, Regan knelt before the little girl. "Hi, Emily! Your stars are very special. I can tell."

Emily nodded emphatically. "Yes. That's what we tell my friends."

Unexpected tears filled Regan's eyes. "What a good idea. I'll have to keep that in mind. I'm so glad I had the chance to meet you. Have a super day!"

As Emily waved goodbye, her mother mouthed, "Thank you!", and they went on their way.

Regan stood and stared out the window, her mind replaying the moment she saw the truck pull out in front of the motorcycle. Life was so full of surprises. A few moments earlier, they could've stopped the bike or turned out of the way.

Dr. Milford came into the exam room. "Hello, Regan. How are we doing today?"

"*We* are not doing that well," Regan said, surprising herself with the sudden feeling of hopelessness that seized her. "I've done everything you told me to do—including icepacks, medication, and all—and I still look awful. And my lips are not normal."

Dr. Milford gave her a knowing look. "Your frustration isn't at all unusual for a patient like you, who's dealing with your new appearance. Sometimes, those feelings change to depression. We don't want that. Let's see what we're talking about with you, shall we?"

Regan sat on the examination table as requested and quieted as Dr. Milford's gentle fingers probed various spots on her face. Then he took off the bandage and examined the long scar under her chin.

"Your face took a beating from gravel and what we think was the sharp edge of a broken shell sitting beside the road. But the scrapes and scratches are healing well, and I think the scar under your chin will heal nicely. There's no family history of keloid scarring?"

Regan shook her head. "Not that I'm aware of. But, doctor, what about my lip? It's drooping on one side. It almost looks as if I had a stroke. Can you fix that?"

"That depends on the nerve healing well. It hasn't been severed, but it's been damaged. I'm evaluating it as a second-degree injury, or axonotmesis, which should recover completely. However, it will be much slower to heal than a first-degree injury, which normally would heal within three months."

"What are we talking about, doctor?" Regan asked, feeling acid rushing to her stomach.

"I'm guessing it'll take three to six months. But we'll be checking it from time to time. The good news is you're young and healthy, and we were able to clean out and suture the wound without doing any further damage to the nerve. Surgery in the neck area can be tricky due to the presence of the facial nerve."

"The scar is so big," said Regan. "It extends up onto my face a little on each side."

"Because of its dark color, it appears much more noticeable than it will after it heals. Then, it should look almost normal. We like to make it appear as if it's a normal crease in your neck."

"And what about the areas where the scar extends onto my face?" said Regan.

"Any scars should fade nicely, and with the use of makeup, it shouldn't be too noticeable," said Dr. Milford. He cleared his throat. "I'm sure it all seems so apparent to you, but I predict, in time, even you will not be so aware of it. As far as the lip goes, time will heal that too."

Regan lowered her head to hide her tears.

"You have plenty of the cream for the scars?" the doctor said quietly. At her nod, he continued, "I want you to keep on using it as directed. If any changes occur, call the office right away. We have coverage 24/7. I'll see you in another month to check on your progress."

He headed for the door and stopped. "Regan, you're going to be fine."

She looked up at him and formed a crooked smile, knowing she wasn't going to be fine at all. She had the awful feeling she didn't know who she was anymore.

CHAPTER TWENTY

DARCY

Darcy dropped Regan off at the front entrance of the hospital and parked the car. She was anxious to see how Brian was doing. Not only on a personal level but because he and his crew were very much a part of the renovation of the hotel.

Inside the hospital, Regan was waiting for her in the lobby area.

"Thought you should know I checked in at the desk, and Brian's already been moved to the rehab area. We can go there together."

"Sure," said Darcy.

They were quiet as they joined others on the elevator. Darcy noticed Regan's attempt to hide her face and filled with sympathy. Regan had always been the beautiful sister, the one everyone compared to Elizabeth Taylor. Now, that image was shattered. At least in Regan's mind. Darcy recalled what she'd read online about patients like Regan getting depressed, and she made a silent vow to keep Regan from falling into that category.

In the rehab area, they were directed to Brian's room. Darcy couldn't imagine he would be happy about having to stay there for any length of time. He was an active man.

Darcy followed Regan into the room. He smiled at them both and then his gaze settled on Regan. "So, you're going to give me my lunch?"

Regan nodded. "I promised I would."

"Let's hope it's better here than on the surgical ward," he said, making a face.

"Next time I'll bring you something from Gracie's," said Regan. "Everybody there is thinking of you."

"Yes, Maggie O'Neill is going to be helping me with exercises, and she's giving me dinner tonight to show me how to manage eating on my own."

Darcy noticed a look of disappointment flash across Regan's face and disappear just as quickly. She turned to Brian. "I'm meeting Austin for lunch and will be back to pick Regan up. Is there anything I can get for you?"

"Besides a way to get out of here? Nothing. But, thanks. I do, however, need to speak to Tony. Will you give him that message? He's been handling things for me."

"Sure," said Darcy. "Any idea how long you'll be in here?"

"Not as long as they say I will," he grumped with a dejected sigh. "I'll do whatever I have to do to get out of here as soon as possible."

She gave Brian and Regan bright smiles and left the room.

Later, talking to Austin at lunch at their favorite Thai restaurant, Darcy expressed the worry that flew at her like a pesky fly. "How is Brian going to keep his business going? It looks like he won't be able to hammer a nail or do anything that requires arm muscles for a long time. Among other things, he was working on the restaurant for us. And, Austin, we need to have Gavin's up and running before Christmas for the income. It's a gamble we took, and we need to win it."

Austin gave her hand a reassuring squeeze. "It'll work out. Isn't Tony running the company for him temporarily?"

"Yes, but he needs to build his plumbing business. Working

for Brian was only part of his workload."

Austin gave her a thoughtful look. "Leave it up to them to work it out, Darcy. Both of those guys are pretty smart."

Darcy nodded her agreement. "You're right. It's just that I don't want anything to go wrong. I want to be able to continue planning our wedding with a sense of ease. I can't wait!"

Austin squeezed the hand he'd continued to hold. "The honeymoon is going to be terrific. I've done a lot of traveling, but being with you will make everything seem like new."

"Oh, Austin, that's so sweet," said Darcy breathlessly. She wondered, as she often did, how she could be so lucky to have found him.

He gave her a grin that made her think of more than sightseeing. Out of pure joy, she laughed.

Darcy was still tingling with pleasure when she entered Brian's hospital room. She stopped in surprise. From photos, she recognized Jill, who was sitting with Brian. Regan was nowhere to be found.

"Hi, Jill! Hi, Brian! Where's Regan?"

Jill gave her a smile that didn't quite reach her eyes. "I told Regan I'd take over feeding Brian. She said to tell you she'd be in the waiting room here."

Still studying the enigmatic expression on Jill's face, Darcy nodded. "Okay, then. See you later, Brian. And, like you asked, I'll tell Tony you want to see him."

He bobbed his head. "Thanks."

As Darcy exited the room, she heard Jill say to Brian, "Darling, why are you dealing with Tony?"

Tightening her lips at Jill's insulting tone, Darcy decided she didn't like Brian's girlfriend all that much.

CHAPTER TWENTY-ONE

REGAN

Regan sat in the corner of the waiting room, anxiously awaiting Darcy's arrival. She'd hated seeing Brian suffer because of something she might have done. Helping him eased her guilt. But when Jill had interrupted Regan and Brian sharing a joke while Regan fed him, she'd looked like a rattlesnake ready to strike. Now, sitting here alone in the waiting room, Regan was glad in a way Jill had forced her to leave. When she was with Brian, her emotions swung between happiness and wariness with such force she felt, as she had always, he was as dangerous as a whirling tornado.

At the sight of Darcy, Regan let out a sigh of relief.

"Ready to go?" Darcy asked.

"Oh, yes," Regan said, jumping to her feet. "Can't wait to get out of here. And it looks like I won't be coming back. Jill and Maggie will be taking care of Brian."

"Maybe it's just as well," Darcy said.

"Maybe," said Regan. "But I'm worried about him. What's going to happen to his business? He won't be able to do any labor for some time."

Darcy put a hand on Regan's shoulder. "I just had that very conversation with a wise, lovely man. He said to let Brian and Tony take care of things. But, I don't think Jill is going to allow that to happen."

"Why?"

"She doesn't appear to like Tony. I heard her question

Brian about working with him." Darcy's lips thinned. "Tony's a wonderful guy."

"Yeah. Good thing Sheena didn't hear Jill say that."

Regan and Darcy shared a chuckle. Sheena wouldn't allow anyone to hurt someone in her family.

They returned to the hotel in time for Regan to rest before meeting Mo to go over their bid for Arthur Weatherman. As she lay on her bed staring up at the ceiling, Regan wondered about her future. Her sisters would attack her and call her foolish, but Regan couldn't help worrying with a scar like hers, no guy would be interested in her. And if her lip didn't heal, things would be even worse. She dug deeper inside herself to where honest feelings lay bare. The truth was, beneath all her talk of annoyance with others for seeing only her appearance, she'd liked being attractive to others. True, she'd wanted more than that kind of attention, but at least she'd suited the role everyone gave her. Now, as she had before, she wondered just who she really was.

At the sound of Mo's voice, Regan awoke with a start. She checked the bedside clock. Four o'clock. Time for their meeting.

Darcy tapped on her door and opened it. "Regan? Mo's here."

"Yes, I know. I'll be right there." With effort, she climbed off the bed and went into the bathroom. As had become her pattern, she avoided looking into the mirror as she went about her business. But she knew she'd soon have to shed her reluctance to do so. As Brian had told her, shit happens, and the result of a ride on his motorcycle would always be part of her life.

She entered the living area to find Mo sitting at the kitchen table, a number of sketches before him.

He smiled when he saw her. "Hey, sweetie! How are you?"

"Better," she said, lying a tiny bit.

"I did a little more work on some of the sketches we put together earlier. Take a look."

Mo moved an empty chair next to him, and Regan sat down.

Looking at the drawings of what they'd present to Arthur, Regan smiled, stiffening when she realized her lip was drooping.

But Mo didn't seem to notice. "Well, what do you think?"

She placed a hand on his shoulder. "I think you're the best interior designer I know." They'd used the floor plans they'd been given for each of the restaurants, and from that, had created 3-D images so they could showcase the murals in each one. Depending on the size of the restaurant, it would contain one or more murals.

Regan and Mo had explained in their presentation the common theme of the restaurants was showcasing the areas in which different kinds of seafood lived. A New England-themed restaurant featured lobster, and the colors for that restaurant were red, white, and blue. For snapper, a Florida theme featured turquoise, yellow, and orange.

"It's different," said Mo, "but I think Arthur is going to like it."

"I hope so," Regan said. "It would be a great way to start a business together. That is if you still want to move forward with it."

Frowning, Mo gave her a puzzled look. "Why wouldn't I?"

Regan hung her head, embarrassed.

"Sweetie, tell me this has nothing to do with your face," said Mo.

She lifted her head, surprised to see anger there.

"Can you imagine all the shit I've had to go through because of my color, my sexual orientation? A scar on a pretty face is not the big deal you think it is." His features gentled. "You get that, don't you?"

Regan nodded, realizing she had to stop feeling sorry for herself. Little Emily had a better handle on it than she did.

"I love you for the person you are, Regan, not your face. Now let's get back to business and finalize everything we've done. I've got an appointment with Arthur in two days."

"Thanks for doing this, Mo. You understand I can't go to the meeting. I don't want Arthur to see me until I've had a chance to heal a bit more. If I can get the job of spokesperson for him, the money I earn could help my sisters and me keep the hotel."

"But aren't the three of you going to get money from your uncle at the end of the year?"

Regan shook her head. "We don't know for sure. It depends on how we're judged on meeting his challenge and just what other tricks Uncle Gavin may have been up to. This whole thing has been one surprise after another."

Mo nodded slowly. "I see. Well, let's get this contract. As you say, it could be a good beginning to our business."

"How's your relationship with Kenton doing?"

A smile crossed Mo's face. "Kenton is moving to Florida to be closer to his sister and will be living near here between gigs. He's thinking of doing a movie, but he told me that even so, he's interested in seeing how things go between us."

"Sweet." Regan studied the glow on Mo's face and gave him a distorted smile. She'd love to see Mo happily settled down with someone.

By the time Mo left with suggestions for the presentation, Regan was ready for some time alone.

Knowing she'd have to wait a few more days before

swimming, Regan headed outside with thoughts of going to the beach. She caught sight of the restaurant under construction. Irresistibly drawn to it, she walked over to the empty building and went inside.

She sat down on a couple of stacked boxes of materials and looked around. In the main dining room, workers had started to install paneling. Before the accident, Brian had assured her and her sisters an opening in mid-December would be possible. She wondered if that was still true.

A voice behind her said, “Hello.”

Regan whipped around.

Graham Howard walked toward her. The smile on his face evaporated when he got closer. “Good God! What happened to you?” he said, giving her a worried look.

At his bluntness, she froze.

“Some kind of accident, I guess,” he said, settling his long-legged body next to her on the boxes. He studied her openly. “Looks like it’s all going to heal okay. What happened?”

“Motorcycle accident,” she responded, fighting the urge to get up and run away.

“Oh yeah. I heard something about that. You and Brian Harwood, right? How’s he doing?”

Regan drew a deep breath. “Not great. Broken elbow, arm, and hip.”

Graham’s shocked look sent a shiver through her. “What’s he going to do about his business? Brian’s building a house for one of my friends.”

“Sheena’s husband, Tony, has been running the business. But, I don’t know if he’s going to continue.” She didn’t mention Jill’s disregard for Tony.

Graham’s brow furrowed. “We’d better not be delayed in getting this restaurant done. I’m counting on a good holiday opening season.”

"Yes, I know," said Regan. Graham's base pay was supplemented by a series of possible bonuses that could mean a lot of extra money. Blackie Gatto had come up with the idea to enable some of the expenses to be shifted into the following year.

"Casey Cochran and I have been creating more, new, specialty dishes to be used at Gavin's. And they're good."

"All your cooking is delicious." Regan smiled, not caring if it was a bit crooked. She felt comfortable with Graham.

"And with Casey handling the management of the restaurant, I won't have to worry about the staff and good service and all of that. I can concentrate on the kitchen and getting good food out." His green eyes lit with excitement. "It's going to be a great team."

Regan nodded with enthusiasm. "I think so too."

Graham rose to his feet. "Guess I'd better go. I just can't resist stopping by on my days off at the restaurant."

"When are you closing it down?"

"The day after Thanksgiving. That will give us time to remove the kitchen equipment of ours you wanted and bring it here. It's good stuff and worth the trouble of moving it." He smiled at her. "I liked what you and Mo have come up with for the interior. It's going to be very handsome."

As she started to rise, Graham held out a hand to her.

"Thanks," she said, taking it. On her feet, she stared at him, feeling as if she was seeing him for the first time.

Unfazed by her scar, he studied her. "Are you and Brian together?"

Regan shook her head firmly. "No, he's back with his old girlfriend, Jill Jackson."

A smile swept across his face, enhancing his rugged features. "Good. I'll call you."

Before she could say anything, he turned and walked away.

She watched his easy gait, realizing she didn't need to worry so much about her appearance. The people she liked didn't seem to have a problem with it.

CHAPTER TWENTY-TWO

DARCY

Darcy tried to tell herself not to be worried, but calls from Ed Richardson, the editor of the *West Coast News*, were always troubling. Especially when Ed wanted a face-to-face meeting with her. Writing a column for the newspaper was a dream come true for her and would never have happened without Nick Howard's encouragement and support. Even though the newspaper was a small, local one, it represented a bright future for her.

Darcy parked Gertie, the '50s Cadillac convertible her uncle had owned, at the newspaper's office and went inside. Jeremy McCarthy looked up from his desk and smiled at her, pausing in his typing of something about sports, no doubt.

She went over to him. "Do you know what Ed wants from me?" she whispered.

Jeremy gave her an exaggerated shrug. "Good luck! One never knows what our *dear* editor has in mind," he said sarcastically.

Worry eating at her, Darcy left Jeremy, and went to Ed's office door and knocked.

"Come in," came a deep, growling voice.

Darcy opened the door and stepped inside.

From behind stacked papers beside a computer on his desk, Ed looked up at her and waved her to one of the wooden chairs facing him.

Darcy lowered herself into one of them, feeling as if she was facing the school principal. "You wanted to see me?"

Ed steepled his hands and studied her. "I really liked your column on the idea of angels supporting others when all hope seems lost. It struck a nerve with a lot of our subscribers."

The tension that had gripped Darcy's shoulders eased.

"You've got a good way of finding material that connects with readers. I think it's time for you to do other things."

Darcy felt her throat tighten. "Do you mean drop my column?"

"Well, let's just say, make it not so regular. I need you to do more. You're capable of it, and I don't want to hire anyone else. A printed newspaper is almost a thing of the past. Everyone wants their news on line. How about it? Willing to become a real newspaper woman?"

A gray cloud of suspicion covered Darcy. "What do you mean? What is it you want me to do?"

"I want you to cover community events," he pronounced in firm tones.

Darcy shook her head. "I don't have time for something like that. My sisters and I are still working on the hotel."

"As I said, I need someone to do that work. I can't afford you and a local events person."

"But I'm bringing in and keeping subscribers with my column. You see all the letters I'm getting," Darcy protested.

"I know. That's the rub."

"Can't Laney do the community events? She's the social editor."

"Laney quit her job. That's another problem I'm trying to resolve. The person who's willing to take over for her says she can't do both."

Darcy fought tears. "Neither can I, Ed. I'm sorry, but I owe it to my sisters to keep doing my share at the hotel. You know how much my column means to me because of Nick."

Ed let out a long sigh. "I'll have to ponder the situation, but I don't think things are going to change. I'd hate to lose you, but my hands are tied by the owners who are struggling with keeping this newspaper going."

Unable to think of anything else to say, Darcy got to her feet.

"Don't do any more columns until you hear from me," said Ed, rising. He came over to her. "You're a good writer, Darcy, with good instincts. No matter what happens, keep writing."

Numb, Darcy merely nodded, feeling as if a giant meteor had just shattered her world.

Later, sitting in Austin's office, she let the tears she'd been fighting roll down her cheeks. "You know how important writing this column is to me, Austin. It's a tribute to Nick."

"And to others," Austin gently reminded her.

"I can't work full-time at the paper. I owe it to my sisters to do my share to meet Uncle Gavin's challenge. You know that."

"Of course. Look, maybe Ed will change his mind, find someone else to take over for Laney."

Darcy gave Austin a challenging look. "And if he doesn't?"

"Publish them yourself," said Austin.

"Me? How?"

Austin gave her a thoughtful look. "How about self-publishing a small, gift book about angels? The wife of one of my fellow graduate students has published a few books of her own. Maybe she could help you."

Darcy sat back in her chair feeling as if she'd been hit broadside by a large, rolling rock. *Could I do something like this*?

Austin chuckled. "I can see your brain churning. It's something to think about. Be sure you have rights to the columns you've written, and go from there."

"I'll have to check, but I think I do have the rights. Blackie Gatto made sure the paper got exclusive rights for only a short period of time. So, after that, they're mine. Right?"

"Sounds like it," said Austin.

Darcy's heart pounded with possibility. "Honestly, do you think I could pull off something like this?"

Austin grinned at her with such affection Darcy's eyes filled. "I think you can do most anything you decide to do."

In a rush of gratitude, Darcy rose from her chair and swept Austin in an embrace. "I love you so much, Austin!"

Laughing, he drew her down onto his lap and wrapped his arms around her. "Love you too, Darcy."

A knock on the door caused Darcy to spring to her feet. Austin rose beside her and went to answer the door.

"Yes?"

"Your next patient is here," said Lucy, the gray-haired receptionist everyone loved. She gave them a look of amusement and closed the door behind her.

Austin turned to Darcy. "Guess I'd better get back to work. We'll talk more tonight."

"Okay," said Darcy. "But I like your idea. This book wouldn't be a novel, but it's a beginning."

She drove back to the hotel full of excitement. She was doing the right thing by refusing to work full-time for the newspaper. She and her sisters had a challenge to meet, and she would do nothing to take away from that. And now she had the possibility of doing something on her own that wouldn't be on anyone else's schedule.

A tingle of excitement threaded through her.

CHAPTER TWENTY-THREE

SHEENA

When Sheena entered Brian's hospital room, she was pleased to see Maggie O'Neill sitting beside his chair, helping him with his lunch. "Having a nice meal?" she asked Brian, smiling at them both.

"Only because Maggie brought me some decent food," he complained.

Maggie helped him take a bite of a grouper sandwich and turned to Sheena. "We're a little grumpy because some of the exercises were painful. But Brian knows he has to keep up with them if he's going to get out of here."

"Yeah, I've gotta get back to work. When is Tony coming to see me?" said Brian. "I need to talk to him again."

"He promised to visit you after work tonight. In the meantime, he had me type up a progress report on each of the projects for you so you wouldn't worry."

Maggie stood. "Sheena? As long as you're here, do you mind finishing up with Brian? We're running a little late today, and I need to get back to the restaurant. Rocky's picking me up right about now."

"I don't mind at all. Sally's handling the registration desk."

Maggie smiled. "That's real nice of you, letting Sally do that for you. She's so happy about it."

"We're thrilled she's willing to do it. She's doing a good job, too."

Maggie gave Brian a pat on the back. "See you tomorrow.

Keep up the good work, hear?"

He rolled his eyes and nodded dutifully. "God! I can't wait to get out of here."

Maggie left, and Sheena took over helping Brian with his sandwich. "How much longer until you can feed yourself?"

"I can do some things for myself now, but I still have to call the nurses to help me with other stuff. It's humiliating, but I have no choice."

"Your right arm and elbow, when are you going to be able to use them?

Brian looked away and then back to her, a glum expression on his face. "That's the problem. I'll be able to move that arm soon. In fact, they'll want me to exercise the elbow as soon as possible, so it doesn't stiffen. But for some months I won't be able to pound a hammer or do any heavy lifting like normal. That's what worries me."

Sheena leaned toward him to give him an encouraging pat on the shoulder.

"What is this?" came a voice behind her.

Sheena jerked back and turned to face Jill, who entered the room and hurried over to them.

Jill glared at Sheena. "What were you doing?"

"I'm helping Brian with his lunch," Sheena replied calmly, though her heart had begun to race at the accusation she saw in Jill's eyes.

"It looked like something more than that," Jill said, standing beside Brian. "I'm here now. You Sullivan sisters don't have to be here all the time. Maggie, Brian's mother, and I are handling the situation."

Sheena blinked in surprise. "I'm here on my husband's behalf."

"And that doesn't need to happen. Right, darling? You're going to talk to my cousin."

Brian eyebrows formed an angry V. "I told you I was handling this, Jill." He gave Sheena an apologetic look. "I'm sorry. We'll talk later."

"I'll walk you out," said Jill, moving quickly to Sheena's chair.

Sheena felt she had no choice but to get to her feet and leave the room.

Jill followed her out the door and then held her back. "I'm sorry if I sounded rude, it's just that Brian and I are trying to rebuild our relationship, and every time I turn around, one of you Sullivan sisters is here. I need the three of you to stay away from Brian."

"You do realize Brian is a friend to us, nothing more. And, like it or not, because we're more or less in business, we'll be talking to him from time to time. And that includes my husband, Tony."

Jill's lips narrowed. "That might not be necessary. Brian and I have been talking about a new business plan for him."

Sheena forced a pleasantness to her voice she didn't feel. "No need for us to be involved. Brian and Tony will work out their relationship themselves, I'm sure."

"Maybe not," said Jill. "Now, I'd better get back to my patient."

Sheena was left alone in the hall wondering how Brian could have chosen a girlfriend as controlling as Jill. He was such a nice, easygoing guy on the surface, but she knew how driven he was to succeed in business and how dedicated he'd been to Gavin. Maybe, she thought with dismay, Brian wasn't the nice guy she'd thought. And maybe Tony would be prevented from working with him and getting his plumbing license to set up his own business.

Feeling uncertain about the future, Sheena headed for the elevator and home. Nine months from now, Michael would be out of high school and heading for college. But how, when, and where remained questions she couldn't answer.

Sheena returned to the hotel and went right to the registration office to relieve Sally of desk duty.

The registration desk was empty.

"Sally?"

"Here," Sally called from the back of the office.

Sheena found Sally going through a number of messages that had come through on the fax machine.

"What's going on?" Sheena asked.

"Cyndi Jansen called to tell us she's planning a late-October weekend here at the hotel with four other couples." Sally beamed at her. "The reservations forms are coming in now. Pretty exciting!"

Sheena returned Sally's smile. "Yes. Let's hope more reservations come in. We're down to three couples tonight, only because of our newspaper specials. We've got to get heads in beds."

Sally's smile evaporated. "It *has* been slow. What else can we do?"

Sheena's heart filled with affection for the little woman who'd been through so much. Sally was proving to be a loyal, flexible co-worker who seemed as excited as she whenever a new reservation came in.

"I've come up with a letter to send to the people who've stayed here, thanking them for their visit. Maybe we should send out letters to those who've made reservations, telling them how excited we are to have them stay with us."

Sally nodded her approval. "Good idea. And send them brochures. Building relationships with clients is important. I learned early on in my old business position." A pink blush covered her cheeks. "I still think of those people who lost their money because of my old boss."

"I can't imagine what you've gone through," said Sheena. She'd been surprised when Sally had asked Darcy to tell Regan and her about her past.

Sally's expression brightened. "But now, I'm able to make good use of all my business experience and help you here. That's how I'll make up for any harm I might have unknowingly caused in the past by not following through on my suspicions."

Sheena gave Sally a smile of encouragement, well aware how tortured the woman was because of her past. "We're so happy you're here with us. Let's get to work on that letter."

Later, after Sally left to help in Gracie's restaurant, Sheena thought of all the good her uncle had done in providing a safe place for Sally and the others in his group. If Gavin really were her father, she'd be proud to say so. But that was never going to happen. Gavin and her mother would have announced such a thing if they'd wanted to, thus ruining the family she and her sisters knew as their own. Some family secrets were best left alone, she decided, content to let the issue of him and the gold coin fade away.

Darcy came into the registration office. "Guess what! I'm going to work on a book of my own."

"A novel? How wonderful," said Sheena.

Darcy shook her head. "No, a collection of my angel stories."

"Angel stories? What about the newspaper? You write the stories for it, don't you?"

"Maybe not anymore. The editor, Ed Richardson, wanted me to work full-time at the paper. I told him no, that I had to help here at the hotel."

"Oh, Darcy! I'm sorry." Sheena knew how much writing that column meant to her.

"It may turn out to be a good thing. I've got the best fiancé in the world," Darcy said. "He's the one who's encouraged me to go out on my own. I'll still be interviewing people as I do for the newspaper columns, but each story will be part of my new book." She clasped her hands together. "It's like a dream come true. A little different from what I thought, but a dream of mine all the same. Cool, huh?"

"Very cool," said Sheena. "Who knew the techie you are really wanted to be a writer?"

Darcy grinned. "The Salty Key Inn has brought a lot of challenges and given us a lot of things to think about, huh?"

Sheena laughed softly. "Has it ever!"

Sheena was slipping a veggie casserole into the oven when Tony called.

"Hi, honey! What's up?"

"I'm going to be late for supper. Like I promised Brian, I'll stop by the hospital to see him."

"Okay, no problem. But, Tony, I think you ought to be aware Jill doesn't like the idea of you and Brian working together. I'm not sure what's going on with that, but she's also made it plain the Sullivan sisters are to stay away from Brian."

"I'm not letting someone like her stop me. Brian and I have business to discuss."

"Okay, hon. See you later." As Sheena hung up, she wondered what Brian had in mind. He'd told Jill he was going to handle it. Was the "it" Tony?

She checked her watch. Michael and Meaghan were due home a few minutes ago. Michael had promised to pick up Meaghan after cheerleader practice. She lifted her phone to call him but placed it back down on the counter. Michael didn't need a reminder. He'd be going away to college in less than a year, and it was time for her to back off.

Regan knocked on the door and entered the suite. "Want to share a cup of coffee, or tea, or more?"

Sheena laughed. "I'll fix you coffee, tea, or lemonade, and I'll have a sip of the 'more.'"

"Guess I need to wait for something stronger until after I finish my meds." Regan sat down in a kitchen chair and sighed. "Mo and I are submitting a bid to Arthur Weatherman, but Mo is doing the presentation of it because I don't want Arthur to see me like this."

Sheena gave her sister a steady look. "There's nothing to be ashamed of, Regan. You were in an accident, and the doctor is very optimistic about the scar healing quickly. With a little makeup, you ought to be able to go forward with the pictures and the rest of the presentation."

"I'm not worried about the scar as much as I am about my lip. That's what would keep me from getting the job of spokesperson. And I had a lot of plans on how we could use the money to keep the hotel going."

Unsure of what to say, Sheena nodded and went about fixing their drinks. She'd just handed Regan her lemonade when Meaghan stormed into the room.

"I'm never speaking to my brother again!" Meaghan plopped herself down in a kitchen chair and crossed her arms, looking like a temperamental two-year-old about to explode.

"What's going on?" Sheena said.

"Michael was supposed to pick me up. Instead, he texted me and told me to walk home, that he wasn't going to make it, he was busy with his girlfriend." She let out an angry puff of breath. "I can't wait until I can drive! Then, when he wants a ride, I'll tell him to walk, that I'm too busy even to care."

Sheena exchanged a worried glance with Regan.

"I mean it, Mom! I'm going to get my permit as soon as I can."

Sheena didn't respond. Though Meaghan would soon be able to get a Learners Permit with the arrival of her fifteenth birthday, Sheena was hoping to hold off her daughter for as long as possible. The thought of her chatty, easily distracted daughter driving was scary.

Sheena lifted her phone to call Michael.

He rushed into the room. "Sorry, I'm late."

Meaghan jumped to her feet. "You were supposed to pick me up, Michael!"

"I couldn't get there, all right?" he shouted at her.

"And why couldn't you pick up your sister?" Sheena asked in a deceptively calm voice.

"Because Kaylee and I were watching the end of a movie," Michael said defiantly. "It was good, too."

"I thought you were studying," Sheena said, finding it harder to remain calm when she had the urge to shake him.

"We did study ... for a while," Michael admitted.

"If something like this happens again, Michael, you'll lose privileges with the car," Sheena said.

"Why is everyone so uptight about a short walk for Meaghan?" he said, stomping out of the room.

Meaghan started to go after him, but Sheena held her back. "Dad and I will talk to Michael after your father gets home. Why don't you start studying? Supper has been delayed."

Meaghan let out a noisy sigh, grabbed an apple from the refrigerator, and left the room with her bookbag to go next door, where she bunked in with Regan and Darcy.

Watching her leave, Sheena was eager for the time when they had a real home in which the four of them could live together as a family.

"What's up with Tony?" Regan asked. "How's he doing with Brian's business?"

Sheena took a seat opposite Regan. "He's extra busy, of

course, and construction on all their projects is continuing. But I'm worried about the future for Brian and him. Jill is making noises about Brian not working with Tony."

Regan let out a sigh of disgust. "For Brian's sake, I've tried to be pleasant to Jill, but I've found her difficult. Money, prestige, and control seem so important to her. And I don't think of Brian being that way at all."

"Opposites attract," said Sheena, "but I don't think it's a basis for a good relationship. And, as you say, Jill is difficult. I've tried to explain to her none of us is interested in him in the way she's thinking, but she still doesn't want you, Darcy, or me hanging around him."

"I don't intend to," said Regan. "Look what trouble it got me into."

Sheena nodded. Maybe it was better if they all stayed away.

CHAPTER TWENTY-FOUR

REGAN

Regan awoke and quietly dressed, careful not to disturb Meaghan sleeping in the twin bed next to hers. Though it was still dark, Regan was too restless to lie in bed, unable to sleep. Today, Mo was meeting with Arthur Weatherman to present their plans for renovating his restaurants.

Thinking of the past when she'd been told in subtle and not so subtle ways she wasn't smart, Regan's eyes moistened. Early on, drawing and painting had been an outlet for her. As she went through school, she'd hoped to be able to use her abilities in that area to study interior decorating, which she found exciting. And when she'd learned about the Rhode Island School of Design, it all fell into place in her mind. But schoolwork and her inability to test well destroyed that dream for her.

Coming to the Salty Key Inn had changed everything. With the possibility of doing some significant work with Mo, she couldn't stop thinking of the presentation. She wanted to be someone who was respected for the ideas she had in her head but couldn't express well on paper.

She slipped out of the room, made herself a cup of coffee, and took a seat on the patio outside. Her thoughts flew to Uncle Gavin's private message to her: "Beauty is in the eyes of the beholder." Had he known how much she liked to make things beautiful? Or was it something about her appearance, which was now marred. He apparently knew a lot more about her and her sisters than they ever suspected.

Regan heard the whisper of the sliding glass door behind her and turned. Holding a cup of coffee in her hand, Darcy gave her a sleepy smile and sat in the chair next to her.

"Couldn't sleep?" Regan said.

Darcy shook her head. "No. I got to thinking about the wedding and realized how much I have to do. And, Regan, I haven't told you about my new idea for a book."

"A novel?"

"No, something a little smaller." Darcy launched into a bubbly description of the gift book on angels she hoped to publish.

Listening to her, Regan's admiration for her sister grew. Like all of them, Darcy was dealing with a lot of changes in her life—good changes.

"It sounds great, Darcy," said Regan. "Mom would be proud of you for doing something like this."

"You think so? I stayed at a job I didn't like because she told me she was proud of the job I had. Funny, huh?"

They sipped their hot coffee in silence, watching the sun come up.

It was fascinating and very reassuring to Regan to think each new day brought light to the world, representing hope to her. Observing the sky brighten and the first signs of the rising sun forming fingers of gold that beckoned to her, Regan decided to stop worrying about the future and to live each day well. That's what it was all about, wasn't it?

She got up and faced Darcy. "Want to take a walk on the beach?"

"Sure," said Darcy. "It'll give me more time to think. It should be a busy day. We have four couples coming in today."

"And three more tomorrow," said Regan.

"I sure hope business will pick up soon," said Darcy. "Too

bad we don't have a small conference area."

"Or a business center, or a lot of other things," Regan added. "That's the hard part of this challenge—trying to be competitive with other properties when we're barely able to offer the basics."

"I'm sure Uncle Gavin had a reason for doing it this way."

"Maybe to give us time to decide what kind of hotel this would be," said Regan. "I think he'd be pleased with our logo, our tagline, and our idea of making it the kind of family place it once was."

Darcy smiled. "The Salty Key Inn—a Quiet Treasure" does have a nice ring to it. Nothing stuffy, just the kind of vacation spot everyone can enjoy."

"The hotel will keep getting better and better if we have the chance to make it the way we want."

"Yes, but that won't happen for some time," said Darcy with a note of frustration. "As Sheena keeps telling us, we can't lose focus. Even though you and I have plans for after the first of the year, we have to concentrate on the hotel."

"Right," said Regan. "Let's hurry to the beach. I'm on the early shift at the registration desk."

As Regan stepped onto the cool, white sand, she marveled at those people already there. Some were carrying flashlights looking for shells; others jogged along the water's edge. She wondered what it would be like to be entirely alone on the beach.

Without speaking, Regan and Darcy headed south, walking side by side companionably. In their younger years, they'd always been at odds—Darcy resentful of the attention she had to pay to Regan when their mother was sick, and Regan hurt because her sister didn't want to be with her. As adults, the two of them had grown close, bonding over the fact that Sheena, as the oldest, was sometimes bossy, and they'd both resented her abruptly leaving the family to get married. Only now did they know how much Sheena had wanted to be a regular college student without the care of their family or her own.

Regan's thoughts were still on Sheena and her family when she turned to Darcy. "Sheena told me she's concerned about Jill's objections to Brian's business and Tony's role in it."

"She told me the same thing," Darcy said. "Personally, I think Brian is making a big mistake in getting together with Jill again. But I can see why he might be attracted to her. She's beautiful and successful."

Regan swallowed hard. Jill Jackson was everything Darcy said. Of course, Brian would be intrigued. She imagined they'd get married and have beautiful babies together.

"You all right?" Darcy asked.

Regan blinked in surprise, realizing she'd stopped walking. "I'm fine." She checked the time on her cell. "But we'd better head back. As we said, it's going to be a busy day."

They'd just reached the boardwalk leading to the road and the Salty Key Inn when a ping on Regan's phone caught her attention. She glanced at the message that had just come in and gasped.

The text read: "I'm sick as a dog. You have to make the presentation today. Sorry. Mo"

Regan stood in front of the mirror in her bathroom and let out a quivery sigh. The makeup she'd applied didn't hide the hideous red scar on her face nor the scabs on her cheeks. And her lip looked and acted as if she'd had way too many shots of novocaine at the dentist's office.

Drawing herself up, she took a last pull of her brush through her long, dark hair and set the brush down. She was fighting for a future she wanted. Nothing was going to stop her.

Regan checked the clock. Five minutes to ten. She was tempted to sneak in another cup of coffee but decided she was too tense even to contemplate adding more caffeine to her jangling nerves.

Sheena poked her head into the suite. "Good luck with your presentation. You'll do just fine."

"Thanks." Regan brushed an imaginary crumb off her floral dress, grabbed the keys to Gertie Sheena offered her, and waved goodbye.

Regan drove into St. Petersburg and into the parking garage near Arthur Weatherman's headquarters, which was in the same building as Blackie Gatto's office.

Standing in front of the building, Regan told herself she could do this, that in some respects it would be easier than applying for a regular job, something she'd always dreaded. She reminded herself she and Mo had worked on this together, and she knew how talented he was.

Gripping the portfolio file closer to her chest, she walked into the vestibule and took the elevator to the top floor. As she stepped off the elevator, the glass door of Arthur's offices offered her a view inside to a reception area. Relieved the décor was classic in nature, Regan entered the office and spoke to the receptionist.

"Regan Sullivan to see Arthur Weatherman." Her voice faltered, but she continued. "He's expecting me."

The receptionist's eyes widened as she studied Regan's face, and then she nodded. "Yes. Please have a seat. I'll let him know you're here."

Moments later, Arthur came walking toward her.

Regan gathered herself together and got to her feet.

"My! What happened to you?" Arthur said, smiling as he held out a hand.

Fingers cold, she took it. "A motorcycle accident."

He looked her up and down. "No broken bones?"

She forced a smile and tried for a little levity. "No, I left that up to Brian Harwood who was driving the bike."

"I see," Arthur said. "I got your message Moses Greene was unable to make the presentation. I'm glad you came in his stead because we're getting ready to make a decision, and I didn't want you to lose the opportunity."

He led her into a sumptuous office that screamed of money. Regan admired the large, designer carpet on the wooden floor, the leather chairs, and the clean-lined, mahogany desk that was neither old-fashioned nor modern.

Arthur bobbed his head toward the long table to one side of the office. "You can use that to display any drawings you have. But first, we'll want to hear your ideas. My wife is someone I trust to help me." At a knock on the door, he smiled. "Here she is now."

A tall, attractive brunette much younger than Arthur entered the room. She gave Regan a cool smile and took the seat Arthur indicated.

He walked over to her side. "Margretta, darling. This is Regan Sullivan. Her partner, Moses Greene, could not attend. Regan, my wife, Margretta Weatherman."

"Pleased to meet you." Wishing her fingers were drier, warmer, Regan shook Margretta's hand.

Arthur sat down at his desk. "Okay, Regan, let's hear it."

Regan drew a deep breath. "When Mo and I first studied your restaurants, we remarked on how similar they were in décor, and yet their menus were quite different. Even though they all feature seafood, we decided to emphasize their differences with color and décor. For the restaurant that features a lobster tank and a number of lobster offerings, we've designed a mural featuring New England landmarks and making the color theme compatible by using red, white and blue."

"Okay," said Arthur.

"We thought that instead of the public's thinking, if they ate in just one of your restaurants they needn't go to another one, with more differentiation between the restaurants, they might be attracted to trying all of them."

Arthur and Margretta exchanged silent glances.

"Okay, let's see what you've got. You made the guest room décor at the Salty Key Inn simple but tasteful. I hope you've done the same with these."

Regan let out the breath she'd been holding. "I think you'll be pleased. No geegaws, just interesting things typical of the areas from which your specialties come."

She went over to the table, opened the portfolio box, and laid out the drawings Mo had worked so hard to create.

"As you can see, the difference between the New England style and that of Florida is very distinctive even with color choices for the décor."

Margretta and Arthur waited until she stepped aside, and then they studied each one carefully.

"You might notice we didn't plan on your replacing all the furniture. Booths and chair seats can be recovered quite easily and inexpensively. Mo knows of someone who can do that kind of work for us. We, of course, can provide you with any furnishings you require, but we're willing to work with the old as well. That's why we've come up with a couple of different financial proposals."

"That's rare," said Margretta in an undertone to her husband.

Arthur smiled at his wife. "I'll show you what Regan has done with the hotel sometime. Very clever."

Regan waited patiently while Arthur and Margretta quietly discussed the different drawings. Finally, they turned to her.

"We like what you and Mo have done, and after reviewing the financials and discussing this with others, we'll get back to you with a decision," said Arthur. "As for the other piece of business we discussed earlier, Regan, I'll have to get back to you on that, as well."

"Of course. Thank you very much for the opportunities," Regan said, carefully masking her feelings as she packed up the drawings to leave behind with the Weathermans. She was elated to think she and Mo might win the bid for the renovation work and depressed over most likely losing the contract to become spokesperson.

CHAPTER TWENTY-FIVE

REGAN

Regan was leaving the parking garage when her cell phone rang. She grabbed it from the seat next to her and clicked onto the call. "Hello?"

"Hi, Regan. This is Maggie O'Neill. I need you to do a favor for me. I'm supposed to help Brian with his lunch today, and I can't leave Gracie's. Your sisters are in a meeting and suggested I call you. Will you please go to the hospital and help him?"

"Is ... is that going to be okay with Jill?" Regan said through a throat gone dry. The word was none of the Sullivan sisters were to be there.

"Jill? Why should it matter to her?" said Maggie.

"I ... really don't know," Regan replied. "Brian and I are just friends."

"I see. Well, I need you to do this for me. Will you?"

"Okay," Regan said reluctantly. "I know you wouldn't ask if you didn't need me."

"Thanks. Gotta go. We're really busy."

Maggie hung up, leaving Regan no choice but to follow through. She turned the car toward Tampa, hoping her being with Brian wouldn't be an issue for either of them.

At the hospital, Regan made her way to Brian's room, reminding herself friends helped each other without judging their actions, and if Brian wanted to get back together with someone like Jill, that was his business, not hers.

Brian's door was half-open as Regan approached it. She heard voices and paused, not wanting to interrupt.

"Jill, I told you I'd take care of the situation. That didn't mean I'd tell Tony he couldn't work for me. It meant quite the opposite."

Jill's voice, sounding as if it were on a speaker phone, came through in sharp, little bites. "Honestly, Brian, you know you can make more money with the deal I've set up for you in the North Carolina mountains. A whole development all for you. No hangers-on, like Tony."

Overhearing this, Regan felt as if her blood had turned to ice. Tony was a hard worker who'd held Brian's small company together while he was recuperating. Didn't Jill understand that? Silently, Regan waited for a response from Brian.

"I know you mean well, but I'm proud of the business I'm building here in Florida, and I trust Tony Morelli to step in while I'm laid up."

"But this deal I'm talking about could be so much more than that," said Jill. "Honestly, Brian, I'm better at this business stuff than you'll ever be. How about trusting me?"

Brian's words came with calm firmness. "Trust is a two-way street. I thought you knew that."

Outside his room, Regan wasn't sure if she should tiptoe away or move forward.

"Look," said Brian. "Maggie should be here any minute. I'd better get off the phone."

"It's not over, Brian. Somehow, I'll knock some sense into your head. Have a good lunch. Talk to you later."

During the silence that followed, Regan knocked on his door and entered.

The bright smile that crossed his face warmed her insides. "I'm substituting for Maggie today. Hope you don't mind."

"Mind? I love it," he said so smoothly Regan suddenly felt shy.

He waved her over to the chair beside him with a bob of his head. "I've waited to order. Help me choose what to eat."

She walked over to the bedside table and picked up the menu the hospital offered.

"How about a sandwich? Or they have a nice selection of salads," she said, reading aloud some of the items.

"Whichever is hardest to eat," he joked. "Then, you'll really have to help me."

She laughed. "Don't worry. Whatever you choose, I'm here for you. I know what a good job Maggie does, and I'll try my best to do as well."

Brian chose a turkey sandwich, chips, and ice cream.

Regan picked up the phone and ordered the lunch for him.

"Thanks." His eyes sparkled. "Having you here makes me feel better. It gets pretty exhausting being with nurses and aides who make me do all kinds of things I don't like."

"Ah, having a little trouble with rehab?" she teased, playing along.

His expression became somber. "I hate having to depend on other people to do things for me."

"I can imagine," she said sympathetically. "In time, you'll be back to your old self."

"That's just it. It might take a couple of months or even more. Simple things like fixing the pillow are things I can't easily do. And I won't go into some of the other stuff I can't do for myself."

"Do you need your pillow fixed now?" Regan asked, noticing it was askew. She reached for the pillow. "Sit up for a moment, and I'll adjust it however you want."

Brian pulled away from the head of the bed that had been raised to give him support.

Regan leaned over and tucked the pillow behind him. "This okay?"

Brian turned his head and looked up at her.

Their eyes met, and Regan had the weird sensation all sound around them faded, along with their surroundings.

"Oh my God!"

The shrill voice that shattered the silence caused Regan to stumble away from the bed.

Jill marched toward them with an expression so fierce, Regan raised her hands to defend herself. "What are you doing here?" Jill demanded of Regan.

"I'm substituting for Maggie. She asked me to help with Brian's lunch. Gracie's became so busy she couldn't leave." Regan was angry at herself for sounding so frightened. She was merely helping a couple of friends. Right?

Jill let out a snort of disgust.

"If you'd like to take over, I can leave," Regan said, unwilling to get into a confrontation with a person she didn't even like. It would be destructive for everyone.

"I can't stay," said Jill. "I was on my way to a meeting and thought I'd take a few minutes to drop these brochures off to Brian." She turned to him. "Here, darling. Here's what I'm talking about. This is a big deal. Don't let it slip by."

Regan moved to the window and stared out, giving Jill and Brian a moment to themselves.

At the sound of heels pounding the floor, Regan turned. Jill was already walking out the door.

Regan and Brian exchanged glances.

"Jill and I have a few things to get straight," Brian said tersely.

Regan remained quiet as she moved to greet the aide

bringing Brian's lunch.

"Thank you," she said, taking the tray from the aide and placing it on the overbed table next to Brian's bed.

"Would you rather eat sitting in a chair?" she asked him.

He shook his head. "If you don't mind, I'm really tired from this morning's workouts."

"Okay. It's no problem to eat right here." She stood by the bed and, taking a knife, carefully cut his sandwich into bite-size pieces.

"Making it easy for me, huh?" Brian said before accepting a piece of the sandwich.

Regan smiled. Watching his jaw move as he chewed, she felt a little uneasy. She stared at the stubble on his chin, the way his Adam's Apple bobbed in his throat as he swallowed and felt an unexpected sense of desire.

His gaze landed on her.

Heat rose to her cheeks as his eyes remained on her. "Why are you staring?"

"I'm waiting for you to give me another bite," he said, amused.

As her cheeks flared with even more heat, she fought for control. "I'm sorry. I got lost in thought."

His knowing grin was playful. "I hope they were good thoughts."

Flustered, she didn't answer, but simply lifted another bite of the sandwich to his lips.

She looked away as he chewed, telling herself her reaction to him was ridiculous. He was simply eating, she wasn't about to get involved with him, and he'd made it clear he was interested in someone else.

"Regan?"

She turned around.

"How about some potato chips?"

She grabbed a couple and lifted them to his mouth.

As he took them in, his warm, soft lips touched her hand. She jumped at the jolt of energy and pulled away.

"Sorry. Did I bite you?" Brian asked with obvious concern.

"No, no," she quickly answered. "Ready for another piece of sandwich?"

He nodded and worked quickly to finish the sandwich.

"Ice cream?" she said when he'd swallowed the last bite of turkey.

"Sounds good. Chocolate is still my favorite."

Regan scooped up a spoonful of the chocolate treat and lifted the spoon to his mouth.

Another frisson of desire swept through her as she watched him take the spoon in his mouth. His lips seemed capable of so many things.

With another spoonful, she imagined what it might be like to feed a baby. One of his. And then, unbidden, an image of a baby that was theirs flashed through her mind.

She dropped the spoon on the table. It bounced off the table to the floor with a clanging sound that sent her scrambling.

"I'm so sorry. I'll wash it off and be right back."

As if he knew her reaction to him, he chuckled softly, making her wish she could simply fly away.

When she returned to his bedside, he smiled at her. "I really appreciate having you here with me, Regan, even though I don't like having you see me like this."

"I understand. I don't like having you see me like this."

"What do you mean? Honey, you're still beautiful. Nothing can change that," he said softly.

She stared at him, stunned by the affection she heard in his voice.

"My God! You don't believe me? Oh, Regan. Too bad we

never could get together. We could have had so much fun."

Regan nodded numbly, pushing away the feeling of wanting to cry.

CHAPTER TWENTY-SIX

SHEENA

When she could wait no longer, Sheena went ahead and fed the kids supper. She'd tried to reach Tony on his cell and was forced to leave him a message. It brought back memories of all the times in Boston when she and the children ate without him because he was tied up with his business. She'd enjoyed his more regular hours in Florida.

"Mom? I've been thinking about my birthday," said Meaghan. "Can I invite a bunch of my new friends here? We could use one of the empty guest rooms for the party and swim in the pool."

"Who are you talking about? Girls from the cheerleading squad?" Sheena asked, taking a bite of the casserole.

Meaghan paused. "And some boys."

"She means Rob Wickham," scoffed Michael. "Rob is part of the younger football group who think they're better than they are. 'Course, the cheerleaders don't care."

"Jealous?" said Meaghan, giving her brother the stink eye.

"What do I have to be jealous about?" Michael retorted. "I've got Kaylee."

"You both better be thinking about schoolwork, not all your social activities," Sheena warned them. "The next year or so will fly by, and then it will be too late to make up for bad grades. Colleges won't want to hear you cared more about having fun than learning."

"Geez, Mom. Lay off it. We're supposed to be able to enjoy

ourselves too," said Michael. "Besides, if you hadn't moved us here, I would never have met Kaylee."

Sheena gave him a steady stare. "Are you trying to blame me for possible bad grades?"

Michael's face turned red, and then he laughed. "Guess not."

Shaking her head, Sheena joined in the laughter. *Teenage boys!*

"Can I, Mom?" Meaghan said.

"Have the birthday party here?" Sheena said. "Let me talk it over with my sisters, and I'll get back to you. We have a couple of weeks before it happens."

"Well, I kinda told everyone about it already," said Meaghan. "Please don't make it seem as if I lied."

Sheena's frustration bubbled over. "Next time, ask first, Meaghan. This is a place of business. We're working toward having more and more rooms filled."

"I know," said Meaghan contritely. "I just wanted my new friends to like me."

"Having parties won't make your friends like you more, Meaghan. It's how you treat them every day that matters."

Michael groaned. "You sound like a Sunday School teacher."

Sheena arched her eyebrows at him. "It's important to talk about things like this. I hope you treat your friends well. How are you and Jésus getting along at football practice?"

"He and I are cool," said Michael.

"Good," said Sheena. At the sound of a call on her cell, she jumped up from the table to answer it. *Tony.*

"Hi, honey! What's up?" Sheena said.

"We've got to talk. I'm on my way home, but maybe there's somewhere we can go to talk privately."

Sheena's heart pounded. "Everything all right?"

"I don't know. I'll be home soon."

After Tony ate a quick, quiet meal, he stood. "Where can we go to have some privacy?"

"We can drive down to the public parking lot at the beach. C'mon, I'll drive. I'm anxious to talk about whatever is bothering you."

He nodded. "Okay, I'll tell the kids, and then let's go."

Outside, Sheena got behind the wheel of her VW Beetle convertible and waited for Tony to get settled in the passenger seat.

"Liking the car?" Tony said, patting the dashboard.

Sheena smiled. "I love it! I still can't believe you bought it for me."

He grinned. "Guess the old guy can surprise you from time to time, huh?"

Sheena leaned over and kissed his cheek. "I love that you do."

"I hope so," Tony said enigmatically.

She gave him a questioning look.

"Let's get parked, and I'll tell you all about it," said Tony.

Sheena pulled into the parking area a half mile down the road and parked her car in an empty space in the corner of the lot.

Turning to him, she said, "Okay. Now, spill."

He let out a long breath. "At the hospital, I gave Brian an update on our projects and gave him a list of all the things we need to follow-up on."

"And he was pleased?"

Tony's brow creased. He stared at her. "What's not to be pleased about? I've run a company before; I can do it again."

"But?"

"But he went on to tell me Jill wants him out of the business in Florida and into a special project in North Carolina—a project that would mean his own, very profitable business set up by friends of hers, wealthy investors."

"And he's going to do this?" Sheena's heart was pounding so hard she almost couldn't breathe. Brian was an important link to her and her sisters' completing the hotel.

Tony shook his head. "No, he doesn't want to move to the mountains. He wants to stay right here. But he knows he can't run the business alone anymore, and he wants me to buy into it."

"Buy into it? How? What money we have is earmarked for a sizeable down payment on the house we intend to build."

Tony simply stared at her.

The reality of the situation hit her like a blow to her heart. "Are you saying if you buy into the business, we can't have our house?"

He drew a deep breath and let it out slowly. "That's the choice we face."

"I see," said Sheena, feeling sick to her stomach. She was more worried about building income in the hotel than she'd let anyone know, and the idea of not meeting Uncle Gavin's challenge was a real concern. And if that happened, would they ever have a home of their own?

Sheena felt the sting of tears.

"I'll give you some time to think about it," said Tony. "In the meantime, I'll work the numbers. But, Sheena, it's an opportunity of a lifetime to become part of this growing business. Brian has a silent partner who helped fund his startup company, but it would be Brian and me running it together. And even if the business goes through slow periods, this would still give me time to meet the criteria for getting my Florida plumbing license."

"I understand you really want this, but I need time to think it over," Sheena said, wishing this had never happened. She wanted to be generous with Tony, but she hated the idea of losing the house she'd already begun decorating in her mind.

The next morning, as soon as the kids got off to school, Sheena hurried down to the beach. She didn't want to talk to her sisters or anyone else until she had time to mull over Tony's proposition. She had to be realistic about the future.

The morning sun was warming the sand under her toes when she stepped onto the broad expanse of white. She walked to the water's edge and lifted her arms to the sky and drew in several deep, calming breaths.

The usual sounds of the surf greeting the sand and pulling away met her ears in a steady rhythm that calmed her racing thoughts. All night long, "what ifs" had played a crazy game of tag in her mind. What if they didn't meet the challenge, what would happen to her family, her sisters, and the hotel? What if Tony invested money in the business and it failed? What if they couldn't afford to send their children to college? On and on, her thoughts had whirled.

Sheena drew in more deep breaths, inhaling the salty tang of the air and listening to the seagulls crying as they circled, climbing through the air and swooping down as if to greet the rolling water beneath them with a kiss.

Apprehension interfered with her normal willingness to let nature take its course. The past few months represented so many healthy changes for her. How could she give up the notion of all that it might bring to her and her family? And was this another instance of her putting everyone else first? She thought of all she'd put her family through by moving to Florida and knew her last question wasn't fair.

As she stood gazing out at the waves rolling into the shore, a calm came over her. Tony was an honest, hard-working man. Gavin had trusted Brian to assist them in meeting their goal. He'd proved to be a constant source of guidance and a huge help in completing large tasks and small. Maybe, she thought, it was time to put her faith in them and, more importantly, in her sisters. They all could meet their goals by working together.

A nasty thought intruded. *And if they didn't?*

We'd survive. Together.

Feeling much better, Sheena ran along the beach, holding her arms out, laughing. When she came to a stop, she turned around and headed home.

CHAPTER TWENTY-SEVEN

DARCY

Darcy was heading for Gracie's when she saw Sheena walking up to the hotel from the beach. She waited for Sheena to get closer and called to her. "Want to have breakfast with me? Regan's working the desk."

Approaching her, Sheena smiled. "I had breakfast a while ago, but I'll sit with you and have a cup of coffee."

They went inside the restaurant and over to their favorite corner table. Maggie came over to their table. "Coffee?" Without waiting for an answer, she poured coffee into their cups and stood by silently, well aware of their usual wishes. "What else?"

"Nothing else for me," Sheena said.

"I'll have a poached egg on toast," said Darcy.

"Sure thing." Maggie started to walk away and came back to them. "Can you do me a favor and ask Regan if she'll do lunch duty for Brian at the hospital?"

"I'll ask her," said Darcy. "Is everything all right?"

Maggie nodded. "I just need her to help me. Bebe's taking a day off, and we all have to pitch in here."

As Maggie left the table, Darcy and Sheena exchanged worried looks.

"I don't know how this small staff can continue handling all their business," said Sheena.

"I agree," said Darcy. "They've added some new people, but it still doesn't seem like a big enough staff to me."

"I'll see if I can talk to Gracie about it."

"Careful," said Darcy. "Gracie runs this restaurant like the captain of a ship, and I wouldn't want to upset her."

"Believe me, I'm very careful around her."

Darcy set down her coffee cup. "Do you think she'd mind if I took advantage of Bebe's being away from the kitchen to try and set up an interview with her for my new book? Bebe and Maggie are the two people in the group I know the least about."

Sheena waggled a finger at her. "Remember, Gavin's people are very private about their past."

"I respect that," Darcy said. "I really do. Maybe, after breakfast, I'll see if I can find Bebe. Now that I've decided to do a book on my own, I can't let any opportunity for an interview pass me by."

Sheena sipped her coffee silently.

"Anything wrong?" Darcy said. "You're awfully quiet."

"I just have a lot on my mind. Also, Meaghan's birthday is coming up. She wants to have a boy/girl party here at the hotel, using the pool and an unoccupied guest room. What do you think?"

Darcy almost choked on the sip of coffee she'd just taken. "Boy/girl party? Guest room?"

Sheena held up a hand. "Not that kind of party. Meaghan thinks being fifteen will allow her a lot of freedom, but you know I'm going to keep a careful eye on her. It seems she has a crush named Rob, and she wanted to impress her new friends by asking them here."

Darcy took a sip of her coffee, letting several thoughts settle inside her as Maggie placed the breakfast she'd ordered in front of her. She'd kept her promise to Meaghan not to say anything about her boyfriend, but now, Darcy wondered if she should've mentioned it to Sheena.

Sheena took a deep breath. "I saw Meaghan give her boyfriend a kiss after they got off the school bus. It seemed rather innocent, but still ..."

"Hey, don't worry about it. Let's set up a girl time—the four of us—and talk casually about things like dating and drugs and all that stuff," said Darcy.

Sheena's expression brightened. "That would be nice. I told Meaghan I'd have to talk to you and Regan about having the party at the hotel. We could talk about the party and then move into a deeper conversation."

"Meaghan's a beautiful girl who's noticed how the boys react to her. I'm glad I'm not her mother."

"Or her father," said Sheena glumly. "It would kill Tony if she did anything stupid."

"All teenagers are a little stupid from time to time," Darcy said, thinking of her own past. "I can't imagine what it will be like going through teen years with a child when Austin and I haven't even had a baby yet."

"You've talked about having a family?" said Sheena.

"Oh yes." Warmth filled Darcy. "Austin says he wants a lot of kids. But we've agreed to start with one or two and take it from there."

Sheena smiled. "Austin is going to make a great dad. I can tell."

Darcy studied her sister, uncomfortable with the need to know. "What about me? Do you think I'll make a good mother?"

Sheena's eyes widened. "Why wouldn't you?"

"Because of Mom and how she left so many things up to you and me. I wasn't always nice when I was babysitting Regan."

Sheena gave her a squeeze on the hand. "Darcy, you were just a kid acting like kids do. I've read your columns and have learned what kind of a woman you are. You'll be a great mother."

Darcy felt a giddy laugh bubble up out of her. "I think Austin and I are going to make adorable babies. He's such a cutie himself."

Sheena chuckled. "Spoken like a woman in love."

They shared smiles, and then Sheena rose. "I've got to go. I have an errand I need to tend to."

Alone, Darcy quickly finished her breakfast and headed up to the second floor of the building, where all eight of Gavin's people had small, private apartments.

Bebe was a large woman who worked by Gracie's side in the kitchen. It wasn't that she was unfriendly, Darcy thought. Bebe was just very self-contained. Even among the group of her close friends, Bebe was mostly quiet. But if Darcy came into Gracie's before it officially opened in the morning, Bebe was the one who hurried to her, offering to make her breakfast.

Upstairs, it was quiet. The rest of the people on the floor were either working in Gracie's or, in Rocky's case, most likely doing some handyman's work around the hotel.

Darcy moved quietly along the hallway until she came to a door marked "Bebe." She knocked on the door, hoping Bebe wouldn't be annoyed by the intrusion. She waited for several seconds and then knocked again. This time, Darcy heard the shuffling of feet, and moments later, Bebe opened the door.

At the sight of Darcy, Bebe's eyes widened. "Hi! Did Gracie send for me?"

"No," Darcy said. "I'm wondering if you could do me a big favor. You know I've been writing newspaper columns, right?"

Bebe nodded. "I've read them all. They're so sweet."

"Well, now I'm writing stories for a book I'm going to publish. Most everyone else in the group here has given me an interview, and I'm wondering if I can talk to you."

Bebe's eyes grew round. "Me? Whatever for? I'm a nobody."

Sympathy welled inside Darcy. "Oh, but that's not true. You're a very important part of the group and in particular to my sisters and me. Gavin would never have brought you here if you weren't someone he respected."

Bebe's blue eyes filled. "Well, my land! I never thought of myself that way." Her voice held a trace of southern drawl.

"Can we talk a little?" asked Darcy, more curious than ever. "Everyone has a story to tell."

Bebe shook her head so fast her full cheeks shook. "My story isn't a pretty one."

Darcy hesitated and then said, "Maybe that's a good reason to tell it. I won't use your name or give any private information away without your permission. I promise."

Bebe stilled.

"And you can stop me anytime," Darcy quickly added.

Bebe let out a long breath. "Okay, come on in. I guess it won't hurt. He's long since dead."

Darcy let the sentence go, but she wondered about the "he" Bebe was talking about.

Bebe's apartment was small but tidy. A queen bed, bureau, and night stand took up half the room. The living area held a large lounge chair, a smaller, overstuffed chair facing it, a coffee table between them, and a couple of standing lamps, along with a large television. A ceiling fan rotated slowly above them, moving the air-conditioned air comfortably.

"Sit down, please," said Bebe, offering Darcy the smaller chair.

Darcy took a seat and waited for Bebe to heft her considerable bulk into the lounge chair opposite her.

"What do you want to know?" asked Bebe. "My real name

is Bertha Baker, as you already know." She held up a hand. "Don't even ask how many times I've been teased by that name, especially because I'm a baker."

"I can only imagine," Darcy said with a little chuckle. She leaned forward. "I didn't know my uncle well. He and my father were, let's say, not very close. Finding out more about the people he liked allows me to get to know him better. How did you and my uncle meet?"

"At one of those meetings where everyone introduces themselves with a reason for being there. In my case, it was AA."

Darcy nodded. "That makes sense. I know about some of Uncle Gavin's troubles."

"Yes, he was very open about the things he'd been struggling with—his son and all. At one of the meetings, I brought in some brownies I'd baked. Gavin made a point of thanking me. From then on, whenever I could, I'd bring him a treat. He had a big sweet tooth and loved everything I made. Over time, we became friends. When Gavin learned why I'd struggled so many years with alcohol and food, he was furious. He promised me I'd never have to be afraid again, he knew of a woman who was going to open a restaurant, and he'd make sure I not only got a job with her but I'd have a safe place to live."

Bebe's composure evaporated. She lowered her head into her hands and sobbed.

Darcy stared at Bebe helplessly, not knowing whether to go to her or give her the privacy she always seemed to want. After a few moments, Darcy rose and wrapped an arm around Bebe's shaking shoulders.

"I'm sorry," said Darcy, not understanding what had happened. She patted Bebe's back and waited for her to calm down.

After Bebe quieted, she looked up at Darcy with red-rimmed eyes. "I'm sorry. I didn't mean to break down like this. I know it's good for me to talk about it, but it brings back so many memories. All of them bad."

Shaken, Darcy said, "I didn't mean to make you feel this way. We can stop right now."

Bebe shook her head with quiet determination. "No, I want to tell you about it. Maybe it can help someone else."

Darcy took a seat again in the chair facing Bebe and decided to let Bebe talk as much or as little as she wanted.

Bebe dabbed at her eyes with a tissue, took a drink of the water from the glass at her side, and began. "As a child, for as long as I could remember, my father abused me. Like all abusers, he told me I could never tell anyone, especially my mother. It wasn't until I was in high school that I told my high school counselor what had gone on. She's the one who got me some help."

"What happened to your father?" Darcy said.

Bebe's laugh was bitter. "When news came out, he was fired from his job. Soon after, he had a heart attack and died. My mother blamed everything on me, of course, and I left home at sixteen. By then, I was very overweight and used to being bullied. I drifted for a while, working in restaurant kitchens, traveling the country, using alcohol and food to soothe myself. Over time, I learned that, by binge eating from an early age, I'd hoped to make myself so unattractive I'd be safe from my father. Still, I kept drinking and eating until I went to AA. There, I had so many friends reach out to me I couldn't disappoint them or myself by continuing with the booze."

Darcy winced at the pain etched on Bebe's face.

Bebe's expression softened. "It was a miracle, really, this reaching out to others."

Darcy felt a lump form in her throat. "And Uncle Gavin was

one of them."

"The best," said Bebe. "He's someone you can be proud of. He always listened carefully to others and, many times, quietly helped them financially or in ways that gave them the confidence to go on with their lives."

"I wish I'd had the chance to know him. I would've liked him too," Darcy said with genuine regret.

"He's the only man I've ever loved." Bebe's cheeks grew a pretty pink. "Of course, I never dared to let him know it."

"I'm sure all those baked goods were a sweet sign of it," said Darcy, seeing Bebe in a whole different way. Bebe might think she was unlovable, but others didn't.

"Thank you, Bebe, for sharing your story with me," Darcy said, her voice shaky with emotion.

She got to her feet and helped Bebe out of her chair.

"Thanks again," Darcy said, and wrapped her arms around Bebe.

They hugged each other. Feeling Bebe's arms tighten around her, Darcy had the unexpected urge to cry.

Darcy sat at her desk nibbling on one of Bebe's sugar cookies, thinking of their earlier talk. She also thought of Nick Howard, who'd led her to the newspaper job. She'd once called him St. Nick, and after hearing Bebe's story, she realized what a gift he'd given her—the chance to see people and life in an entirely new way.

She began typing.

> Angels come in all sizes and shapes with gifts as varied as they. It is up to the rest of us to recognize when such a gift comes our way. How do I know this? Because I met an angel today. Abused as a child,

bullied for her size, this angel is able to put love into the sweet things she makes for others. Some angels are gentle; some are strong and brash. Others are survivors who move beyond their past to become the people they were meant to be—loveable and loved. These angels are sometimes the hardest to see, but, believe me, they are there.

How do I know?

Because I fell in love with an angel today.

CHAPTER TWENTY-EIGHT

SHEENA

Sheena entered Brian's hospital room to find it empty. Unsure as to whether she should stay or go, she was suddenly aware of someone walking toward her. She turned to see Brian heading her way. An aide held onto his left arm encased in a cast. He gingerly moved his right leg forward.

Holding back a gasp of dismay at his sad condition, Sheena forced a smile. "Hi, Brian!"

He groaned at a painful step and looked at her. "What brings you here?"

"I thought we could talk for a few minutes. Do you have the time?"

"I've got too much fucking time here," he snapped and immediately looked contrite. "Sorry. Don't mean to take it out on you. It's just that I can't wait to spring out of here."

"Believe me, I understand. For an active man like you, this has to be hell," Sheena replied honestly. She couldn't imagine Tony in the same situation.

The aide helped Brian into a chair. "Best to eat lunch here," she said quietly and left the room.

Sheena sat in the chair next to Brian's and drew a breath, wondering where to begin.

"Tony tell you about my offer?" Brian said, saving her the worry.

"Yes, that's why I'm here. I need to know your offer to Tony isn't just a temporary fix, that you're in this for the long haul.

Jill has made it very clear to my sisters and me she doesn't want us or Tony involved with you."

Brian's eyes widened. "She said that?"

"She did, and I don't want Tony hurt. He's very happy working with you, and frankly, my sisters and I have come to think of you as family. You've been great about helping us."

"Jill actually spoke to you that way?" Brian said with such quiet firmness Sheena was relieved she wasn't the one who'd have to face his wrath.

"Let me assure you I run my business, not Jill," said Brian. "I've come to depend on Tony, and I trust his instincts and business judgment completely. My men like and respect him, and I'd be honored if he'd consider becoming a partner of mine."

Sheena sat back in her chair as a sigh of relief escaped her. "Okay, I believe you. Considering all we're facing, this would be a big step for Tony and me to take. Before I could agree to it, I had to make sure this was the case."

Brian's brown gaze bored into her, demanding her sole attention. "I made a promise to Gavin I'd be there for you Sullivan sisters, and I don't break any promises. Understand?"

"Yes, I do." Sheena rose, leaned over, and gave him a quick kiss on the cheek. "Thank you." She turned to go and then faced him. "By the way, Regan is going to stand in for Maggie again today. She'll be here a little later to help you with lunch." A devilish thought entered her mind. She spoke before she could stop herself. "Regan might also be able to help you with some of your exercises. Ask her. She's a very good swimmer."

A grin spread across Brian's face. "I just might."

CHAPTER TWENTY-NINE

REGAN

Regan adjusted the purse on her shoulder and gripped the bag in her hand a little tighter before knocking on the door to Brian's hospital room. Sheena had warned her Brian was getting restless about the stay in rehab and needed someone to boost his spirits.

"If that's the leader of group therapy, go away!" came Brian's voice.

Regan pushed the door open. "It's only me, and when you see the lunch Gracie packed for you, you're going to be happy."

Brian looked up from the chair in which he was sitting and grinned. "Sounds a lot better than more exercises."

Regan walked across the room, laid out his lunch on the overbed table, and wheeled it over to Brian's chair.

"What do you have there?" Brian asked, trying to see.

Regan lowered the table and pushed it closer to him. "Fried chicken tenders, fresh corn, green salad with lots of tomatoes like you usually order, and lemon cake."

"Mmm. Tell Gracie I'll give her a big kiss if I ever get out of this place."

"She and everyone else at the hotel are rooting for you, Brian," said Regan. "I am too." Her eyes stung with tears. Embarrassed by the unexpected emotion, she swiped at them and looked away. "I'm just so sorry this happened to you."

"Me, too," said Brian. "Will you ever forgive me?"

Regan turned to face him. "I should be asking the same

thing of you. How soon until you come home? Will you be able to keep your business? When can you go back to work?"

"I won't be able to work like I did for some time. That's why I've invited Tony to go into business with me."

"You have? What about Jill? It's apparent she doesn't like Tony."

Brian let out a sigh and closed his eyes. Angry color filled his cheeks. When he opened his eyes, they snapped with frustration. "*I* run the business, not Jill. Why don't people get it?"

Regan kept quiet. The less she said about Jill Jackson the better. *Brian deserved someone who knew how kind, how wonderful, how sexy ...*

Brian coughed.

Regan snapped back to the present moment so fast it made her feel dizzy. My God! What had she been thinking?

"Are we ready to eat now?" Brian asked, giving her an enigmatic look.

"Oh, yes," she said, lifting a forkful of chicken to his lips.

An aide knocked and walked into the room. "Anything I can do for you, Brian?" she asked in a voice that sounded way too breathy to be real.

Annoyed, Regan studied the voluptuous young woman. *Someone else totally wrong for Brian,* she thought.

"I'm taking care of lunch for him," Regan said sweetly.

"And she's going to help me with my afternoon exercises," added Brian, surprising them both.

"Well, you know I'm here day or night to help you." The aide winked at Brian and sashayed out of the room with an extra wiggle to the right and a wiggle to the left that signaled an invitation.

"Seriously?" mumbled Regan as she scooped up a spoonful of corn.

Brian laughed. “Andrea just broke up with her boyfriend.”

Regan fed Brian the corn and went about spearing lettuce leaves, her thoughts whirling. When had she become so protective of Brian? Answering her own question, she realized seeing him like this was disturbing enough to make her feel that way. He was a big, brawny guy who was always on the move. Or, had been.

“Think you could speed it up?” Brian said.

Regan looked down at the fork in her hand and wondered how long she’d been staring into space, lost in thought.

“Sorry. I’ll do a better job,” she said sheepishly. “I promise.”

They worked in tandem, content to be silent as food was passed, delivered, and eaten.

“Okay, time for dessert,” Regan said. “Bebe baked this cake last night especially for you.”

“Her lemon cake is one of my favorites.” He gave her a teasing grin. “Hurry up, woman!”

Regan forked a piece of the cake edged with the tart, buttery icing Bebe was known for and slid it into Brian’s open mouth. She watched his lips clear the fork of the icing in sexy swipes.

Brian closed his eyes and sighed, and chewed slowly as if capturing flavor for each of his tiny taste buds.

Observing the way his mouth worked, hearing his soft groan of pleasure, Regan was transfixed by the sensual sensations that rolled through her.

He opened his eyes. “Delicious!”

As he continued to stare at her, sending silent messages, Regan realized Brian was no longer talking about the cake. Longing surged inside her. Though she knew nothing could come of it, she wanted the kiss he seemed to be offering her.

“Regan?” he said, his voice low, seductive.

She jumped to her feet. "I can't. Jill ..."

"Dammit!" he said, struggling to get up and falling back in his chair. He sighed as she continued to stand away from him. "Guess we'd better finish the cake."

Regan sat back down and forced herself to continue feeding him, wondering how soon she could take leave of this man who had so much power over her.

After Brian had eaten the last bite of cake and had been given water, Regan packed up the dishes to go back to Gracie's.

"You *will* help me with exercises, won't you?" Brian asked. A devilish grin crossed his face.

"Right now?" Regan said.

"In a little while. I need to lie down for a bit first."

"I don't know if I should stay. Maybe they'll need me at the hotel."

"Call Sheena, if you want, but I don't think she'll mind."

Regan frowned at him. "What aren't you telling me?"

He smiled. "Sheena and I have already talked about it. You're the perfect one to help me." He paused. "I'm sure it will make you feel better about the accident."

Regan shook her head. The man was not above using sly tactics to get his way. Well, Jill be damned! She'd do exactly what he asked.

Regan didn't realize she'd fallen asleep in the chair next to Brian's bed until she heard the sound of his voice calling to her.

She sat up and stared at Brian groggily.

"Can you get the nurse for me? I pushed the buzzer, but she hasn't shown up, and I need to pee like a race horse."

"Sure. Hold on," said Regan, wide awake now. She

scrambled to her feet and went into the hallway. A nurse was headed toward her.

"Can you help Brian go to the bathroom?" Regan said, going up to her. "He needs you right away."

The nurse nodded and hurried toward the room.

Regan followed the nurse into the room and watched as she carefully helped Brian out of bed and walked beside him into the bathroom.

Feeling like an intruder, Regan turned away and headed out of the room as Brian stood at the toilet and began to relieve himself without even bothering to close the door. In the hallway, she waited for an indication Brian was through.

"Regan? You can come in now," called the nurse.

Regan stepped inside the room.

"This would be a good time to help Brian walk the halls. He needs to walk several times a day," said the nurse. "I understand you're going to be helping him. It's good if you two can get a steady routine going. We all know how anxious he is to go home."

Regan and Brian exchanged glances.

"I'll help him for as long as he wants," Regan said.

The nurse smiled. "Good. Now, Brian, walk as long as you can to strengthen those muscles that have already begun to weaken."

Looking miserable, Brian nodded. "Okay."

Regan went to his side. "Tell me what you want me to do."

The nurse said, "If you support his left arm, he can walk on his own. Later, when his right arm is stronger, he may be able to use a walker, but, at the moment, while we want to have him moving his right elbow as soon as possible, we don't want any weight on it until it's able to take it." The nurse clucked at Brian with sympathy. "A pretty grim situation for you, I know, but you can handle it."

"Yeah," Brian said, looking as if he wanted to cry.

It struck Regan then how much effort Brian had put into keeping his spirits up. Now they were definitely drooping.

"C'mon! Let's take a walk," Regan said brightly. She offered her arm, and he grabbed hold of it with the ends of the fingers the hard cast on his left arm hadn't covered.

Brian's pace was steady as they slowly moved to the end of the hall. But by the time they returned to his room, a light sheen of sweat covered his face, and Regan knew the effort it had taken him to make this walk.

After Brian was settled in his chair, she said, "I'll be here every afternoon to help you. Together, we'll get you ready to come home."

His eyes moistened. "I hate for you to see me like this. I feel like a goddamn baby."

Regan shook her head. "You're no baby." Impulsively, she leaned over and kissed him on the cheek.

He tried to grab her arm as she pulled away. Looking up at her, his lips curved. "Can you do that again?"

Regan let out a soft laugh. "See? You're feeling better already! Sorry, but I really do have to go. See you tomorrow!"

She turned and forced herself to keep walking so she wouldn't run back to him for another kiss—one that wasn't as sisterly.

CHAPTER THIRTY

SHEENA

Sheena was at the registration desk later that Saturday morning when a young couple entered the office. The girl was obviously pregnant. The man beside her looked not much older than Michael.

"Hello," Sheena said politely. "Can I help you?"

"We don't have reservations," the young man said, "but we're looking for a place to celebrate our honeymoon, and we liked your sign. Do you have any openings?"

"As a matter of fact, we do." Sheena smiled and handed him a brochure.

He looked it over and nodded. "Okay, we'd like to stay one night."

"All right. Let's get some information from you, and we'll give you one of my favorite garden rooms where you can have all the privacy you want. Unless you'd rather face the pool."

The couple exchanged shy glances and shook their heads.

"Okay, then, let's get you registered."

She typed in the information from their Alabama drivers' licenses and then asked them to verify their addresses.

"We're apartment hunting, so we don't have a Florida address. But you can use my home address," said the girl, who Sheena now knew as Lindy Sue Brown. Bobby Stroehler, Lindy Sue's new husband, was broad-shouldered and handsome, a football jock, Sheena guessed.

"Okay," said Sheena, trying not to judge them for their age, shabby suitcase, and other signs of a runaway couple. They were both over eighteen and Lindy Sue, a pretty brunette, wore a delicate, gold wedding band on her left hand.

After taking all their information, including Bobby's credit card, Sheena led them to the far end of the Egret Building.

"It's a slow weekend for us, so please make yourselves comfortable at the pool and by the bay." Sheena smiled. "Think of it as your own private place."

Inside the building, Sheena opened the door to their room, handed Bobby the room key card, and stepped back.

"Wow! I love it," said Lindy Sue. "This is perfect for us."

"Enjoy," said Sheena. "There are two free bottles of water in the small refrigerator and a whole bunch of coupons for the place next door and several other restaurants nearby. And everyone loves Gracie's, the restaurant on the property. It's open until three. Would you like me to make a reservation for you?"

Bobby glanced at Lindy Sue. At her nod, he said to Sheena, "How about two o'clock? That'll give us some time alone."

Sheena hid a smile at the blush that crept up Lindy Sue's cheeks. "Okay, I'll make sure you're set there. Now, would you like me to fill your ice bucket?"

Lindy Sue and Bobby glanced at each other and shook their heads.

Realizing they just wanted to be alone, Sheena tipped her head and said, "If you need anything, anything at all, please call the registration desk. The extension is posted right by the phone."

As she strolled back to the registration office, Sheena thought of the young couple as a version of Tony and her, and her heart opened to them. On a whim, she stopped by Gracie's to not only make the reservation but talk to Bebe.

###

Darcy entered the registration office a short while later. “I’m here to relieve you. Any new guests?”

Sheena told her about the young couple. “I’ve asked Bebe to make them a small cake. I have a feeling they didn’t have one. Looks like an elopement to me. “

Darcy grinned. “Oh, Bebe will love the idea! I interviewed her, and she, like the rest of Gavin’s people, has had a tough life. Baking is her way of healing.”

Regan’s arrival interrupted their talk. “What’s going on?”

“Young honeymoon couple is in the house. I gave them garden room E-100,” said Sheena. “For privacy. And I’ve made reservations for them at Gracie’s at two o’clock with a special surprise. Join me there.”

“Perfect,” said Darcy. She turned to Regan. “How’s Brian?”

“A little depressed. I said I’d help him for as long as he wanted. Any way we can schedule me away from the office for his lunch and an hour or two of exercises?”

Sheena glanced at Darcy and nodded. “Don’t know why not. I think it’s good you’re helping him. I know how guilty you’ve felt about the accident.”

Regan nodded. “As long as Jill doesn’t make a fuss. Brian was furious to think she didn’t want him to offer a partnership to Tony.”

“Wha-a-a-t!” said Darcy. “A partnership? When did this happen?”

“Last night,” said Sheena. “Tony and I haven’t officially announced it, but I’ve decided to tell Tony I’m okay with it. And I have the feeling what Jill Jackson thinks is of little consequence to Brian. I give her less than forty-eight hours to enjoy having the title of ‘his girlfriend.’”

Sheena noticed the bright expression that filled Regan’s face but decided to say nothing about it. Time, she was sure, would play a part in determining if Regan would see Brian for the great guy he really was.

When Sheena returned to her family's suite, there was a handwritten message waiting for her on the kitchen counter.

Mom, came home for a snack. Going to special football practice. Won't be home until late. Michael

Sheena set down the note and sighed. The high school years, filled with the kids' activities, were hectic.

Meaghan came into the room and sank into a kitchen chair.

"What's going on?" Sheena said. "Are you all right?"

Tears streamed down Meaghan's cheeks. "Rob Wickham is a jerk."

Sheena sat down in a chair next to Meaghan. "What happened?"

"He told me he's not inviting anyone to the Halloween dance this year. I thought he was going to ask me."

"Halloween is more than a few weeks away. Maybe he'll change his mind."

Meaghan shook her head. "No, all the JV football players are going stag."

"Well, then, what's the worry?" Sheena said.

Meaghan jumped to her feet. "You just don't get it!"

Sheena watched helplessly as Meaghan stormed out of the kitchen and went next door. Hopefully Regan would be able to "get it," thought Sheena sourly.

She was still on edge when Tony arrived home for a late lunch. He looked around. "Where are the kids?"

"Meaghan's pouting next door, and Mike's at football practice." She pulled herself up out of the kitchen chair, where she'd be doing some personal budgeting. "Sorry to be so grumpy, but it's been a long day already."

"Have you had time to think about Brian's offer?" he asked, reaching inside the refrigerator for a cold beer. After popping open the cold drink, he turned to her with a questioning look.

"I have. In fact, I went to see Brian early this morning. After talking to him, I feel a lot better about his offer. Jill Jackson is not going to be an issue."

Tony shook his head. "I can't see Brian with her. Not in the long term." He came to her side and lowered his lips to hers. "So, Mrs. Morelli, what is it going to be?"

She looked into his brown eyes, seeing the uncertainty there, and realized if she really objected to it, he wouldn't take Brian's offer. Her heart surged with love for him. "I want you to be happy and successful, doing something you want to do. We have a home of sorts here, at least until the end of the year."

"Wow! Put that way, it makes this whole scene a little shaky, huh?"

Sheena smiled at him. "Like life. Uncertain."

He set down his beer and swept her up in his arms. "Yeah? Well, I've never been uncertain about you, Sheena Sullivan Morelli."

Sheena nestled against him, not minding his T-shirt was a bit smelly. He was her man, and she would do almost anything to make him happy. He'd given her the chance to meet Uncle Gavin's challenge. Now, she would give him the opportunity to make it a go with Brian's business.

Sheena's cell phone pinged with a text message. She checked it. "Michael wants to go out with the guys after practice."

"As long as he gets home in time for his curfew, it's okay with me," said Tony.

Sheena answered Michael's text and started to put the phone down when it rang. *Darcy*.

"What's up?"

"Lindy Sue and Bobby just went into Gracie's. Let's give them fifteen minutes and then meet me there. I'll call Regan."

"Okay, I'll be there. Tony, too."

Tony frowned at her as she clicked off the call. "Where am I going?"

"To Gracie's. We have a surprise planned, and there's a special reason I want you there. Once you see them, you'll know why." She checked the clock. "We have fifteen minutes."

"Be right back. I'm going to take a quick shower," said Tony. "We're done for the day, and Gracie wouldn't like me in her restaurant like this."

Sheena laughed. "You're right. Hurry and change."

Fifteen minutes later, Regan and Meaghan knocked on their door.

"Ready?" said Regan.

Meaghan stood behind her. "I love surprises."

"Me too," said Sheena, pleased to see the change in Meaghan. She sometimes forgot how easily hormones could wreak havoc for Meaghan, changing her from sweet and loving one minute to another person entirely in the next.

Tony emerged from their bedroom, his dark hair still wet and curly from the shower. Sheena's attention lingered a moment on his body, which had become tanned and muscular from his construction work. He'd turned into what Darcy would call a real hottie.

"Okay, we're ready to go," said Sheena, following Regan and Meaghan out of the building with Tony.

"What's going on, Sheena?" Tony said as they walked

across the hotel grounds.

"It's a surprise for a young couple that reminds me of us—only we were a lot luckier than these young kids seem to be."

When Sheena entered the restaurant, she noticed Lindy Sue and Bobby seated at the corner table of the restaurant where the family normally sat. It had been reserved for them.

Sheena walked over to them. "Good afternoon. How is your lunch?"

"Delicious," Lindy Sue said.

"Yeah, Gracie's fried chicken special is as good as it says," added Bobby, patting his stomach.

"Ready for dessert?" Sheena said. "We have something special for you."

Lindy Sue's eyes rounded. "You do?"

Sheena bobbed her head at her sisters.

Regan and Darcy and Meaghan approached the table with Bebe. In Bebe's hands was a plate holding one of the sweetest wedding cakes Sheena had ever seen. Scallop shells made of white icing were interspersed with pink rose buds atop the pale-yellow icing that covered a sizeable cake.

When Lindy Sue saw the cake, she clapped her hands to her mouth and turned to Bobby, who looked just as surprised as she.

As Lindy Sue started to sob, Bobby rose and went to her side. "We couldn't have a fancy wedding ceremony. Not with things the way they are."

"Hold it right there!" said a photographer who rose from a nearby table.

"Better stop crying, honey," said Bobby. "They're taking pictures of us."

Bebe set the cake down in front of Lindy Sue and stepped away.

Doing her best to smile, Lindy Sue dabbed at her eyes with

her napkin and then she smiled at Bobby.

The flash went off at that moment.

CHAPTER THIRTY-ONE

DARCY

Darcy gave Skip Namath, the photographer at the *West Coast News*, a thumbs-up sign. She hoped he'd take a lot of pictures like he'd promised, because she was going to use it for their advertising campaign. In fact, she was thinking of using Skip to do her wedding pictures. He was that good.

At Sheena's urging, everyone in the restaurant gathered around the table. "We all want to share our best wishes for the two of you," she said to Bobby and Lindy Sue.

"Yes," said Regan. "Congratulations and all the best for a wonderful future!"

"I wish you many years of happiness," said an older woman who smiled at the couple. "Maybe, if you're lucky, you'll be as happy as Joe and me."

"Hear! Hear!" cried another guest, moving among the others with an empty coffee cup, asking for donations.

Gracie and the other staffers joined the group around the table as the coffee cup, now full of bills, was handed to Bobby.

Sheena watched his face work with emotion as he tried to hold back tears. "Thanks, y'all. Won't you have some of this delicious-looking cake?"

Someone shouted out, "Good idea."

Another started singing, "*For he's a jolly good fellow,*" and the whole restaurant joined in with giddy camaraderie.

Darcy thought of the stories she'd written about different angels and knew it would take more than a lifetime to tell them all. She caught Bebe's eye.

"Thank you," she mouthed.

Bebe nodded and smiled.

After the spontaneous party came to an end, Darcy joined her sisters in the kitchen.

"Thank you all so much," Sheena said, "for your participation in making this a special time for Lindy Sue and Bobby. More than that, it shows what we can do together. As a family."

Gracie wasn't the only one who dabbed at her eyes. Darcy, too, filled with tenderness as she observed the bunch of people who others might disregard, but people their uncle had saved.

While she still had a fresh picture of the event in her mind, Darcy left the others and hurried into her office to write her impressions. If she were lucky, Ed at the newspaper would publish the story.

Two days later, Darcy posted the article on the bulletin board in the registration office. A photograph of the couple, taken at the moment Lindy Sue had looked up at Bobby, graced the front page of the newspaper.

"This is terrific," said Regan, standing beside Sheena in front of the bulletin board. "We've received a call for a reservation already. I've been thinking we might want to turn that guest room into a bridal suite. When the restaurant opens, we can offer wedding receptions there, and it would tie in nicely if we reserved a suite for those occasions."

Sheena placed a hand on Regan's shoulder. "How'd you get so smart?"

A pretty pink flush crept up Regan's cheeks, which were clearing of the superficial cuts and scratches.

Darcy smiled, knowing what a compliment like that meant

to her sister. "Hopefully it will bring in more business. Nicole should be here in the next couple of weeks. As soon as possible, I'll meet with her and see when we can look at the ad campaign she's working on for us."

"You mentioned she still hadn't found an apartment or a job. She's welcome to stay here for as long as she needs, in exchange for a lot of ideas," said Sheena.

Darcy tapped Sheena's shoulder. "How'd you get so smart?"

The three of them laughed together. Moving this project forward would take the talents of all three of them.

CHAPTER THIRTY-TWO

REGAN

Several days later, Regan headed into Brian's hospital room as she did every day. As the nurse had suggested, she and Brian had developed a good routine. She helped him with lunch, assisted him with his long afternoon walk, and then counted as he did some basic exercises to keep his muscle tone.

Because Jill had spoken to her, asking Regan to respect her wish to build a relationship with Brian, Regan did her best to ignore the attraction she felt for him. The minute his gaze lingered on her, she glanced away. And when the exercises were done, she pulled away from him, ignoring the emptiness she felt inside.

On this day, Regan brought in fresh spice cookies from Gracie's.

As she entered his room, he looked up at her from his chair with expectation. His attention swung to the paper bag she carried, and he smiled.

"Treats for me?"

She laughed at his eagerness, like a puppy with a fresh piece of meat. "Oh yes. Gracie and Bebe are making sure you know everyone there is thinking of you."

He accepted the cookie she handed him and sank his teeth into the soft treat. "Mmm. Tell them I'm never sure enough. They'll have to keep reminding me like this."

She laughed with him. "Ready to order lunch?"

"I already did," he said. "A hamburger. I ordered you a glass of iced tea too. Lemon, no sugar, just like you usually order it."

"Thanks."

She sat down in the chair next to his. "You know that article about the young bride and groom in the paper a few days ago? It's brought in some new business for the hotel. Nice, huh?"

"Great. Every little bit counts."

Regan took a deep breath. "I've come up with an idea to take the downstairs garden room and turn it into a bridal suite. What do you think? It shouldn't take much money to convert the bedroom into a sitting area. Especially with the furniture deals Mo can come up with."

"Good idea, Regan. With the beach so accessible to the hotel, you can cater to the wedding business and brides who want beach ceremonies. By the way, how's Mo? You haven't talked about him lately."

"Mo is doing well," said Regan. "He's busy with small projects." She wasn't about to tell him Mo was in love again.

"I like the guy. He's very clever. When we complete a couple more houses in the development I'm working on, I'd like you and Mo to decorate the one I intend to use for a show house."

"Thanks. That would be great," she said, pleased he trusted them.

His expression changed, became somber. A long sigh rumbled from his chest. "I've got to get out of here."

Sympathy filled her. Most days he was pretty cooperative with the people helping him, but Regan had learned enough about him to know it came at a cost. Inside, he was howling like a banshee at being penned up like this. She reached out to pat his arm, realized what she was doing, and pulled her hand away.

His right arm moved so quickly his fingers brushed her hand. “Don’t,” he murmured. “I like it when you touch me.”

“But Jill ...”

“Last night, I told Jill it’s over between us. I’ve tried to let a few irritating things go, tried to tell myself her attitude would change, but it all added up to a very bad relationship. I have to concentrate on getting better. No serious relationships stopping me. It’s up to me to heal quickly so I can help Tony keep the business going. Understand?”

Regan nodded. “It’s a good idea. I feel the same way about relationships. I have to think of the hotel and the business I want to set up with Mo.”

“Good. We agree on that.”

“Yes, it makes this situation of working with you much easier,” Regan said, hiding her disappointment.

“Any word from Arthur Weatherman?” Brian asked before taking a bite of another cookie.

Regan shook her head. “Mo and I should hear by the end of the week. Their decision was postponed because his wife wanted more time to think about all the proposals for their restaurants. I think it’s because a friend of hers submitted a bid for the work.”

“Hopefully, that won’t knock your proposal out of the game.”

“I know. I really want that job.” Regan liked that she could talk to Brian this way.

“And the job of spokesperson?”

Regan shrugged and looked away.

“Your face is healing nicely,” said Brian. His brown eyes filled with tenderness. “You’re always beautiful to me.”

As his smile settled on her, demonstrating feelings neither of them could risk, Regan shifted in her chair uncomfortably. She never knew what to say to him when he talked this way.

The first time he'd said something like it to her when he first met her at the airport, she'd told him to fuck off. It had surprised her as much as it had him. But guys' come-on lines had always bothered her for sounding fake and being self-serving.

"Regan, I didn't mean to upset you. The words just came out," Brian said quietly.

Regan studied him. He was still the guy everyone seemed to fall in love with, but now, there was a vulnerability to him she liked even more than the brash, charming man he usually was.

"Thanks." She'd once taken her beauty for granted, something she had come to resent. But with the accident, she realized how vain those feelings were.

A knock at the door indicated Brian's lunch had, no doubt, arrived. Regan got to her feet to collect it.

The young aide smiled at Regan as she handed over the tray and then leaned around her to call out to Brian. "Hello, Brian? I brought you a nice lunch today."

He looked up at her and chuckled. "Thanks, Tracy."

Regan forced herself not to roll her eyes. Brian was a magnet to the young, single girls on the staff who subtly flirted or acted like love-struck teenagers in front of him—another reason to keep things on a friends-only term.

She helped Brian with his hamburger, taking care not to let ketchup dribble on his chin, though, in her mind, he used an outrageous amount of it on the burger. She'd warned him about it, but he insisted on having it his way.

After Brian finished his meal, they took their normal after-lunch walk, this time, going the length of the corridor and back three times. The progress on his hip was remarkable, but he had yet to use the walker, due to the injury to his right elbow and the fractures of his left forearm.

As she was about to leave, a young man wearing a light-blue scrubs top knocked on the open door and entered. He glanced at Regan. "Ah, we finally meet. You're the elusive lunch server I hear about."

Regan's eyes widened in surprise and then she laughed. "You must be the mean guy who makes Brian do all kinds of painful things." She held out her hand. "Regan Sullivan."

He took her proffered hand. "Adam Reston. Stick around, and I'll show you just what a good professional physical therapist can do to him."

"Why are you two talking as if I'm not here?" Brian grumbled, looking from Adam to her.

"I'd rather talk to this beautiful woman, but I guess we'd better stop and get to work on you," Adam said pleasantly. "I have to leave early today."

"Hot date?' said Brian with envy that couldn't be missed.

"Should I leave?" Regan asked.

Adam shook his head. "No, I was serious. Stick around because I'm aware you'll be the person most likely to help him with his exercises after he's released. We need to start slowly, building movement without disturbing the bones or the nerves while they heal."

"It's a lose-lose situation," said Brian. "The longer we wait, the more difficult. Either way, it's not fun."

Regan pulled up a chair next to Brian's and sat quietly while Adam worked on Brian's arms, gently showing him a variety of exercises for mobility of his arms, hands, and wrists. He removed the soft cast around Brian's elbow and went to work, massaging the area lightly before exercising the arm. Each time the forearm was raised and lowered, Brian's face turned white, but he didn't cry out.

"Can't let the joint stiffen," Adam explained to her.

Regan nodded, unsure how Brian would react to her

conducting the obviously painful exercises.

Adam stood. "There are a number of other exercises Brian can do that don't involve the injured elbow or forearm. Simple things like shoulder rolls and stretches. I've left a list of them, along with photos. Make sure he does those too. Where possible, we don't want him to lose muscle tone."

"How about hugging?" said Brian. "All that reaching and squeezing should be good for me." He gave Regan a teasing smile.

Adam laughed. "That's a good exercise for anyone. I've got to go." He turned to Regan. "Nice to meet you." His eyes twinkled. "No wonder Brian can't wait for lunchtime."

Regan glanced at Brian and turned away at the scowl he sent Adam.

CHAPTER THIRTY-THREE

DARCY

On a pleasant morning in mid-October, Darcy dressed for the luncheon Sheena had arranged for her sisters and Meaghan. As Sheena and she had once discussed, this would be a girls' time to talk with Meaghan about a lot of things.

Standing in front of the mirror, Darcy tried to envision what Austin saw in her that others hadn't. She had the same unruly red hair, blue eyes, and figure she'd always had, though, now, there was a certain glow on her face Austin had brought out in her.

Regan came into the bathroom. "Help me with my makeup?"

Darcy turned to her with a smile. "Sure."

With gentle fingers, Darcy worked the makeup into and around the scar beneath Regan's chin and on her face. The surgeon had done a great job of making a lot of the ugly line disappear beneath her chin, but he hadn't been able to hide the ends that curled up to Regan's jawline. The scar on her forehead looked like a thin stress line, but Regan insisted on covering it. The one thing that couldn't be hidden was the droop on the right side of Regan's lip. It hadn't improved, and they wouldn't know for several weeks, possibly months, if it ever would.

Sheena came into the room. "You two ready? Meaghan and I are set to go."

"Just have to put on some lipstick," said Regan. "Not that

it'll help the lip very much."

As Darcy followed her sisters and Meaghan to Gertie, she studied Regan. She and Austin had tried to buoy Regan's spirits by inviting her out with them, but Regan had politely but firmly told them no. She spent all her time working at the hotel, with Mo, or with Brian, with whom she had an agreement to be only friends.

Regan climbed into the front passenger seat as Darcy slid behind the wheel. Sheena and Meaghan sat in the back.

"We're off to Sammy's!" Darcy cried, starting up the engine.

Sheena turned to Meaghan with a smile. "It's a great restaurant. Perfect for a special lunch with some of my favorite people."

Darcy put the car in gear and pulled the '50s Cadillac out of the garage in the main building where it normally sat.

Driving down the highway, Darcy remembered the first time they'd taken Gavin's Gertie for a spin. They'd been so disappointed by everything else about the hotel this car was a pleasant surprise to them. Since then, they took great care not to abuse the car and usually left it behind. But once in a while, for a special outing like this, it felt good to be seen driving the classic car.

"I can't believe it! Two more weeks and I get my learner's permit," said Meaghan happily.

Darcy smiled at the silence from Sheena. She knew her sister was dreading the time Meaghan would get behind the wheel of any car. Darcy couldn't blame Sheena. Meaghan was a social butterfly who'd pay more attention to her phone than to the road ahead of her.

"It can be a process," Darcy warned Meaghan. "Just take it one day at a time. You'll be driving soon enough."

They pulled into Sammy's. Situated close to St. Pete Beach,

the gray-shingled building offered a beautiful view of the water to those inside. The bar and grill was known for its excellent seafood and enjoyed a brisk business for both lunch and dinner. Darcy found a space in the crowded lot and parked the car. She got out with the others and inhaled the aroma of good food cooking. Her mouth watered. Thinking of her wedding in February, she'd already begun to watch her weight more carefully than normal. But, today, she decided she'd enjoy every morsel of food.

Inside, although Sammy's kept a traditional beach décor with fishing nets, sand dollars, and other beachy accents, the atmosphere was more sophisticated than most others. Turquoise-linen tablecloths were accented by pink-rimmed water glasses at each place. In the middle of each table, a single sprig of bright-pink bougainvillea nestled in a white bud vase.

Darcy was pleased when the hostess led them to a table in the corner where they could have some privacy.

"Nice," commented Sheena. She turned to Meaghan. "This is really an early birthday luncheon for you."

A smile crossed Meaghan's lovely face. "Presents and everything?"

Sheena frowned and shook her head. "The presents are the presence of your aunts and me."

Darcy grinned at Meaghan. "Who could ask for anything more? We Sullivan women are the best."

Meaghan nodded and smiled. "Okay, I get it."

After they were all seated, they were handed menus.

When their waitress finally came to the table, they quickly ordered. In the silence that followed her departure, Darcy said, "So, Meaghan, what's going on with you?"

Sheena shot Darcy an appreciative glance and leaned forward.

"Well, I'm excited about my party at the hotel. Rob and the other guys on the team have promised they'd come, and all my cheerleading friends will be there, of course."

"You think they can handle keeping things nice at the hotel?" Darcy said. "No funny stuff going on with each other or any substance abuse?"

Meaghan let out a sound of disgust. "Aunt Darcy, they're not like the kids at my old school. Everyone is too busy with sports and everything to get into drugs, or alcohol, or anything else."

"Good," said Regan. "We wouldn't want any trouble with them."

Meaghan shot daggers at her mother. "Is this why you set up the lunch?"

Sheena shook her head. "No, but it's good we can all be honest with one another. Now, let's talk about the birthday party. There are lots of ways you can do this."

Their food came, and as they ate quietly, Darcy thought about bringing up the topic of sex and decided not to.

As if she knew what Darcy had been thinking, Meaghan smiled at her. "Rob and I are back together. Nice, huh?"

"Yes," said Darcy, "as long as you're not too serious."

Meaghan's surprise turned to a frown. "You sound just like my mother."

Darcy laughed. "I hope not. But, really, Meaghan, it's important not to rush things in that department. You've talked to me about going into the hotel business one day. Don't end up going into the baby business instead."

Darcy looked up from her private conversation with Meaghan to find Regan's and Sheena's gaze on her.

"Anything we all should talk about?" Sheena asked.

"It's private," said Meaghan, giving Darcy a silent plea to keep quiet.

"Well, then," Sheena said smoothly, "let's talk about the birthday party. I figured a late afternoon start would give you all a chance to swim before refreshments."

"Does the hotel have a volleyball set? Some of the guys want to play beach volleyball," Meaghan said.

"Great idea," said Darcy.

"Yes, the hotel can use something like that," said Sheena. "What do you say?"

"I say we go for it," said Regan. "It's a good family thing."

"We could even hold volleyball contests!" Meaghan said with enthusiasm.

Listening to her, Darcy's concerns for her niece lessened. Meaghan was a good kid who wouldn't be foolish.

Together they set a time for the party, the menu, and some rules for handling other hotel guests.

"I can't wait!" said Meaghan. "It's going to be so cool. I'm going to get Bebe to make a special cake for me."

"She'll like that," Sheena said. "It makes her feel like a part of our family."

"Speaking of family," Darcy said. "I've got some news. I talked to Dad the other day, and I think he's going to try and make it down here for Thanksgiving."

"Really?" said Regan. "Is he bringing Regina?"

"Yes, of course. They haven't made the move to California, but I think he still intends to marry her." Darcy grinned. "And he's promised to be here for my wedding in February."

"I can't wait to be in your wedding, Aunt Darcy," said Meaghan. "I've already told my mother what dress I want." A happy smile creased her face. "It almost makes me look like a bride."

"Hold on, missy," said Sheena. "We're not ready for any weddings from either you or Michael."

"Awww, Mom!" Meaghan replied, and they all laughed.

CHAPTER THIRTY-FOUR
REGAN

Regan was sitting at the registration desk when she got a call from Arthur Weatherman. With trembling fingers, she clicked onto it.

"H-hello?"

"Hi, Regan. Arthur Weatherman here. Sorry to take so long to get back to you, but after much consideration, I'm pleased to inform you that you and Mo have won the bid to refurbish the restaurants. Go at it, you two! We're delighted to have you on board. I'll sign the paperwork and give it to Blackie, who, I understand from you, is going to be handling the financial end of this project for the two of you."

Regan gripped the edge of the desk, feeling weak with relief. "Thank you so much, Arthur. I promise we'll do a wonderful job for you. We'll get to work on it right away and have sample fabric groupings ready for your review within two to three weeks."

He chuckled. "I love your enthusiasm."

"Thanks again," said Regan. "Talk to you later."

"Hold on, Regan. I need to discuss something else with you."

Regan gulped nervously, awaiting the rejection she knew was coming.

"Margretta and I have done a lot of talking to each other and others about the advertising campaign. Specifically, about you as our spokeswoman. You can certainly understand why."

Tears blurred Regan's vision as she stared out the window. "Yes, Arthur, I can, and I'm sure you've found someone to represent your company better than I can do. No apologies are necessary. It was an intriguing thought, but not possible now. I get it."

"Regan? Will you stop a moment so I can tell you that you did get the job? We decided we wanted a real person to represent us. You're a beautiful, young woman just the way you are."

"But my scar, my lip ..."

"You will be a model for all young girls the media and advertisers have led to believe they have to be perfect. They're not, you're not, and I'm not. We're real. Don't you see the importance of this?"

Regan's shocked mind flew to little Emily who'd been told her "stars" were special. "I see what you mean. Let me think this through and get back to you. And, Arthur, bless you. I really appreciate the offer."

"Talk to you soon, I hope."

Regan hung up and collapsed into the desk chair, trembling. Being spokeswoman for Arthur would mean she could help ensure no matter what happened with the challenge, she and her sisters might be able to go forward. But it would also mean everyone would be introduced to her scarred face, her drooping lip. Since the accident, she'd been hesitant to show her face. She was terrified now.

As soon as Sheena came to relieve her, Regan left for the beach. There, she hoped to find the calm she sought.

Regan moved with determination along the sand edging the water, her feet pounding the hard surface as she marched along. Little sandpipers and other birds scurried out of her way as she worked through the thoughts whirling in her mind. They all came down to the one thing she'd been questioning all along. Who was she?

She turned and faced the water rolling in to greet her. The timelessness of the waves' movement slowed her breathing. She lifted her face to the sky and watched clouds drift by like marshmallows atop the cocoa she used to love as a child.

Where was that child now? She asked herself, knowing the answer. That child, who felt misunderstood, dumb, and unloved, had morphed into a woman who was still trying to shape herself. Of all the things she'd taken for granted through the years, the image of her face had made her feel she was worth at least something. Now, she'd even lost that. Or so she'd thought.

A laugh erupted from her. My God! She got it! By accepting herself as she was, imperfections and all, she was free to be who she wanted to be. She lifted her arms to the sky and shouted for joy, not caring if her smile was crooked or not. Those people who really mattered to her didn't care if she was perfect. Regan started running along the sand, splashing in and out of the water's frothy edges, feeling as if she was leaving her past behind.

When she finally slowed, she breathed the salty air deeply, loving the way the warm air caressed her skin like a hug. Excited by the changes in her, she ran home to call Mo and to tell her sisters Arthur's good news.

A couple of weeks later, Regan sat back in her desk chair in Mo's office and gazed at the stacks of fabric. "I love them all. Thanks for scouting around for them."

"I think the choices we've made for each of Arthur's restaurants are perfect. I'll give them to Lance, and he can work his colors from there."

Lance Everett, an artist friend of Mo's, had agreed to paint the murals for the restaurants at the price they offered. It was a winning deal for them both—Lance would get the notoriety, and they would get a high-quality product.

Mo gave her a penetrating look. "Kenton is flying in today, and he's eager to meet you. He knows I love you like a special sister."

Regan's eyes teared. She loved him too. Mo was a gift from above—a treasured friend, mentor, and, other than her sisters, her biggest supporter.

"How about having dinner with me tonight to meet him?"

"Okay, I will," Regan said quietly, already feeling her nerves come to life at the thought.

That night, waiting for Mo's arrival, Regan checked the clock on the wall for the umpteenth time. In order to keep their relationship quiet, Mo and Kenton had agreed to arrive at the restaurant separately and to share a private booth in a corner of the restaurant.

Regan had taken care to dress, hoping to make a good impression on Kenton. She wanted him to know how much she cared for Mo.

Darcy knocked on the bedroom door and called in to her. "Your date's here."

Taking a deep breath, Regan moved out of the bedroom to greet him and stopped in surprise. Kenton Standish, the brawny star of the television show, smiled at her.

"Mo and I figured it might be better if I showed up at the restaurant with you. Keep the talk down. Hope you don't mind."

Regan drew in the breath she'd let out in a gasp and smiled.

"I don't mind. Thank you."

"See you later," said Darcy, giving Regan a wide grin.

Kenton offered his arm, and Regan took it, feeling tiny next to his tall, broad frame.

He led her to a black Mercedes and waited while she got inside before going around the car to slide in behind the driver's wheel.

"You look lovely, Regan," Kenton said, gazing at her before starting up the engine.

"Thank you."

"We're going to meet Mo at a place up the road called Gills."

"Nice. I've been there before. The food is good, and the way it's set up, you and Mo will have some privacy." Regan hesitated and then spoke. "Kenton, I want to make sure you won't hurt Mo. I'm sure you can have the choice of many people in your life. You won't find anyone sweeter, kinder, nicer than Mo."

Kenton chuckled. "Mo told me you'd question me. For all the reasons you just mentioned, I intend to keep Mo in my life. It's not a casual thing for me at all."

Regan smiled, and suddenly realizing how the smile might look to Kenton, she stopped.

He noticed and shook his head. "Don't apologize to me or anyone else for your injury. You're a beautiful, sincere woman, Regan. Let that natural beauty show. God knows, it's rare, especially in Hollywood, where fake appearances are just as fake as behavior."

Regan was surprised at the bitterness she heard in his voice.

"You don't think I've taken a few arrows to the heart?"

Regan observed pain in his expression and placed a hand on his arm. "I'm sorry."

"Aw, I don't know why I'm suddenly confessing this to you. Maybe because I know from Mo what an open person you are."

Regan stared out at the water and remained quiet, thinking that, like Darcy, she was finding most people had a lot going on beneath the surface. It made her realize how superficial she'd been to worry so about her looks.

At the restaurant, Kenton quickly ushered her to the back room and to a table provided privacy by the tall potted palms strategically placed near it. Mo rose when he saw them. The smile on his face when he looked at Kenton made Regan's heart clutch with tenderness. She turned to Kenton and found such a look of affection it took her breath away.

My God! she thought. *This is what love looks like.*

Her thoughts turned to Brian. He was the only man who'd ever made her feel that way. Too bad it wasn't reciprocated.

The evening was as pleasant as Mo promised it would be. Kenton was an interesting guy. Regan listened to his stories with interest.

Built like a football player, Kenton had always been thought of as the perfect son who would, of course, succeed in sports, win scholarships for college, and be a proud representative of his family. Early on, however, he'd proved to be on the clumsy side and not at all willing to spend all his waking hours playing rough with the other guys. His heart was never in it, but he did enough to cover up his sexual orientation.

"It was only when I was drafted into doing a school play I realized what I really wanted. You can imagine how well that went over with my father. But, as soon as I graduated, I did what I'd promised all along and headed out to the west coast and Hollywood."

"You've done so well," said Regan. "And playing a Scottish hero must be fun."

He laughed. "Swinging silver swords and fighting to save the world *is* fun." He winked at Mo. "But I'm a homebody at heart."

Mo smiled. "Kenton bought a place on the water close to the Don and is fixing it up. It's going to be lovely. He's already asked me if you and I want to decorate it."

Regan's eyes widened. "Really? That would be great. I'd love to help you, Mo."

Kenton looked from her to Mo and grinned. "Deal. We'll draw up a contract."

Regan was almost sad when the evening drew to an end. Mo and Kenton were so easy to be with. They shared a quiet sense of humor she liked. And with that much affection in the air, they'd all relaxed. Regan wondered if she'd ever find a love so perfect for her.

Brown eyes and a saucy smile appeared in her mind, but she pushed those images away. Reality could be cruel, and she knew dreaming about Brian would only bring pain.

CHAPTER THIRTY-FIVE

SHEENA

The next morning, Sheena went to her sisters' suite to check on Meaghan. She greeted Sheena with a warm smile. "Okay if Tara and Maria come to the hotel after school today? We want to practice volleyball before my party and then go for a swim."

"As long as you don't disturb hotel guests, it's fine with me. Remember, our hotel guests take precedence over our family's wishes."

"I know," said Meaghan. "Thanks, Mom. They'll get off the bus with me."

Meaghan gave Sheena a kiss, grabbed her backpack, and hurried out the door.

Regan looked up at her from where she was sitting at the kitchen table. "I'm glad to see Meaghan with so many friends. They seem like a nice group of kids."

"I agree," said Sheena, pouring herself a cup of coffee and sitting down. "Michael's girlfriend is another matter. I've tried to talk to him about spending time with other kids, but my words are ignored."

"Typical, I guess," Regan said.

"By the way, I'm glad you're here," said Sheena. "Holly Harwood called me last night."

"Brian's mother called you? Why?"

"It seems she's wondering if Brian could bunk into one of our suites for a while. It will be hard for him to climb the steep stairs up to his apartment over the bar, and she thinks it would be good for his attitude if he didn't have to do that for a while. He's at that grumpy stage of healing when he's realizing how limited he's going to be for another month or so. I can't say I blame him."

Regan gave her a thoughtful look. "I can help get it ready if you wish."

"Oh, I do. In fact, I'm asking you to decorate it as best you can. I'm sure Rocky and his crew can help move furniture and do whatever work you need."

"Sure. What's the timing?"

Sheena gave her a sheepish smile. "That's just it. Immediately."

Regan laughed. "Sounds like him."

Sheena studied her sister. "What is it with the two of you?"

Regan tried to hide the heat that rose to her cheeks. "What do you mean?"

"It's obvious you like each other. You spend a lot of time with him, and the work you're doing with him is paying off. At one time, I thought you two might be in love."

Regan shook her head emphatically. "No. We've agreed to be only friends. That's the way he wants it. And that's fine with me. You know he can have anyone he wants. You ought to see the way nurses at the hospital make up excuses to stop by. It's disgusting."

"I see," said Sheena, wondering how her sister could be so dense. It was obvious to her the two of them had something going on neither would acknowledge.

Darcy came into the room, yawning and stretching. "What a lazy morning. I can't remember when I've slept in like this."

Sheena checked her watch. Eight o'clock. "Darcy, grab some coffee and then I need to talk to both of you. As you know, I've been going over numbers and financial projections.

We need to talk about a couple of things."

"Okay, boss," said Darcy agreeably, filling her coffee cup and taking a seat at the kitchen table.

"What's going on?" Regan asked.

"It's the restaurant," Sheena said, sighing.

"Gavin's? What's wrong with it?" said Darcy, frowning. "I thought we all agreed on how it's going to be."

"Yes," said Sheena. "But we haven't generated enough money to pay for everything to open it."

"It's supposed to open December 15th," said Regan. "That gives us less than two months to complete it. We've already ordered materials, decorative items and such."

"I know, and that's the problem. We don't have the money to pay for all of that and the finish carpenters too. Brian and Tony have agreed to carry the cost for a week or so, but then they need to be paid."

"Oh my God! What are we going to do? Graham has already agreed to act as chef. We can't let him down!" Darcy gave her a pleading look. "Can we?"

"Absolutely not," Sheena said with a firmness that erased the worry from Darcy's face. "I have a plan. But I need the two of you to go along with it."

"Okay, spill," said Darcy.

Sheena took a breath for courage and began. "The money from the insurance settlement for the fire was meant to rebuild the house. When we got permission to change it from a house to the restaurant, Archibald Wilson, who oversees Gavin's will, agreed to a small adjustment in cost for what we thought would be a small but nice restaurant. Since then, we've changed the scope of it to include the upstairs function room for weddings, and we've added space to the original footprint of the building. Then, with Graham providing upscale meals, we dressed up the interior."

"What are you talking about in dollars?" Regan said. "Mo and I have done our best to keep costs down."

"And a good job it was. But, to proceed as we've now planned and to keep from failing, we need to do this right. The bottom line is we need to borrow money. A lot of it."

"Who in the hell is going to give us money?" scoffed Darcy. "We're in no position to get money from anybody."

Sheena paused, studying each sister. "How about from Uncle Gavin himself?"

"What? How can we do that?" said Regan.

"No way," said Darcy. "What if we fail?"

"I suggest we meet with Blackie and talk to him about it. He'd have to be the one to approach Archibald. That man would turn us down for sure. Okay if I ask Blackie to meet us here?"

Darcy and Regan looked at each and turned to her.

"Okay," said Darcy. "Let's do it."

"As Darcy says, we can't fail," Regan said. "We've made it this far. We have to do our best to make it to the end of the year."

Sheena got to her feet filled with both dread and excitement. "I'll call Blackie and work on a presentation for him. This has to be done as professionally as possible."

The next day, Blackie met with Sheena and her sisters in the small office behind Gracie's restaurant.

After greeting each one of them, he took the seat they offered him. He smiled as they formed a circle around him.

"Feels a little bit like a firing squad taking aim," he joked. "What's going on that you had to see me right away?"

"It's the restaurant," Sheena replied before launching into the reasons they needed a loan. "As we've developed the concept for Gavin's, which is something he, himself, wanted, things have changed. With the newspaper article about the bride and groom staying here, we've received requests for weddings, which has brought about the idea of the large function room at Gavin's—something that wasn't in the original plan.

"And Graham Howard's food offerings require an upscale interior," said Regan. "Mo and I have done a lot on a short budget, but we can't perform miracles on top of miracles."

Blackie nodded. "Arthur is very happy with what you're doing for him, but, you're right. Gavin wouldn't have wanted anything that wasn't the best. Go on."

"The restaurant is bigger than the original house," said Darcy. "And rightly so."

"Yes," said Sheena, "and in adding space, we've added garden views and water views, making it the kind of restaurant we think Gavin had in mind. We've ordered supplies and hired the crews to do the finish work, but now, we need to pay them, fit out the kitchen, and furnish the extra facilities upstairs."

Sheena handed Blackie a spreadsheet. "This shows you the money allotted to us for this project, the expenditures, and what other money we need."

Blackie studied Sheena and then each of her sisters. "I must say, I admire your guts. It takes a lot of them to come up with a plan like this."

He turned his attention to the analysis Sheena had handed him. In the silence that followed, Sheena felt her stomach curl. Had she overplayed her role?

When he looked up from the paper, he said, "You realize how much $200,000 is. Right?"

Sheena swallowed hard. "Yes, we do."

He shook his head. "Well, I'm not going to ask Archibald

for that amount of money for you."

Sheena and her sisters exchanged looks of distress.

"I'm going to ask for $250,000 instead. That will cover any unforeseen expenses, and, as you know by now, there will be a few."

He sat back in his chair. "Sheena, remember Gavin's note to you? 'Sheena, you're more like me than you think.' You've proved that over and over. This is the type of scheme he would've come up with. Just be sure you show some success with it before the year is up. Got it? If you don't, Archibald Wilson won't be kind to you."

Sheena felt a little sick as she nodded. "We'll do our best."

"Damn right," said Darcy.

"The Sullivan sisters will always stick together," Regan added, giving Sheena's hand an encouraging squeeze.

Blackie got to his feet. "Gavin would be proud of you. I'll make the call to Archibald on your behalf and let you know."

Sheena walked Blackie out of the room and to his car.

"Thank you, Blackie. The friendship and help you gave to Uncle Gavin and now, to us, is genuinely appreciated."

"I know that, sweetheart. I'm doing it for all of you." He smiled. "I'm behind you all the way. Let's hope Archibald is."

CHAPTER THIRTY-SIX

REGAN

Regan got up early so she could talk to Rocky before he got busy with other projects. She'd begun to work on the space for Brian, and she needed Rocky's help in arranging the furniture she'd scrubbed clean in another suite while a crew shampooed the carpet in the suite next to hers for Brian's use. They had received the new mattress and box spring they'd ordered, so the bedroom Brian would use was almost ready for him. She'd supplied the kitchen with enough pots, pans, kitchen utensils, glassware, plates, and silverware for him to get by. When he was able to move back to his apartment, they'd use them in one of the other suites they would renovate for guests one day.

Holly Harwood had brought in new sheets and other bedding for Brian, along with towels and supplies for both his bathroom and the kitchen.

Regan entered Gracie's.

"Can I get you something for breakfast?" Maggie asked her. She and the others in the group were sitting at tables, eating a quick breakfast before the restaurant opened.

Regan smiled with gratitude. "A cup of coffee would be nice."

"Coming right up," Maggie said, jumping up from her seat.

When Maggie returned, she handed Regan a cup of steaming-hot coffee. "How's our boy Brian doing? I've been going in to check on him in the evenings, but I stay just long enough to see if he needs anything."

"He still wants me to come in at lunchtime, but now that he's able to feed himself, I'm not really needed."

"Oh, but he needs you there. I've noticed on the few days you haven't been able to visit him, he's depressed." Her eyes twinkled. "It's amazing what love can do."

"What are you talking about?" said Regan, taken aback. "Brian and I have agreed we're just friends. He and I are different people, and we each have our work."

Maggie stared at her. "Is that how the two of you are playing it? Really?"

"Maggie, I appreciate your interest, and I know you mean well, but this idea of yours is totally crazy."

Maggie started to say something, then stopped when Rocky approached them. "You wanted to see me, Regan?"

"Yes, I'm wondering if you can help me move furniture into the suite we've set up for Brian. He's hoping to move into it this afternoon after he's released from the rehab center."

"Sure thing. Ready to do it now? I promised I'd go into Ybor City to take care of things, but I can give you some time before I go."

Regan set down her coffee cup. "Okay, let's do it now." She turned to Maggie. "Thanks for the coffee. See you later."

"Have a good day," Maggie said. "And by all means, say hi to Brian for me. I'll try to get over to the suite to see him in the next day or two."

Regan gave her a little wave and hurried out of Gracie's with Rocky.

An hour later, Regan stood back and studied the living area of the suite she'd set up for Brian. A table and chairs like the ones in the two suites her family used sat by the kitchen. Both they and the kitchen had been scrubbed clean and now sparkled from the attention. A reconditioned couch sat along one wall facing a television Holly had donated to the cause.

Two overstuffed chairs in different colors sat on either side of the couch, along with end tables holding lamps. From a decorator's viewpoint, the décor was a disaster. But everything was clean and comfortable. And that's what counted. Brian hoped his stay there would be limited to just a couple of weeks until he was easily able to handle the stairs up to his apartment. While the doctor wanted Brian to strengthen the muscles around his hip, he didn't want him to abuse the hip, causing a setback. Wires and screws were what held it together, and the bone needed more time to heal.

Darcy came into the room. "Things look pretty good for Brian. You did a great job on such short notice."

"It's pretty basic, no real decorations to speak of. I thought I'd try to hang a picture or two to make it seem homey."

Darcy grinned at her. "A little nest for the two of you?"

Regan placed her hands on her hips and glared at Darcy. "What are you talking about?"

"You and Brian," said Darcy. "You'd be great together."

Regan let out a puff of disgust. "You and everyone else better get such thoughts out of your mind because Brian just wants to be friends. I agree with him. You know how he is."

Darcy cocked an eyebrow at her. "And exactly how is he?"

"He's a flirt who can make any woman believe she's the one for him. I know better. I've seen him in action. There isn't a nurse on the floor that isn't at least a little bit in love with him. That's not the kind of guy I'm looking for."

"Whoa!" said Darcy agreeably. "I just thought I'd ask. When is he moving in?"

"Sometime this afternoon. I'll find out more when I see him at noon."

"Okay," said Darcy, giving her an enigmatic smile. "See you later. I'm off to interview Maggie, if I can get her to talk to me."

Later that morning, Regan pulled into the hospital parking lot, so familiar now, and parked the van. Determined to ignore the excitement of seeing him, she walked inside, ready to begin their normal routine.

Outside his door, she took a calming breath, telling herself it was no use being bothered by other people's expectations of her having any romantic relationship with him. She wanted nothing more than a nice friendship with a friend of the family.

She entered Brian's room and silently stood aside as a nurse's aide jumped up from the chair next to Brian's.

"Hi, Regan! Brian was just telling me he's going to live at your hotel temporarily until he can handle the stairs to his apartment again."

"Yes," said Regan. "It's ready for him anytime."

"It is?" said Brian.

Regan nodded. "Rocky helped me with the furniture this morning. Everything else was all set."

"Okay, Jeannie, I need your help," Brian said to the aide. "Make sure the release papers for me are signed. Okay, hon?"

She beamed at him and gave him a mock salute. "You got it."

After she left, Regan sat down in the chair Jeannie had vacated. "Ready to order lunch?"

"Yes, but let's order for both of us as a way to celebrate my last meal here. All right?"

"Okay. That sounds like a good way to end your stay. I know how anxious you are to leave."

His brown eyes flashed with appreciation as he smiled at

her. "The only good thing about being here was all your visits."

"That's what friends are for—supporting each other. Like Mo and me."

He studied her for a moment. "Yeah, I guess that's it. Good friends." He took her hand in his, clasping it with fingers that had grown stronger with exercise. "But, Regan, I always feel better when you're around."

The sensation of electricity traveling from his fingers into her hand silenced her. She looked up at him with confusion.

He dropped her hand. "Okay then. Get the menu and let's order. I'm hungry. I want to eat, and then I want to get out of here."

Regan retrieved the menu from the bedside table and sat down. "I feel as if I have this thing memorized. What do you want?"

Brian ordered his favorite—ham and swiss cheese sandwich. Regan decided on a green salad. The food was better than some other hospitals', but after eating at Gracie's so often, Regan felt few commercial kitchens could equal theirs. Still, to satisfy Brian, she placed the order.

As they waited for the food to arrive, Regan went about gathering Brian's things. Holly took care of seeing he had fresh clothes to wear, so the bundle Regan put together was small—a book or two, an electronic game, and his cell.

Their food came. Regan set the sandwich and his drink on the table for Brian and placed her salad and iced tea beside it. They ate quietly, and then Brian said, "I'm going to miss these times with you. I'm glad I'm moving in next door, so we can continue to do things like this."

"Sometimes we'll be able to do this, but not always," said Regan. "We'll each be busy. You'll be even more involved with your business and working with Tony. I'm working with Mo on a new, secret project, and we have the restaurant project as well." She couldn't tell anyone about Kenton's house. Not yet.

"Oh, yeah, right, you and Mo," said Brian, giving her a long look. "I guess that's the way it is."

Ignoring a longing she couldn't define, Regan nodded. "Yep. Guess so."

An aide, someone different from Jeannie, came into the room. "Okay, the doctor has signed your release papers. You can go." She smiled at Brian. "We're all going to miss you so much. Keep in touch. Hear?"

He returned her smile. "You can always find me at The Key Hole. Come say hello anytime."

"Okay," the aide said brightly. "That's a promise."

Regan stared out the window, hating the feeling of jealousy that stabbed at her heart and clouded her vision.

CHAPTER THIRTY-SEVEN

DARCY

Darcy entered Gracie's as the staff was cleaning up after the lunch rush. She went right over to the table Maggie was wiping down.

"Any chance we can talk? I'm putting together some interviews for my book."

Maggie gave her a steady look. "Anyone besides me decide not to talk to you?"

"I've spoken with everyone else. They trust me not to use names or specifics, but to use the story behind the person like I did for my newspaper columns. I'm pretty excited about doing the book, and I hope you'll let me interview you." Darcy could hear the pleading in her voice, but couldn't stop herself from saying, "Please, Maggie. It would mean so much to me."

"Okay," Maggie said with reluctance. "I suppose I owe it to Gavin."

Maggie headed for the table in the corner of the restaurant and sat down. Darcy followed and lowered herself into a chair opposite her. "As I said earlier, Maggie, I will respect anything you say to me. No names, no identifying circumstances will be mentioned. Everyone has a story, and I'm interested in yours as it relates to my uncle. In a way, this whole book is a tribute to him."

Maggie's eyebrows shot up, forming arcs above her eyes. "Oh. Well, in that case, I'm happy to help you."

"How did you know my uncle?" Darcy said, taking out her

notebook and pen from her purse. She waited to see if Maggie would object, and when she didn't, Darcy opened her notebook and waited for Maggie to begin.

"Gavin and I met in the county courtroom. He was there to attend the hearing of a friend and happened to be there when I was sentenced to two years of probation and the loss of my nursing license." Tears came to Maggie's eyes. "It was such a difficult time for me."

"I'm sorry," Darcy said and waited for Maggie to continue.

"My father was dying of cancer and had come to live with me. I wanted to call in hospice, but he begged me to help by giving him something to speed the process along."

Darcy remained still while Maggie looked away, lost in memory.

"I told him I couldn't do it, I was a nurse who was trained to help people in other ways, and I would be there for him until the end. But he persisted, telling me of all the things he'd sacrificed for me to go to nursing school. He sobbed and threatened to haunt me to my dying days if I didn't help him. His was a very painful cancer, and although his doctor had prescribed pain medication, it still wasn't enough. He wanted just a little more of what the doctor had already prescribed. Don't you see?"

Darcy nodded with sympathy.

Maggie continued. "He cried out in pain for days until I couldn't stand it anymore. One night, I went back to the office where I worked and got enough medicine to do as he asked. I knew I'd done the right thing for my father. But I also knew it would be the end of my nursing career." Maggie gripped her hands together. "How I wish he'd never asked me."

"Those are hard decisions," said Darcy. "The laws are changing, but it's a very difficult situation for everyone involved."

Maggie studied her. "I hope you don't ever have to go through anything like it."

"After you met Gavin, what happened?" Darcy said quietly.

"He told me he'd put together a group to help him restore a hotel he'd bought, and he needed someone smart and capable to help him give these people a happy home. He asked me if I would keep watch over the others, guiding them with any medical problems that might arise. He said it might be a beginning for a whole new life for me, living and working with these friends of his and caring for them. I have no other family, and the house where my father lived was to be sold to pay for medical expenses, leaving me with no home. I gladly accepted Gavin's offer."

Darcy realized Maggie wasn't all that much older than Sheena. "Do you intend to stay with the group, or do you want to do something different?"

Maggie sighed. "Gavin and I talked about it. I'm committed to staying at the hotel until the end of the year. Then, if I choose, I'm free to go elsewhere, do something different. But I've found a pleasant existence here and on my own. And in the evenings, I've met some people who've become good friends. So, my options are open."

"Nice," said Darcy, wondering how she and her sisters could make better use of her talents.

"Even if I end up doing something different, I'll never abandon Gavin's people. That's a promise I'll keep." Tears flooded Maggie's eyes. "Just like I promised to take care of my father."

As Maggie began to sob, tears filled Darcy's eyes and spilled over. She reached across the table and squeezed Maggie's hand. "You're a good woman, Maggie. Thank you for telling your story."

"No names, right?" Maggie said.

"Absolutely," said Darcy, knowing she'd never look at Maggie in the same way again. She was another angel with a story of her own.

As was her pattern following an interview, Darcy sat in her office typing up Maggie's story.

When she was through, she glanced through it, made first-round edits, and started to read it once more

> Angels are all around us. Sometimes angels are hard to find because someone's age, size, shape, or color need not play a part, as angels are discovered by their acts, not their appearance. How do I know this? Because I talked to an angel today who acted out of love, knowing it would hurt her. Selfless acts are too often disregarded or sometimes not understood. But angels do what they must to help others.
>
> How do I know this?
>
> Because I cried with an angel.

Darcy laid down the paper and thought of Nick Howard and all he'd done for her. He was her private angel, someone she'd always love, though he wasn't around for her to tell him so.

Her thoughts shifted to Austin. He was another angel of hers who'd yet to know the depth of her love for him. She couldn't wait until they were married, and she could share every day and every night with him. She picked up her phone and typed a simple message to him. *I love you!*

She giggled happily when he immediately replied. *Me too you!*

Darcy stood and stretched, feeling good about the way her interviews were piling up for her book. On a whim, she called Cyndi Jansen.

Cyndi answered her call with a cheery, "Hello, Darcy! What's up? Calling about our reservations?"

"No, but we'll be very glad to see you and your friends. The reason I called was to check on the progress of your book. How are your interviews coming along?"

"It's amazing. The spouses of the men and women in Tom's recovery group have so many good ideas about surviving the trials of having spouses with Post Traumatic Stress. We'll talk more when I see you."

"Great," said Darcy. "See you soon."

Thinking of the group coming in, Darcy placed a call to Nicole Coleman. She was supposed to have moved to Florida by now, but Darcy hadn't heard a word.

Darcy couldn't reach Nicole on her personal number. Taking a chance, she called Nicole's place of business and was put through right away.

"Nicole? It's Darcy. When are you coming to Florida?"

"Oh, I've decided not to come after all. My boss put together a package for me here that was irresistible. I'm staying."

Darcy swallowed a gulp of dismay. "What about the advertising package for the Salty Key Inn?"

Nicole chuckled. "That, my friend, is on its way to you. I sent it off this morning. Sorry for the delay, but everything was in a state of flux here. Darcy, if you guys ever go big, I want you to remember me. I'd love to have you as a client of mine."

"If we make it as big as we hope, I'm sure my sisters and I would love to use you for our advertising campaigns. Nicole, thank you so much for setting this up for us. We can really use it."

"No problem. I like you, Darcy, and I hope you and your sisters do well."

"Thanks, Nicole. You too." Darcy paused, then couldn't resist. "How's Alex?"

"I don't know," said Nicole. "After I got back from our visit to Florida, I decided to spend some time at home. And when my new position here at the company came up, I decided to buy a small condo of my own. Right now, I'm sharing it with my old boyfriend."

"Rick?" said Darcy, pleased for her. Rick Darrow was a tall, lanky guy who was a straight shooter. Darcy had always liked him.

"Yes. He never did like Alex, which was one reason we drifted apart. But, Darcy, I think our relationship has moved to a whole, new, healthy level."

"Tell you what," said Darcy. "If you guys ever marry, I'll give you a super deal for a beach wedding."

Nicole laughed. "From your mouth to God's ears. Thanks. Gotta go."

Darcy hung up the phone and stood a moment, gazing out the office window at the swaying palm tree nearby. Sometimes, she thought, life had a way of making things right.

CHAPTER THIRTY-EIGHT

REGAN

Regan stood beside Sheena as Brian slowly made his way into the suite next to hers. "I hope you like it," Regan said to Brian, feeling a little nervous.

"She's worked very hard at turning this place into something comfortable for you," Sheena said, sounding like the protective older sister she was.

"A real show house, huh?" said Brian looking around.

"No-o-o, but hopefully a comfortable place where you can continue healing," said Regan. In her mind, she could already see how beautiful these suites could become if they had enough money to do a proper renovation.

Holly Harwood joined them. She gave Brian a kiss on the cheek. "Glad to have you nearby, son. You'll heal much better here, where you can be out in the sun and relax."

"Mom, you forget I have a business to run," Brian all but growled.

"Oh, I know, but you need your rest too." Holly turned to Sheena. "I'm so glad Tony is now Brian's partner."

Sheena smiled at her. "Brian's done very well, and Tony is pleased to now be his partner. Thank you, Brian."

Brian's earlier irritation was erased by the wide smile that spread across his face.

Observing this interchange, Regan realized how sensitive Brian had become about not being able to work. He was a man used to physical labor and managing his business.

Regan checked her watch. "I have to relieve Sally. See you later, everyone. And, Brian, if there's anything I've forgotten in setting up the suite, please let me know."

"There might be a couple of things we need to discuss," he said, giving her a teasing grin.

"Gotta go," she said and hurried away before the others could sense from the way her cheeks had heated she couldn't help responding to the sexy look he'd given her. The thought of having Brian so close was both exciting and scary. But as she crossed the lawn to the registration office, Regan reminded herself, as she often had to do, Brian's teasing was part of the game he played with all women.

Sally greeted her with eyes shining with excitement. "I just checked in another couple who read the recent article in the newspaper about the newlyweds. They're staying with us for just two nights, but they want to talk to you about having their wedding here."

"Nice. And did Mr. Rushman and his family come in?"

"Yes. He and his wife seemed pleased with their rooms, but I'm glad we placed them at the end of the building. Their children aren't well-behaved. They may be a problem."

"Maybe the sun, sand, and surf will wear them out," said Regan.

They laughed together. "Need S's" had become a code for describing kids who were difficult.

Regan checked the registration list for the day. Two more couples were due to come in, and then over the Halloween weekend Cyndi and her group would add to the numbers. Still, it was slow going.

Hoping for more business, Regan sent out a few brochure packages requested through their website. They were caught in an almost impossible position of having a lovely property that wasn't up to par. Gracie's, the bar next door, coupons, and the magnificent beach made up for some of the things lacking, but it bothered Regan things were not the way she wanted.

After straightening the office, seeing details were taken care of, and registering the last two guests, Regan hung the "closed" sign on the door and headed for her suite, hoping for a quiet evening.

She opened the door and stared inside with surprise. Brian, Holly, Sheena, Tony and the kids sat in the living area with Darcy.

"I thought we'd have a little party to celebrate Brian's being part of our suites group," Darcy said, beaming at her.

Regan gave a good attempt at curving her lips. Inside, though, the thought of Brian's being such a part of her life was disturbing. How could she maintain just a friendship with Brian when he was constantly around her? She'd seen stronger women, even married women succumb to his charm.

Brian seemed to see inside her whirling mind. "Don't worry. I'll give you and everyone else enough space to miss me when I'm not around."

The others laughed at his good-natured joke, and Regan joined in. The guy didn't realize how unforgettable he was, not that she was about to mention that to him or her sisters.

"When are we going to eat?" said Michael. "I promised Kaylee I'd pick her up from the library tonight."

"Call and tell her you might be late," Sheena said in an undertone. "This is a family celebration."

Michael made a face, rose from one of the chairs, and went into Regan's bedroom for privacy.

"We asked Brian what he wanted for dinner, and he chose Borelli's pizza," Darcy explained. "It should be here soon. Austin is picking it up."

"I've made a tossed salad with Rosa's special dressing," said Sheena.

Regan's mouth watered. Sheena's mother-in-law, Rosa, was a good cook. Avoiding the looks Brian cast her way, she accepted a glass of wine from Tony and sat in one of the folding chairs the family used for parties.

The light red wine slid down her throat and soothed her nerves. She felt some of the tension leave her shoulders.

Michael checked the clock on the wall. "When is Austin going to get here?"

"He's here now," said Darcy, rising to meet him at the door.

Regan observed the happy glow on Darcy's face and saw the way Austin looked at Darcy with open adoration, and a twinge of envy flashed through her. She wanted to find a good man like him or someone like Tony.

As Regan turned her attention back to her glass of wine, she found Brian's gaze on her.

Ignoring him, she rose. "I'll help you serve, Darcy. It smells wonderful."

The aroma of garlic, tomato, and sausage filled the air as she walked into the kitchen.

Chatting happily in anticipation of the meal they were to receive, the others moved to chairs at either the kitchen table or the folding table that had been set up.

After they'd all served themselves the pizza and had passed the huge salad bowl around, Tony lifted his can of beer. "I'd like to propose a toast to Brian. Here's to a speedy recovery. We all miss you at work and can't wait to have you back ordering us around."

Brian laughed. "Thanks. I've been practicing my ordering abilities with the nurses at the hospital."

Silence reigned as they dug into their meals.

"Great pizza," said Michael. "May I have more?"

"Why don't you serve the rest of us?" Sheena suggested.

Michael jumped out of his seat and came back to the table

carrying one of the boxes of pizza.

The women held back while the guys quickly helped themselves to more. Looking around at the people closest to her, Regan felt a sense of gratitude. Her family life in Boston hadn't been that happy, but being here in Florida, living and working together reminded her of how special family could be.

After another round of pizza for those who wanted it, Michael looked to his father. "May I be excused?"

Tony nodded. "Yes, son, but be home at the regular time. Hear?"

"But ..."

Tony cut him off. "You can abide by our rules, or you can stay home."

To Regan's surprise, Michael did nothing more than scowl. Tony and Sheena were strict with their children, and it seemed to be paying off. Michael's sassiness of last spring seemed to be gone.

Holly got to her feet. "I've got to get back to the bar. Thank you so much for including me in Brian's welcome home dinner." She turned to Brian. "Want me to walk you to your suite?"

"Sure. I don't want to wear out my welcome here."

Regan noticed the lines of fatigue on his face and realized it would take some time for Brian to build up his strength again.

After Brian and Holly left, Tony excused himself. "They're replaying some of the World Series games, and I don't want to miss seeing the Red Sox games I missed. Want to join me, Austin?"

"Yes," Austin said. "I couldn't get away from work to see the day games."

Meaghan got to her feet. "I've got homework to do, and

then I promised I'd call Tara."

Alone, the three sisters looked at each other and smiled.

Darcy retrieved the wine bottle from the kitchen. "I say this calls for a little more wine. It's hard to have time alone, and I want to tell you about my call with Nicole."

Regan lifted her glass so Darcy could pour her more wine. "What's going on with Nicole? Is she working on our advertising campaign?"

Darcy finished pouring Sheena's wine and turned to Regan with a grin. "It's on its way."

"Great. Where did she end up working?" said Sheena.

"She's not coming to Florida, after all. In order to keep Nicole, her boss apparently gave her a raise and a promotion. She's bought a small condo and is living with her old boyfriend."

"Wow! Where's Alex?" said Regan.

Darcy's smile grew wider. "After their trip here, Nicole moved out of the condo she was sharing with Alex. They haven't seen much of one another since then."

Regan exchanged glances with Darcy. They'd both been victims of Alex's mean snobbery.

"I've promised Nicole a huge discount on any wedding she wants here at the hotel," said Darcy.

"That's the least we can do," said Sheena. Her smile disappeared, replaced by a frown. "I thought we'd hear from Blackie by now regarding the loan."

Darcy's face lost a little color. "What if we don't get it?"

"I don't know. Without additional funds, we can't do justice to the restaurant. We might even have to delay opening it," said Sheena. "And that worries me."

"We owe it to Graham to open it," protested Regan, well aware of how excited he was by the prospect of overseeing its kitchen.

"Tomorrow morning, I'll call Blackie," Sheena promised. "We're running out of time."

"Cyndi and Tom Jansen and their friends arrive this weekend," said Darcy. "Let's make sure they have a good time."

"I hope Meaghan's birthday party won't interfere with them," said Sheena. "There's no way I can cancel it now."

"Of all people, I'm sure they and their group will understand," said Darcy.

"Right. We advertise the Salty Key Inn as a family place," added Regan. "This weekend will be a good test of it."

They finished their wine, and then Sheena said, "I'd better get home."

"I'll go with you," said Darcy. "I want to spend some time with Austin."

"Then, I think I'll go for a swim in the pool," said Regan. "My muscles feel knotted with tension. Trying to run this hotel is harder than I'd ever dreamed."

"I'll keep an eye out for you," Sheena said. "No one should be swimming alone. Not even one of us."

"Yes, mother," Regan teased, and both Darcy and Sheena laughed. Sheena's bossiness had been a bit of a problem when they'd started out the year together, but now they could joke about it.

Regan opened the gate to the empty pool and set her towel down on a chair, happy for the privacy. She pulled a bathing cap over her head and dove into the clear water, slicing the water cleanly. She rose to the surface and let out a gasp at the water's coolness.

She struck out along the length of the pool, her limbs stretching, pulling, or kicking with each stroke, and she soon became lost in the rhythm of it.

After a few laps, she stopped to catch her breath. At the unexpected sight of a large shadow sitting nearby, she cried out.

"Sorry to scare you," said Brian. "I didn't know you could swim like that. Very good."

"Yeah, well I don't get a chance to do it privately like this very often," Regan said.

"You should take the time. You're a beautiful swimmer."

Regan hesitated to get out of the water. The bathing suit she'd put on was her tiniest bikini, and she knew Brian would tease her.

"Need help getting out?" he said.

Regan removed her bathing cap and felt her long hair tumble to her shoulders. And then, drawing a deep breath, she climbed the steps out of the pool.

Brian stood and held out her towel. "Need this?" He was wearing shorts and no shirt.

As they stared at each other, a frisson of energy raced through her and tightened her stomach. She tried not to notice the bulge in his pants, but it was impossible to miss. Trembling, she held out a hand to take the towel.

"Cold?" he said gently. "Here." He wrapped the towel around her and brought her close.

She thought of resisting and then laid her head against his bare chest, feeling the tickle of chest hairs against her cheek.

"Better?" Brian murmured.

She inhaled his manly scent and nodded.

He stepped away and gazed down at her. With great tenderness, he gathered a strand of her hair and pushed it away from her face. He trailed his finger along the scar under her chin and studied her lip.

She started to pull away, but he drew her closer. Knowing

what was coming, she closed her eyes and let out a sigh when she felt his lips on hers. A surge of longing deep within her thrummed with the beat of her racing heart. When he indicated he wanted her to open her mouth to his tongue, she happily did so. His tongue stroked hers in a sexy dance until she felt her knees go weak. Trying to catch her balance, she stumbled away from him and faced him breathing hard.

"You okay, hon?" he said softly.

She nodded, but she wasn't okay at all. She'd never wanted a man more than she wanted, no needed, Brian at this moment. And it scared the shit out of her.

"I've got to get back to my room," she said, unable to hide the tremor in her voice.

He laughed softly as she turned and sprinted away from him.

CHAPTER THIRTY-NINE

SHEENA

Sheena waited anxiously for Blackie to take her call. So much depended on Archibald Wilson's relaxing some rules, and good ole Archie seemed to be such a stickler for them.

"Sorry to keep you waiting," Blackie announced brusquely through the phone. "It's been a hectic morning."

"I understand," said Sheena. "You're a busy man. My sisters and I were wondering if you've been able to talk to Archibald Wilson on our behalf."

"Yes, as a matter of fact, I just hung up from a call with him."

Sheena's stomach clenched. "And?"

"And I think he's on board. We had a long discussion about Gavin. The fact that he told me to be open to any moves from you Gavin might have tried himself makes a compelling argument for going ahead with a loan for you."

"Wonderful!" cried Sheena, jumping up from the kitchen chair in which she'd been sitting. Unable to hold back her excitement, she did a little dance.

"But, Sheena, it comes with a price," cautioned Blackie. "If you fail with the challenge, you and your sisters will still be liable for either the entire loan or a part of it, depending on your success at the end of the year."

Sheena's excitement faded. "And what exactly does that mean?"

"It's not as ominous as you might think, provided you and your sisters move forward. However, if the restaurant should flop, it won't be good for you."

"We've got to do it," said Sheena. "It's a gutsy move, but it's the only way we can pull off this challenge of Gavin's."

Blackie laughed. "Good for you! I told Archie you'd say that. You're Gavin's girl, all right."

Sheena's heart stopped beating and then sprinted forward in shock. "What did you say?"

"Just that you and your sisters are like Gavin. He'd be so proud."

Deflated, Sheena sank down into the chair. She might never know the true story of the gold coin Uncle Gavin had given her. She'd treasure it as much as she now treasured her relationship with her sisters.

Blackie continued. "I'm having the agreement between you women and Gavin's estate drawn up now. I'll email it over for your signatures as soon as possible. I understand you're on a time crunch here."

"Thank you, Blackie. I don't know how we'll ever be able to thank you for all you've done for us."

"Just win this challenge. Gavin and I were both betting on it."

Blackie hung up, and Sheena was left to wonder if she and her sisters could do what their uncle wanted. She texted Regan and Darcy to meet with her in the registration office as soon as possible and then headed there herself.

Regan was on duty when Sheena walked in.

"Got your message," she said, looking up at her from behind the registration desk. "What's going on?"

"It's about the agreement we need to sign with Archibald Wilson and Gavin's estate. Let's wait for Darcy, and I'll tell you all about it."

Regan nodded and then studied Sheena. "How did you know Tony was the one for you? Were you ever worried you'd made a mistake by choosing him?"

"I think I know what this is about," Sheena said quietly. "Sometimes you have to follow your heart. I know Mom made you think everything had to be perfect before committing to someone, but life doesn't come up with perfect situations. It didn't for me, as you know. But my life has worked out very well."

"Hey, there!" Darcy cried, entering the office. "What's up? Did we get the deal?"

"Yes, but it's not as simple as you might think." Sheena explained the situation to her sisters. "Blackie is emailing the agreement for each of us to sign. And we need to check in with Brian and Tony right away. We'll need their cooperation in scheduling finish carpenters, painters, and everyone else, to get the job done on a timely basis."

"And that means giving Mo and me time to do the interior," said Regan. "I'll call him to set up an appointment to meet and discuss the upstairs function room we're adding."

"Nicole's package should come today," Darcy said. "But she was unaware of our destination wedding concept, so I'll get to work on that. I'd better call Graham too."

Sheena studied her sisters. Their time working with one another had brought them together in more ways than one. For the first time that morning, she thought the three of them might be able to pull off this new idea of theirs, after all.

That afternoon Sheena led Tony up the stairway of the restaurant to the function room. Brian slowly climbed the stairs behind them, holding onto Regan and Darcy for support.

The room, unfinished, lay in front of them, full of possibilities.

"This is where we envision functions of all types, though we'll be pushing the wedding business," Sheena said.

"We'll need room for dining, along with restroom facilities and a room I would call a bridal suite—a place where brides can change their clothes, or entertain their wedding party, or have private moments with the family," said Regan.

"And if it's large enough, small private parties could be held there, too," Darcy said.

They turned as Mo and Graham joined them.

"Glad you're here," said Sheena. "We've been talking about how to use this space." She told them what had been discussed and turned to them. "What do you think?"

"Could be very lucrative," said Graham. "But only if we make it special and then charge a decent price."

"I envision a nice open area, versatile, and attractive without overdoing it," said Mo. He looked up at the roof. "How about adding some skylights for lighting during the day and a little romance at night."

"The kind with the retractable sun screens," said Regan, smiling at him.

"Okay, everybody, make a list of features for this room so I can give you an estimate on what it'll cost to complete it," said Brian.

"Right. We need to come up with a list of materials, and then I need to be able to budget time for the men," Tony said, receiving a nod of approval from Brian.

"We need measurements so we can work out what furnishings we'll need," said Mo. "Regan and I would like to design the bridal suite."

"Right," said Regan. "I have a picture of it in my mind."

"Window seat looking out over the bay?" said Mo.

Regan laughed. "Exactly."

"And when it's not used for brides, it can be a nice, small dining room," said Mo.

"We want a small service kitchen to handle meeting groups, though our main kitchen will handle food production and the large functions. I'll start working on menus," said Graham. "I wonder if Bebe would consider making the wedding cakes?"

A look of delight crossed Darcy's face. "I bet she'd love it. I can talk to her and Gracie about it."

Sheena stared at the members of this group, realizing life had taken another sharp turn, and maybe, just maybe, it would save them.

CHAPTER FORTY

REGAN

Regan and Mo left the restaurant building, arm in arm, chatting companionably about various possibilities for decorating and designing the space. As they crossed the lawn to the Sandpiper Suites Building, it seemed natural to Regan to share moments like these with Mo. As she often had, she wished she could find another man who made her feel so comfortable, so accepted for who she was.

"How are things going with you and Kenton?" she asked him.

Mo's dark eyes sparkled. "Things between us are good. We know we can't live together for a while, but whenever he's in Florida taking care of business or seeing his sister, we meet."

Regan beamed at him. "I'm so happy for you, Mo. Everyone needs love."

He angled an eyebrow at her. "How about you? Anything happening between you and Brian? I noticed the two of you hardly looked at each other in the meeting like you were trying not to. What's up with that?"

She took a deep breath. "It's complicated."

He stopped and studied her. "Oh my God! You love him! Does he love you?"

"That's the thing. I'm not sure how he feels about me. I know he's attracted, but I have no idea about the possibility of any real future with him. I made a commitment to myself to be careful about any relationships, and Brian is hard for me to figure out. He likes everybody, and everybody likes him. But when it comes to long-term arrangements, he seems to back off. I guess that's why he's single."

"If you're talking about backing away from Jill Jackson, that was a smart move," said Mo.

"Yes, but at his age, he could've had many other opportunities, and he's still alone."

Mo snorted with disgust. "Because he's ten years older, it doesn't mean he can't commit to anyone. It just means he hasn't found the right person while he's been building his business."

Regan swallowed hard.

"Look, sweetie," said Mo kindly. "I think it's you who is afraid to make a commitment. Think about it. You turn away every guy who shows interest."

"But all they want is to go to bed with me," Regan protested. "You have no idea how many guys I've fought off after I told them 'no.'"

Mo squeezed her hand. "I can well imagine. But here, you're in a healthier situation with family and friends around you. Maybe it's time to reassess."

"Do you really think so?" Regan said, knowing she was asking a bigger question than that.

He nodded. "Sweetie, I do. I want the best for you. I really do."

Regan gave Mo a hug. "Thanks."

Brian and Tony approached them.

"What's this?" Brian said, smiling.

Mo stepped away from Regan. "Just a heart-to-heart talk." He gave Brian a meaningful look that made Regan wish she could magically join the seagulls circling over the beach.

"Regan, you two will let us know about your requirements as soon as possible. Right?" said Tony, oblivious to her discomfort. "Brian and I have taken some measurements, and we'll get some drawings done."

"I can make some sketches for you," Mo said. "In fact, Regan and I planned to work on them this evening."

"Good," said Tony. "I'll probably be working on stuff tonight too."

Regan took Mo's arm. "C'mon. Let's hurry and get started."

"Running away so soon?" Brian said, resting beside his walker.

Regan gave him a little wave and headed to the Sandpiper Suites Building.

"See what I mean?" Mo said as they walked along.

"What?" said Regan, knowing exactly what Mo was talking about.

The next couple of days flew by as everyone concentrated on finalizing details of the function area in the restaurant.

Cyndi and Tom Jansen arrived with four other couples. Regan helped to see everyone was settled in their rooms. She and her sisters had decided to purchase some additional equipment for the handicapped rooms to help the other two men who still coped with disabilities.

With each new guest in the hotel, Regan learned what additional features would make for a more comfortable stay. Watching the ex-military men work with their post-injury disabilities, she was reminded how hard Brian had worked to overcome his. Though it would be some time until his bones healed for a full recovery, he continued exercising the muscles around them.

She'd just delivered warm cookies from Gracie's to each room when she saw Brian sitting on a chair by the pool. She waved and went on her way back to her suite. She and Mo were making final choices on the light fixtures and carpeting for the function room, and then she was on duty at the registration desk for the rest of the afternoon.

In her suite, she looked again at the photos of the light fixtures. She and Mo had narrowed it down to two. She liked the idea of strategically placed, recessed lighting in addition to three chandeliers that would hang in a row from the center of the high, cathedral ceiling. She and Mo had gone back and forth about the style of the chandeliers, trying to decide whether to keep to a funky, Florida theme or to select something more elegant. Even though it would cost more, they were going with crystal chandeliers, which meant they had to keep that tone throughout the upstairs. But Regan and Mo couldn't resist the idea of sunlight coming through the skylights and landing on the chandeliers, refracting rainbows throughout the room.

Choosing the carpet was a little more difficult. Floral prints were a possibility, and the choices were endless. Regan was going to let Mo take the lead on that.

Mo arrived out of breath. "Sorry to be late. My grandmother called, and I didn't dare cut short her conversation."

Regan laughed. No one would dare dismiss Carlotta Beecher, Mo's grandmother, whom Regan had met earlier in the year. She was as regal as the Queen of England.

They lugged the carpet samples and the lighting fixtures book to the restaurant. Downstairs, crews were working on several projects. Upstairs, the electricians were finishing the wiring of switch boxes and outlets so the drywall could be installed, taped, and mudded over before painting.

Mo laid several carpet samples next to each other on the floor. Regan stood by Mo's side as they studied them.

"I like the smaller patterns better," Mo said. "It's more

suitable for the room."

"I agree," said Regan. "And I think the green tones suit the room better than the reds."

"Yup. They have a cooler feel to them, which is nice for a room that will often be crowded." Mo grabbed two of the samples and moved them beside the sliding door leading to the balcony overlooking the back garden. He stood back. "Ah, just as I thought. The darker color plays nicely with the outdoors. What do you think, Regan?"

"I like it. How fast can we get it?"

"That answer will take a phone call and a lot of begging."

Regan's sigh was filled with worry. Opening the restaurant meant a lot of people had to come through with their promises.

"Okay, let's choose the chandeliers, and then I have to go to the office.

It took no time for them to choose the chandeliers they wanted. The choices for lighting for the wall sconces, ceiling fixtures, and the bridal suite easily followed.

"All right," said Mo, picking up the carpet samples. "I'll place the orders and get back to you. I'm also checking on the orders for Arthur's places. I'm meeting with Lance later today, and he'll give me a schedule for the murals."

"Arthur is still waiting for the work to begin after the New Year, right?" said Regan.

Mo nodded. "He doesn't want anything to interfere with the holidays." He gave her a shy smile. "I'm hoping by then we can work on Kenton's house."

At his excitement, Regan grinned. "Me too!" Her heart swelled with affection for this beloved friend.

When Regan arrived at the office, an older couple was

checking in. Darcy handed them a key to the room and said, "My sister, Regan, will be happy to take you to your room. Regan, this is Mr. and Mrs. Webster, here from Alabama.

"Welcome," Regan said smoothly, accustomed to the duty they all shared of showing guests to their rooms.

As she led them to the Egret Building, Regan explained the hotel was at one time noted for being a family place and was now under renovation.

"The setting is lovely," said Mrs. Webster. "We're here at my granddaughter's request. She's going to be married next spring and wanted us to look at the hotel. A friend of hers living in Boston told her about the Salty Key Inn."

"How nice," said Regan. "We definitely have plans for destination weddings. If you'd like, I can talk to you about it and show you what we have in mind."

"That would be very nice. Bill and I are paying for their small wedding as our gift to them."

"Think it's a lot to ask of us, but we're happy to do it," grumbled Mr. Webster. "Family issues and all."

Regan smiled. For all the gruffness in his voice, he wore a look of pride.

After showing them to their room, explaining the facilities to them, and making sure they had coupons, Regan left them to return to the office.

"Glad you're here," said Darcy. "I've looked at Nicole's package. We need to set up a meeting for tomorrow. Right now, Austin is going to pick me up for a very late lunch, and then we're going to look at furniture for the condo." She let out a happy sigh. "I can't wait until I can officially move in."

"Just a few more months, and we'll know what's going to happen to all of us," Regan replied. Of the three of them, she was the least settled, and it bothered her. She thought of Mo's remarks to her about Brian and wondered if she could find the courage to follow her heart.

She had no more time to think of it because the phone rang as Darcy left the office. And then, when she finished her call, she looked up to find Brian heading into the office.

"Hi," she said. "What can I help you with?"

His eyes gleamed with mischief. "I have a deal for you. I'll take you to dinner if you'll help me exercise in the pool tonight. I'm going to use the pool to help assist with my recovery. It's much easier to do the exercises here than at the rehab center."

"Okay. Deal. Do I get to choose the restaurant?"

He shook his head. "Nope. I'll pick you up at your door at seven, but you'll have to drive. Okay?"

She laughed. "Okay."

As he left the office, Regan watched him walk across the lawn. The walker had been replaced with a cane, but even so, it was a slow process.

At seven, Regan heard the knock on the door to her suite and hurried to answer it. When she opened the door, Brian's gaze traveled from her face to her feet and up again. A wide smile lit his face. "My God, Regan, you're so beautiful."

Trying to shake off her shyness at his remark, she blurted out, "You don't look so bad yourself."

He chuckled. "Sounds like it's going to be a great evening."

"Let me get the keys to the van, and I'm ready to go," said Regan. She grabbed the keys and her purse, and they headed outside.

Regan waited patiently as Brian took a few moments to get into the van, and then she walked around behind it to get in on the driver's side.

"Thanks for driving," said Brian. "It's a little awkward with me restricted like this."

"Not a problem," Regan said sincerely. "Now, where are we going?"

"The Key Pelican. I know it's the inspiration for Gavin's, and I wanted to look at it from a guest's point of view with you."

"Nice," said Regan. "Their food is delicious too."

Regan drove to the turquoise building that held one of the most successful, upscale restaurants in the area and waited for a valet to help her out of the car. She handed the young man the keys to the van and went to Brian's side.

When they entered the restaurant together, the hostess beamed at him. "Hello, Brian. Long time no see. What happened to you?"

"My girl, here, and I got into a little motorcycle accident, but I'm getting better."

Taken aback by his words, Regan thought back to how annoyed she'd been when Chip suggested they were together. But no such feelings rose in her now, and Regan realized how much she liked the idea of being with Brian.

They were seated at a table by the window overlooking the outside garden, lit by lights strategically hidden among the foliage. The effect was stunning.

After the waiter filled their water glasses and placed the wine menu in front of Brian, he asked, "Is this a special occasion?"

"Yes," said Brian, winking at her. "We're celebrating our recoveries."

The waiter glanced from him to Regan and smiled. "Very nice. I'll leave you to make your wine choice and will be back to tell you about our specials."

"Should we do something like champagne?" Brian said. "I think this occasion calls for it."

"It sounds very festive," Regan said, unwilling to admit she'd had champagne only one other time at a friend's wedding and had awoken with a headache the next morning.

"Okay, let's do it. I like *Bille-Cart Salmon*, a brut rosé. I learned about it from one of my mother's wine distributors. I think you'll like it too."

"Thanks," said Regan, amused by his enthusiasm. She'd always thought of Brian as a beer kind of guy and was pleasantly surprised by this side of him.

Regan watched as the champagne was ordered, opened, and served. After Brian had tasted it and nodded his approval, the light-pink wine was poured into a stemmed tulip glass for her and then for Brian.

The waiter quietly slipped away as Brian raised his glass to her. "Here's to us! We've come through quite a time together. May the future be brighter for us."

"Yes, here's to us!" Regan said. She took a sip of the champagne and giggled as the bubbly liquid tickled her nose.

Brian reached across the table and brushed a finger across her nose. "I love to hear you laugh like this."

She smiled at the tenderness in his expression and told herself to relax, though his touch had sent a sudden rush of nervous energy through her.

As they were perusing the menu, Brian said, "I told Graham we were coming here, and he asked us to order as many different things as we could, as a kind of taste test. You go first, and I'll follow."

They were laughing by the time the waiter took their order—escargots and calamari for appetizers, rack of lamb and snapper for their main courses, and two different kinds of salads—one with pears and blue cheese and another with parmesan croutons and mushrooms.

"This is lovely," said Regan, glancing around the room,

seeing the happy faces of customers, and hearing the soft buzz of conversation. "I hope we can do as well with Gavin's. It might mean the difference between winning or failing in our quest to meet Uncle Gavin's challenge."

"Your restaurant is going to look very nice, and Graham is an excellent chef. He's put together a nice team for the kitchen."

"And Casey Cochran is helping him manage the place. If the challenge is met, we'd like him to manage the entire hotel for us."

Brian studied her. "So, you're happy here in Florida?"

"Oh, yes," Regan said. "I have no plans to live anywhere else. And both my sisters feel the same way. The two of them are nicely settled."

"And you? Are you nicely settled too?"

Regan looked away from his penetrating stare. "I suppose. Mo and I work well together."

"What about the other parts of your life? I saw Chip the other day, and he told me he wants to get back together with you."

Regan's nostrils flared. "He and I were never really together, and I have no intention of being with him."

"I see." Brian's lips curved into a satisfied smile.

Their talk returned to the hotel and progress on the restaurant. Regan was pleased to learn how dedicated Brian and Tony were to getting the work done. They'd even started scheduling evening crews during the week.

By the time dessert was served—apple crisp and vanilla ice cream for Brian and crème brulée for her—Regan felt content with life, with Brian, with herself. They'd talked and talked about a lot of things. Relaxed together like this, Regan realized how much she liked Brian.

They left the restaurant arm in arm.

As she drove them back to the hotel, sexual tension filled the quiet between them. She snuck a glance at him, observing his strong jaw and broad shoulders. Even injured, he was a handsome guy.

At one point, he clasped her hand in his and trailed a thumb over her palm, sending tingles racing up her arm.

She glanced at him, saw the longing in his eyes, and nervously retrieved her hand.

When she pulled into the parking lot, Regan felt a sense of relief wash over her. Brian Harwood was trouble and she knew it, wanted it.

Brian got out of the van and faced her. "Okay, now you have to help me in the pool. You promised. Remember?" His brown-eyed stare silently spoke to her, causing a wave of desire to roll through her. "Well?" he said softly.

"Sure. A promise is a promise. I'll get changed and meet you outside, though it's not good to swim on a full stomach." At the smile that crossed his face, her stomach felt more fluttery than full.

The cool night air felt pleasant against her skin as Regan remained next to Brian while he made his way across the lawn to the pool. He used the cane only to help keep his balance, but she saw how hard he worked to keep from leaning too heavily on it because of arm injuries.

She stopped and looked up at the stars that sparkled in the inky night sky like promises of wishes about to come true. Smiling, she turned to Brian and pointed to the sky. As he looked up, his foot hit a depression in the lawn, and slowly, as if in slow-motion, he tumbled to the ground.

Gasping with shock, Regan raced over to him. "Oh my God! Are you all right?"

Brian lay on his back and stared up at her, his lips thin with frustration. "Goddammit! I hate having you see me like this!"

"Are you hurt?"

At the shake of his head, she held out her hand. "Come on. I'll help you up."

She took hold of his upper arm and braced her feet against the ground as he hefted himself up.

Wincing, he said, "Maybe I better go back to my room."

"I'll go with you to make sure you're all right." Regan's concern caused another sound of disgust to escape Brian. Studying his face, Regan recognized how humiliated Brian was by the fall.

"Look, Brian ..." she began.

He cut her off. "Don't say anything."

Understanding how he felt, Regan was quiet as they made their way back inside the building and to his suite. She held the door for him, and he walked into the living area and over to the couch.

"Would you like some water? Do you need aspirin? What can I do for you?" Regan asked him, feeling helpless.

He smiled and patted the couch next to him. "Just come here and sit with me for a while."

Regan lowered herself onto the couch and studied him. "Are you really all right?"

"Yeah, just feeling stupid. I wanted to show you how much better I am, then I go and fall on my face. No wonder people don't want to be around me like this. I feel like a damn baby."

Regan knew self-pity when she heard it. She took hold of his hand. "Brian, I'm not people. And I want to be with you."

His face brightened. "You do?"

"Yeah," she said, feeling her cheeks grow warm. "I do." His gaze reached deep inside her to where her heart pounded with an un accustomed emotion.

"Good." Brian put an arm around her and drew her to him.

She settled her head against his broad chest and heard the pounding of his heart. His racing heartbeats matched her own.

Brian tilted her chin up and sighed happily. "I've wanted this from the moment I first saw you."

"Even after I told you to fuck off?"

He laughed. "That did surprise me, but I could tell you were as shocked by that as I was."

"I was just so tired of guys flirting with me. I wanted to be someone different, try new things, have a better life."

"Regan, you're perfect as you are. You're bright and beautiful and kind, and I've wanted you for a long time."

She focused on his sensual lips and uttered a small sigh as they came down on hers. His mouth and tongue told her how much he wanted her. She responded in kind, letting her emotions rule her behavior.

His hand cupped a breast, and instead of pulling away like she often did with others, she leaned into his fingers, thrilling to the sensations racing through her.

When they finally pulled apart, Brian stared at her breathing heavily. "I love you, Regan, and I always will. Trying to work things out with Jill when I knew you weren't interested made me realize I could never be happy with anyone else. I've waited for you to give me a chance."

He cupped her cheek with his broad palm. "With you, I share such a special connection. And I know I can trust you and depend on you. You're the one who's been with me through one of the worst times of my life, and now I don't want to lose you."

Regan looked at his leg and the cast on one arm, the sling around the other. She couldn't hold back her feelings any longer. With Brian, she came alive in a way she never had with anyone else. She held onto his hand, needing to feel his warmth, his strength.

"My feelings for you sometimes scare me. I'm way out of your league. Women all love you. I thought you were looking for a casual relationship. And even though guys have wanted it, I've never had sex with anyone before. I've been waiting for the right man like my mother asked me. I know it sounds silly, but I made a promise to myself and ...

Brian leaned toward her and kissed her gently on the mouth. "We can wait for that. I'm just happy you'll give me the time to show you what I feel. I'll let you tell me when you're ready for more. Okay?"

"Okay," Regan whispered, blinking away tears. She felt like such a child.

"No need to cry," Brian said with such tenderness she wanted to break down and bawl. He drew her up against his side, and she lay in his arms.

Regan awoke with a start. Glancing at the kitchen clock, she blinked in surprise. Three A.M.

She carefully moved away from Brian and studied his face. He was breathing deeply, his mouth open in a soft snore. Seeing him like this, she smiled. Not willing to wake him, she got up and tiptoed out of his suite.

Inside her own suite next door, she quietly went into her room, undressed, and fell into bed. She tossed and turned restlessly, unable to go back to sleep. Tonight, she'd wanted Brian like nobody before. And if the time came for them to make love, she'd be ready, because her heart would tell her it was okay.

CHAPTER FORTY-ONE

SHEENA

Sheena looked up from her computer when Darcy came into the kitchen, a mischievous grin brightening her blue eyes.

"What's up?"

"I happen to know Regan did not come in from her date with Brian until three o'clock this morning. Looks like things may be heating up between the two of them."

Sheena smiled with delight. "That would be great. Two of my favorite people together."

Darcy plopped down into a chair at the kitchen table. "Yeah, the two of them are good together. Anyone can see how they feel about one another."

"I've tried to talk to Regan about following her heart," said Sheena. "Maybe she listened to me."

"Mom laid a trip on her about not letting any man get close to her unless she wanted to be with him for the rest of her life," Darcy said.

Sheena sighed and nodded. "Probably because of me."

"But you and Tony are great together and happy after all these years," protested Darcy. "Mom knew that."

"Yes, but it could've turned out so differently," Sheena said. "Mom knew very well some marriages aren't the happiest."

"True," said Darcy. "Austin is such a good guy I have no worries about being with him for the rest of my life."

Sheena squeezed her sister's hand. "I'm so happy for you.

Hopefully, Regan will find that kind of happiness too."

Regan arrived, holding a note in her hand. "Sorry, I'm late. I just got Darcy's note to meet you here."

"Late morning, huh?" Darcy teased. "Or was it a late night?"

Regan's cheeks reddened. "It's not what you think. Brian and I fell asleep watching television."

"Gee, I was hoping for more than that," said Darcy, continuing the tease.

"Really," said Sheena in an attempt to ease Regan's discomfort, "if you and Brian are getting serious, we'd all love it."

"You would?" said Regan.

"It's obvious you two are attracted to each other," Sheena said.

"Yeah, those smoldering looks between the two of you could sizzle a slice of bacon," said Darcy grinning.

"Oh, wow," said Regan. "I thought I hid my feelings well. I was so confused about him."

"And now?" prompted Sheena.

A crooked smile broke out on Regan's face. "I'm following my heart. Brian and I talked a lot last night. He told me things about himself I never suspected. Did you know his father left him and his mother when he was just a small child? He's had to be the man of the house since then. It hasn't been easy for him." She sighed. "That's why he's struggling so hard now with his inability to work. He feels useless."

"I can well imagine that," said Sheena. "Poor guy."

Regan's eyes filled. "I love him. I really do. But I'm afraid I may spoil it. I've never been with a guy ..."

"Don't worry. It'll all work out." Darcy rose from her chair and gave Regan a hug.

"It's about love as much as anything," added Sheena,

touched by the tenderness between her sisters, recalling how hateful they'd been to one another in the past.

"Well, we'll see what happens," said Regan. "But as Mo said, I've got to stop running away from my feelings for Brian."

"Mo said that?" Sheena grinned. "I love that guy!"

"Me, too," said Darcy and Regan together. At their verbal duet ringing in the air, they broke into laughter.

"Okay, let's get to the meeting," said Sheena. "Darcy, let's go over the materials Nicole sent. Does she have a good marketing plan for us?"

"I think so," Darcy said happily. "I've read through everything she sent and have made some notes for us. First of all, she loves our logo and our tagline, so that makes it easy. However, she said wherever we could, we need to place both of them together, so people become familiar with them. We need to include them in newspaper ads and articles."

"What did she say about ads?" Sheena said.

"She said we have to spend money on ads, and we need to get a continuous campaign underway." Darcy held up a list. "That means running ads every week in the local paper, putting ads on travel sites and even on Facebook. We'll direct people to our webpage and build a mailing list."

"When are we going to have time to do all that?" Regan said.

"And how are we going to pay for it?" said Sheena. She quickly checked her computer and brought up the budget for the restaurant. "We do have some money budgeted for advertising for Gavin's. Maybe we can juggle some funds there."

Darcy shook her head. "Nicole didn't know about our plans to draw in destination weddings. That's something we'll have to work on ourselves."

"I think advertising for weddings should say something

about treasures or treasured, similar to our tagline," said Regan.

"I've got it," said Darcy. "A Treasured Time."

"How about extending it to 'Treasured Times,' and then we can list weddings, anniversaries, and family plans under that umbrella," said Sheena.

"I love it," said Regan. "We can list military family plans there too."

"Okay," said Darcy. "I'll have to completely revamp our webpage, but I think it's fabulous."

Sheena gave her sisters a high-five, loving how they'd learned to work together.

After they drew up a list of duties for each of them, Darcy got up. "I'd better get to work right away."

"Regan, you're going to help me with Meaghan's birthday party, aren't you?" Sheena said.

"Sure, I'll meet up with you later. First, I want to check on Brian. Maggie is going to help him with some of the exercises, but I promised I'd work with him in the pool."

Sheena exchanged smiles with Regan and stood. "I've got to talk with Bebe about the cake she's making for Meaghan."

"See you later," said Regan.

As Sheena walked over to Gracie's, she thought of Gavin's people. She knew most of their stories and found it touching Gavin had brought them together. And as Blackie had once told her, they all served a purpose she hadn't foreseen. Sally was now handling the registration office; Maggie was helping Brian with his injuries; Bebe was doing special baking projects and would continue to do so; Lynn assisted Gracie in the restaurant. Rocky, Blackie Gatto's brother and a previous sailing buddy of Gavin's, Clyde, a mentally slow young man, and Sam, whom Gavin had rescued from prison, did a variety of projects around the hotel and in the restaurant.

Sheena entered the restaurant and went into the kitchen.

Bebe looked up from where she was icing a cake and smiled at her. "Thought I'd try a couple of butterflies near the flowers."

Sheena clapped with delight. "Oh, Meaghan will love it. It's gorgeous! Thank you so much!"

Bebe smiled. "Nothing's too good for our girl, right?"

"Right," said Sheena, giving Bebe a quick hug.

Sheena had just left the restaurant when Meaghan came racing toward her. "Rocky and Sam put up the volleyball net. It's great! Thank you so much!" She threw her arms around Sheena, hugging her tight. "It's going to be the best birthday ever!"

Sheena laughed, delighted Meaghan had made such good friends in a short period of time. The girls she hung out with were nice and down-to-earth. From hard-working families, they didn't exhibit the entitled attitude of Meaghan's old friends. For that reason, among many, Sheena was glad her family had moved to Florida.

She and Meaghan walked together back to the suite.

"Are you done putting together your prizes for your guests?" Sheena said.

Meaghan nodded. "I've got prizes for best volleyball team, best sport, best girl player, best guy player, and a whole lot of other prizes—enough for all twelve of us."

"Sounds good. I just checked your cake. It's beautiful."

Meaghan smiled. "Maybe someday Bebe will make my wedding cake. Hers are the best."

Sheena laughed. "Let's not rush things. You're turning fifteen." She watched with affection as Meaghan skipped on ahead of her. Meaghan was fifteen going on twenty-five. Oh, to be that young again.

Later, watching the kids play volleyball on the beach, shouting, teasing, and laughing together, Sheena was pleased. In a while, they'd serve the kids dinner and the cake, but for now, it was a quiet moment for Regan and her to talk.

"Did you help Brian with the pool exercises?"

Regan shook her head. "The pool was busy. I'll help him tonight when we can have the pool to ourselves."

Sheena nodded. "Makes all the sense in the world."

"When you're with Tony, does he make you feel as if you could fly with happiness?" Regan asked shyly.

Sheena filled with tenderness for the sister who'd never believed she was as wonderful as she was. "If that is how Brian makes you feel, that's special, Regan. Don't let him go. And yes, with Tony, I sometimes feel as if we both have wings."

CHAPTER FORTY-TWO

REGAN

It was quiet and dark as Regan and Brian, with his walker for stability, made their way to the pool. Cyndi Jansen's group had settled down for the night, leaving the pool empty. Behind the hedge of oleander and hibiscus, the pool was protected from view by guests in the Egret Building, giving Regan and Brian the privacy they sought.

Regan unlocked the gate and held it open for Brian. He moved beyond her, tossed his towel onto a chair, and took off his T-shirt. Leaving the walker behind, he made his way to the pool and held onto the railing, waiting for her.

Watching him, Regan admired the shape of his body, the width of his shoulders, and the muscles hard work had built. He was as handsome a man as she'd ever dated, and much nicer. When she'd apologized for sneaking away from him, he'd given her a roguish look and said, "Hopefully, next time, it won't be so easy for you to leave me."

Even now she smiled at the memory of those words.

"Ready?" Brian called to her.

She slid off the T-shirt that covered the top of her bikini and set down her towel.

Brian watched her every move as she came closer. "Have I told you lately how beautiful you are?"

In the cool air, her body heated at the sexy look he gave her.

He held out a hand, and she took it.

"Time to get to work," she said, leading him into the water, then diving through it, away from him.

He laughed and struggled to follow her.

She swam to end of the pool and back and stood beside him. “Okay, hold onto the side of the pool with one arm and then carefully stroke through the water with the other arm. The booklet the doctor gave you said they did not want you to strain any joints, but simply to work on the muscles around them. If you feel any pain at all, stop. I’ll count the strokes. When you can’t do any more, we’ll switch arms, and then we’ll work on your leg.”

“Yes, nurse,” teased Brian.

Forty minutes later, Brian sat on the steps taking a break.

Regan swam over to him. “You had enough?”

“For now.” He caught hold of her arms and gently tugged her into his lap.

She faced him. “You’re doing very well. That’s hard work.”

“I’m just trying to impress you,” he said smiling and brushing the hair away from her face.

Her heart thumped in anticipation as his mouth met hers. His warm lips were inviting. Regan relaxed, letting herself be carried away by the pleasure of the kiss. Soon it became apparent Brian was ready for more.

Groaning, he pulled away from her. “Want to go back to my suite?”

Regan nodded, well aware of what he was asking. “Yes. Let’s go.”

Regan stood by as Brian climbed the steps of the pool and accepted the towel she handed him. Even after wrapping the towel around himself, it was evident how aroused Brian was. She tried not to stare, but couldn’t help noticing the size of it. A frisson of excitement rolled through her at what lay ahead.

They moved together across the hotel lawn.

“Christ,” said Brian, thumping his walker down on the

ground. "This is so annoying. I'd run if I could."

"I'm not going anywhere, but with you," said Regan, realizing that's exactly how she thought of the future now—with him.

They made it to his suite and closed the door behind them.

Brian dropped his towel and pulled her into his arms. His hands cupped her face, and he kissed her with such longing her stomach tightened. His hands slid over her body as if he was memorizing her shape. When he unhooked her bra, her breasts tumbled free.

She moaned as his lips touched their tender skin.

He pulled back and studied her. "Are you ready for this? We agreed you'd let me know."

"Oh, yes," she cried, unable to ignore the pulsing inside her body.

Brian's smile was so loving, so tender, tears came to her eyes.

"Let's go into the bedroom," he said. "That will be much more comfortable."

He led her into the room and helped her remove her wet bathing suit bottom. And then he freed himself for her full view.

Suddenly nervous, Regan stared at his manly shape.

Brian moved to her, wrapped his arms around her and rubbed her back. "I love you, Regan. I have from the first time we met. I just couldn't make you believe me."

"Oh, but I do believe you now," she said, reaching for him.

"Words aren't enough," he whispered. "I'll be gentle, I promise. Follow my lead, and we'll work around my injuries to make it the best for you."

She nodded, trusting him.

###

Later, as she lay beside him, her eyes filled.

"My God! Did I hurt you?" Brian said, taking a thumb and wiping away the tears that spilled onto her cheeks.

"No," she said. "It's that I'm so happy I finally got to know what everyone else has been talking about. It was better than all the romance novels I've read."

He grinned. "Did the earth stop for you for a moment?"

"I felt as if the earth was spinning with happiness," she said with a smug smile.

Brian cupped her cheeks in his broad hands. "Ah, Regan, you're the best thing that's ever happened to me. I want you with me forever."

She gazed at him, uncertain she'd heard correctly. Was he asking her to marry him?'

His lips came down on hers. As their kiss escalated into a need for more—a need she was only too happy to fill—she knew if the time came when he did ask her, she and her heart would say yes.

CHAPTER FORTY-THREE

DARCY

As the days raced toward Thanksgiving, Darcy focused on carrying out the ad campaign, Regan concentrated on the construction and decoration of the restaurant, and Sheena worked the numbers, trying to figure out how to get the most for their money. With the ads they'd put together, they were starting to get calls from people interested in booking winter weddings, as well as a couple of people wanting long-term winter stays.

One morning, the three of them sat in Sheena's kitchen going over the special items they'd need for weddings and receptions. They studied brochures from other hotels, trying to come up with ideas unique to the Salty Key Inn. Even in their partially renovated state, the inn had some things in their favor—the wide expanse of white beach across Gulf Boulevard in front of the hotel and Gavin's, which was turning out to be even more stunning than they'd dreamed.

They talked to one of Brian's landscapers and came up with an idea to build an arbor that could be used as the backdrop either for wedding services in the back of the lot beside the bay or for wedding photos. A gazebo would come later, they decided.

While talk of weddings and hotel guests was first on their list of topics, their father's forthcoming visit was always on their minds. Patrick Sullivan was in many respects like his brother Gavin—big, booming voice, a fondness for beer, and a bit of a jokester. But he had a dark side to him they suspected Gavin didn't have. The darkness came from Patrick's time in Vietnam and the fact that though he'd done very well in his job as a fireman, he'd never felt it was good enough. And now, they knew, his marriage to their mother had had its disappointments.

Sipping coffee together one morning, Darcy spoke of her nervousness. "I hope Dad will not get out of control like he sometimes does. I want Austin and his family to like him. He promised to give me away at my wedding."

Sheena reached over and gave her hand a comforting pat. "I understand. My concern is his resentment over Gavin's success. I hope he doesn't find fault with everything we've done here after we've worked so hard to make it."

"I want him to meet Brian," said Regan. "When I was little and at home, he always told me he'd fight any man who wanted to take me away from him. I think he was kidding, but still ..."

"Well, he's been invited here so we're all going to have to deal with it," said Sheena. "We'll have a special dinner at Gracie's, and that should take care of a lot of problems. He'll love the food."

"We can have a small, private reception at one of our suites before dinner," said Regan. "Nothing fancy, of course, but we can make it nice."

"I wonder how Regina will handle the family," said Darcy. "I've never cared for her."

"Regina O'Brien makes Dad happy, and that should be important to all of us," Sheena said, sounding like the big sister she was. "The day they come in, we'll have a simple meal in my suite. That'll give us a chance to get comfortable with one another."

Darcy and Regan exchanged silent looks.

CHAPTER FORTY-FOUR

REGAN

Regan looked into the mirror and smiled. The scar that had horrified her after the motorcycle accident would always be a reminder of a time she dared meet a challenge from Brian—a challenge that had brought out the love between them. What she saw now was not a face that was marred, but a face that had found love, and for that, she'd always be grateful.

"Come on! Are you ready? We can't be late to pick up Dad," said Darcy. "You know how airports are the day before Thanksgiving."

Regan pulled a brush through her long, dark, shiny hair and turned to her sister. "Okay, let's go. Where's Sheena?"

"In the van," said Darcy, hurrying Regan along.

The atmosphere inside the van was tense as they made their way into Tampa. Regan understood. Her sisters were as uptight as she. Their father could be unpredictable, and even as adults, they wanted his approval for all they'd accomplished.

After Sheena parked the van, the three of them went inside the terminal to the baggage claim area where they'd promised to meet Regina and their father.

"Remember, be kind to Regina," Sheena said.

Regan rolled her eyes at Darcy. Another big sister moment.

"Oh, here they come now!" said Darcy, running toward them, waving.

Regan and Sheena hurried after her.

Their father saw them, lifted his hand, and beamed at them. "Well, well!" he boomed, his face flushed with emotion. "Here are all my girls! Just look at you, all tanned and beautiful!"

"Welcome to Florida," Sheena said, giving him a welcoming embrace.

"Glad you're here," said Darcy, hugging him.

Standing back, Regan felt suddenly shy. Her father hadn't seen her since the accident.

"What? Don't I get a hug from you?" he asked, opening his arms.

Feeling like a little girl again, Regan ran into them. Her father patted her back and lifted her chin. "Got quite a scar there, honey, but you're still my beauty."

She stepped away, uncertain she wanted that role again. Sheena had always been the reliable one, Darcy the sassy one, and she, the beauty. In Florida, they'd tried to shake those roles up, be the people they wanted instead of being pigeonholed like this.

Their father turned to Regina standing aside. "Come here, honey, and say hi to the girls."

Regan studied the overdressed woman who'd replaced their mother. Regina was of average height and, like her father, carried a little extra weight. Brown hair streaked with gray surrounded a pretty face that now looked uncertain as she strode toward them.

Sympathy filled Regan, and she, like her sisters, rushed forward to greet Regina.

After they'd gathered the luggage, Regan followed the others out to the van.

Their father stopped outside the van and studied the logo. "So, all of this is real. Hard to believe my brother would do this for you, but then he and I never got along. Not after ..."

Sheena placed a hand on his arm. "Dad, you're here to enjoy the time with us."

"And we want to show you what we've done," said Darcy. "It's been a hell of a lot of work."

"We're not done yet," said Regan.

"But we're on our way," Sheena said, giving her a father a warning look.

Regan was glad when her father nodded. "You're right. Let's just have a good time."

They climbed into the van, and after getting settled, Sheena said, "I'll drive along the coast. It may take a little longer, but it's much more scenic."

"I'm anxious to see it," said Regina politely. "My daughter lives on the California coast, so I've seen that, of course."

"Regina wanted us to move to California, but we're not doing that just yet," Patrick said. "Right, honey?"

"He says we should stay in Boston," Regina said with resignation.

Regan and Darcy, sitting on either side of her in the backseat, glanced at each other but said nothing. Their father was old-fashioned that way.

As they came closer and closer to the Salty Key Inn, Regan's nerves twanged uncertainly. They'd worked hard to make the entrance to the property attractive, and she hoped her father wouldn't denigrate it with nasty comments.

"Here we are!" Sheena said moments later. She drove through the entrance and around to the parking lot by the Egret Building.

"We've put you in what is one of my favorite garden rooms," said Darcy. "You'll have quiet privacy there."

"Not by the pool?" Patrick said.

"The garden room will be lovely," Regina said with a

quietness that brought Patrick's protest to an end.

They got out of the van and, heart pounding with apprehension, Regan led her sisters, Regina, and her father to their room. She'd made Sheena and Darcy promise not to say anything about what she'd done until after he'd seen the accommodations for himself. But she'd be crushed if her father didn't like her work.

With trembling fingers, she unlocked the door and stood back.

Regina entered the room, followed by Patrick .

"Lovely," Regina exclaimed.

"Yeah, nice," said Patrick, and Regan let out the breath she'd been holding.

Darcy and Sheena followed behind her, showed their father the hotel's brochure, and handed him a bunch of discount coupons.

"I'll get you some ice," Darcy said. "Cold water and sodas are in the refrigerator. And, Dad, we put in a six-pack of your favorite beer."

Their father smiled. "I could use a Bud about now. Thanks."

Sheena placed a hand on Regan's shoulder. "Dad, I want you to know Regan is the one who designed and decorated the rooms. She and Moses Greene work together on projects like this."

The surprise etched on her father's face was telling. Fighting the old feeling of being the beautiful but dumb sister, Regan straightened and said what Mo had told her to say. "I was going to wait until after the new year to go into business with Mo, but we've already contracted a huge project for the Florida's Finest Restaurant chain."

"Really? Wow, Regan, that's something." Her father gazed at her as if seeing her for the first time. "You always were a good artist. Who knew you'd turn it into a real business?" He wrapped his arms around her. "I'm proud of you, honey. Beauty and brains."

Regan couldn't stop the tears that filled her eyes. She'd waited all her life to hear something like this from him.

"Hey, what'cha crying for?" her father said, his own eyes filling.

"It just means a lot to me to hear you say that," said Regan.

"We're all proud of her," Sheena said, as Darcy returned to the room. "And wait until you see what Darcy has done with the website and our advertising campaign."

"I'll show you later after you've unpacked and relaxed a bit," Darcy said, receiving a grateful smile from Regina.

"And what about you?" Patrick said, studying Sheena.

Before she could answer, Regan spoke up. "Sheena's our financial person. Blackie Gatto, our financial advisor, says she's clever, like Uncle Gavin."

Their father's lips thinned. "She'd better be a lot more honest than he was. He cheated me out of some money. Told me the investment he talked about was going to make me rich." Gazing around, he shook his head. "Don't know how he could've afforded all this."

Regan glanced at the stricken look on Sheena's face and drew herself up, furious their father had hurt her feelings. "Dad, I don't know what happened between you and Gavin, but I don't think you knew your brother at all. And if you'd accuse her of doing anything dishonest, you apparently don't know Sheena either."

Their father's jaw dropped, and his cheeks turned bright red. "Oh, no! I didn't mean that like it sounded." He turned to Sheena. "I'm sorry. It's just that Gavin always made me crazy, and now, being here, it brings it all back."

"You'd better get over it," warned Darcy, "because we

invited you here to show you and Regina a good time."

A look of surprise crossed their father's face. "Well, I'll be! I never thought I'd see the day when you would band together like this. Look, I'm sorry if I got off on the wrong foot here. I'm proud of the three of you, and I'll do my best to keep quiet about Gavin."

"Okay," said Sheena. "Now that we have the ground rules established, let's all enjoy one another."

"Hear, hear!" said Regina, sending a message to her father in a nice, but firm way.

Watching the sheepish look on her father's face, Regan decided she liked Regina after all.

CHAPTER FORTY-FIVE

DARCY

Darcy joined Regina and her father and the rest of her family for cocktails and dinner in Sheena's suite. Knowing the big meal that awaited them the next day, the three of them had decided to do something informal on the property instead of going out to a restaurant. Besides, she and Regan liked the idea of a quieter setting in which to introduce the men in their lives.

Darcy kept checking the door, waiting impatiently for Austin to show up. He'd had a dental emergency to handle and told her he'd come along as soon as possible. Even so, she was nervous. Her father hadn't cared much for Sean Roberts, and though she'd been touched by her father's eagerness to participate in her wedding, Darcy hoped he and Austin would get along.

From across the room, she watched her father talking to Brian and Tony. No doubt they were talking business. Funny, how things had turned out—Gavin's dependence on Brian, the accident, and Tony buying into Brian's business. It all seemed part of a greater scheme.

Austin arrived, and Darcy hurried over to him. "Hi, darling! Everything set?"

He smiled and kissed her. "Just had to reset a crown. I couldn't let the poor guy go through the holiday being uncomfortable." He lowered his voice. "How's it going with your dad?"

"Like always, he's a little unpredictable, but I think he's pleasantly surprised by the three of us and what we've accomplished. Come. I want you to meet him."

Austin nodded. "Okay, let's do it."

As they approached, her father's attention landed on Austin. He smiled and held out his hand. "You must be Austin. I'm Patrick Sullivan."

"Pleased to meet you, sir," Austin said, shaking his hand. "You have a lovely daughter."

Her father grinned. "You are a brave man taking her on. But I'm glad to see you two together. Happy to have given you permission," he said, winking at them both, "and I'll be very happy to give her away."

Darcy laughed, understanding where she got some of her sassy wit. "With or without you, it's going to happen, and both Austin and I are glad you'll be part of it."

"Yes, it means a lot to Darcy," said Austin, putting an arm around her.

"To all of us," said Sheena, joining them. She handed Austin a cold beer. "Thought you might like this."

He grinned. "Thanks."

Brian asked Austin how he was doing, and hearing the conversation between the men, Darcy eased away, glad to see how easily Austin became part of the family group.

CHAPTER FORTY-SIX

REGAN

Regan forced herself to stay away from the men's group, knowing how important it was for her father to get to know Brian. If the time came when Brian proposed, she wanted her father's approval given as easily as he'd given it to Austin.

Meaghan came over to her. "Brian's so cute. When I get older, I want someone like him."

"What happened to Rob?" Regan replied, amused.

"Now he likes Tara, and I like Devlin."

Chuckling softly, Regan wrapped her arm around the niece she loved. "I suspect you're going to have a lot of boyfriends before you're ready to settle down, but when the time comes, I hope you find someone as wonderful as Brian."

Meaghan gazed up at her with shining, hazel eyes. "You guys are really in love. I can tell."

"Oh, how?"

"By the way you look at it each other—like Mom and Dad, and Austin and Darcy."

Happiness surged through Regan. She looked up to find Brian staring at her and felt her lips curve.

"See?" said Meaghan, giggling as she waved at Brian.

Regan couldn't help laughing. Meaghan had been a conquest of Brian's the first time she met him. At the time, it had bothered Regan, but now she thought it was charming.

She walked over to Brian and took hold of the hand he

offered her.

"So, you two getting married?" her father said, glancing from one to the other.

Regan blinked in surprise, stunned her father would say this. "Da-a-ad!"

Austin and Tony moved away, leaving her with Brian and her father, who appeared to be sizing each other up.

Though Regan wanted to choke her father, she didn't want to make a scene. "Dad, please ..."

"What?" her father said. "A lot has happened in these last months, and I'm just trying to catch up with all of you."

"When the time comes, you'll know." Brian smiled at her father and gave her hand a squeeze.

"I like you, so when the time comes you have my blessing," her father said agreeably. "Now, how do I get another beer around here?"

"I'll get it for you, Dad," Regan said, needing a moment to collect herself.

"What happened?" said Sheena, when Regan entered the kitchen. "I saw you talking to Dad."

"I could die of embarrassment. Dad came right out and asked Brian if we were going to get married. Now, he wants another beer."

Sheena reached into the refrigerator and pulled out a can of beer. "I'm sure, by now, Brian understands how Dad can be."

"But I hate for Brian to have been put on the spot like that," Regan protested. "We've talked about the future, but it's so unfair Dad asked him. It places us both in an awkward situation. God! I don't want Dad to scare Brian away."

Sheena placed a hand on her shoulder. "Honey, have you seen how Brian looks at you? Like Darcy says, the two of you sizzle."

Regan drew a deep breath and headed back to her father, who was still talking to Brian. As she reached them, Brian pulled his phone out of his pocket. "Sorry, but I've got to see my mother about something. I'll try to get back here for dinner, but you know how the bar business can be." He turned to her. "I'll be back. I promise." He gave her a quick kiss and moved away.

"Ah, here's my beer," said her father. "Thank you, my beauty."

Regan placed her hands on her hips and faced him. "Did you say something to scare Brian away? All this talk of marriage ..." She fought the sick feeling swirling inside her. "Brian isn't somebody to make a commitment lightly. He needs time."

Her father let out a puff of breath. "Sorry if I messed things up for you. Why don't you go catch up to him? I'll explain to Sheena."

"Do you think I should?" Regan said, aware of her father's discomfort.

Her father grimaced and nodded. "After the private conversation I had with him, I think you'd better talk to Brian. Clear things up."

Regan's eyes widened. "Oh my God! It's that bad?"

She didn't wait for an answer. She hurried out the door.

In the growing dusk, Brian was walking toward The Key Hole.

"Wait!" Regan called, racing across the lawn to meet him. "Brian, we have to talk."

He turned to her, his expression grave. "We certainly do. Let's go down to the bay where we can be alone."

Trying to hold back tears, Regan went with him to the cleared area next to the water, where they'd set up a few comfortable chairs. The arbor they'd recently constructed shielded them from view. Regan was glad for it because if Brian was about to break it off with her, as her father had indicated, she was going to shatter.

"Look, I'm sorry if my father pressured you ..." Regan began, stopping when she saw Brian starting to kneel in front of her.

He looked up at her with a smile. "Regan Sullivan, will you marry me?"

Regan's heart beat so fast she felt faint. "Wait! Aren't you going to break up with me?"

"Not if I can help it," Brian said, laughing. He pulled a small velvet box out of his pocket, and opened it. A large marquis diamond winked at her from a platinum band.

"It's beautiful," Regan gushed, still trying to get her head around the fact he was actually proposing to her.

"Will you, Regan? Will you marry me?" His gaze settled on her with such love she immediately started crying.

"Regan?"

"Yes, oh yes!" Regan cried, throwing herself at him. In slow motion, they gently rolled to the ground.

Looking up at her atop him, he grinned. "I like your response, lady, I think you're going to have to help me get up."

Laughing, she got to her feet and grabbed hold of him. Then, she watched as, with shaking hands, Brian slid the ring onto her finger. The happiness on his face reached inside her, comforting the fear that had almost felled her. "I've waited a long time for you, Regan. I love you, and I always will."

"And I love you, Brian Harwood," she said, her voice quivering with emotion. "I never really meant that horrible thing I said to you at the airport. Looking back, I was afraid of the sensations you caused in me even then, and it scared me to death. Thank you for being patient and teaching me what it is to love with not only my body but my soul."

"It's only just begun," he whispered, lowering his lips to hers, melting away the world around them.

As they walked back to Sheena's suite, Regan kept glancing at the ring on her finger. It meant more than a symbol of their love; it meant she was finally free to be herself in a way she'd always dreamed. The man beside her loved her for who she was—not her face, but the person inside who was still learning she had a lot to give.

Outside the door to Sheena's room, Regan stopped and clutched her hands. "I can't wait to tell them what's happened."

She opened the door and stepped inside to find her family gathered around, staring at her.

"Well, did it happen?" her father asked Brian.

Brian laughed. "Yes. I admit I was going to propose later this evening, but suddenly I couldn't wait. Thank you, Patrick, for helping to make this happen now."

Regan's jaw dropped. "Do you mean you knew about this?"

Her father laughed. "Like I told Darcy, I'm happy to give away my daughters."

Brian tugged her to his side. "I'd planned something like this all along. I just needed a little help to get you outside."

Sheena and Darcy hurried to her side and swept her up in their arms, forming a circle.

"Congratulations, Regan. We're so happy for you," said Darcy.

"Can't believe Dad did this. He's so pleased with himself," said Sheena. "And for once he did something right."

"Am I going to be in your wedding too?" said Meaghan, coming to them and taking hold of Regan's hand and studying the ring.

"Of course," Regan said, still startled to think now that she was engaged, she'd have to start thinking of a wedding.

She turned as Holly Harwood entered the suite.

Holly hugged her son and turned to Regan smiling, even as tears shone in her eyes.

"Congratulations, Regan. You're the perfect wife for Brian and the perfect daughter for me. I'm so glad he finally proposed."

"Finally? But we've been together for just a couple of weeks."

Holly smiled and cupped her cheek in one hand. "But he's loved you for much longer than that."

Brian came to her side and wrapped an arm around her, bringing her closer to him. "It's true, Regan. Everyone knew it but you."

She smiled up at him, loving him more than words could say.

As if reading her mind, he leaned down and whispered, "Later."

She laughed and, on tiptoe, kissed his cheek, feeling as if she was the luckiest girl in the world.

The next day, Regan and Brian walked into Gracie's together for the special, private Thanksgiving dinner Gracie had prepared for both the hotel family and theirs. Every one of Gavin's people already knew about the engagement, and at the sight of Regan, two of them rushed over to her.

"Congratulations," said Lynn, leaning over for a closer look at the diamond.

"Pretty! Pretty!" said Clyde, tapping her hand.

Bebe emerged from the kitchen and, smiling, came over to her. "Looks like I have another wedding cake to bake."

Regan grinned. "We'd be honored if you would." She turned to Brian, but he'd left her to go with her father and the other men standing in a corner where drinks had been set out.

Gracie, wearing an apron, approached. "Such wonderful news, Regan! Brian is one of our favorites, and you are too. You're going to be happy together. I just know it."

"Thanks." Regan gave Gracie a quick hug. Gracie wasn't usually comfortable with shows of affection, but she hugged Regan back.

Maggie and Sally joined the group around her, extending their congratulations. Touched by all the good wishes, Regan couldn't help the tears that stung her eyes. She was still feeling like a princess in one of the stories she'd always loved.

Sheena and Darcy waved her over to the long table that had been set up for their dinner.

"Is Mo coming?" Sheena asked, arranging place cards on the table.

Regan shook her head. "He flew to California this morning. I'm disappointed, but happy for him. Where's Regina?"

"She's taking a tour of the kitchen," said Darcy. "Both she and Dad have gotten an earful about how great Gavin was. I think it surprised them both."

"Gracie told me Dad and Gavin look an awful lot alike," Sheena said. "Odd how two brothers could be so different."

"Maybe they're not so different," Regan said, watching her father laugh with the other men. "Only time will tell."

Sheena said, "Time will tell us a lot of things, including whether we get to keep the hotel."

"We're going to pull this off," said Darcy. "I feel it in my bones."

"Of course, we are," said Regan, feeling a surge of confidence rush through her. "We're the Sullivan sisters!"

Smiles filled Sheena's and Darcy's faces as Regan squeezed

them tight. She didn't know exactly how they'd win Uncle Gavin's challenge, but they'd learned, together, they could do almost anything.

Regan gazed across the room at Brian. He noticed and sent her a tender look that filled her senses. Of all the joys the Salty Key Inn had brought her, finding love with him was the best of all.

Note to my Readers

My apologies for not being able to end the series here, but as I was in the middle of writing Book 3, I realized I couldn't deprive you, my readers, of the full story of the Sullivan sisters, and a final book would be necessary to complete the series. *Finding Family,* Book 4 of The Salty Key Inn Series, has just been released!

Thanks for understanding. Love my readers!

Thank you for reading *Finding Love.* If you enjoyed this book, please help other readers discover it by leaving a review on Amazon, Goodreads, or your favorite site. It's such a nice thing to do.

Enjoy an excerpt from my book, *Finding Family*, Book 4 in The Salty Key Inn series.

CHAPTER ONE

SHEENA

Sheena Sullivan Morelli stood outside Gavin's, the new restaurant at the Salty Key Inn on the Gulf Coast of Florida, feeling as festive as the mini-lights wound around the trunks of the palm trees that softened the outline of the building. She was dressed in her finest on this unusually warm, mid-December night, and the tropical Gulf breezes felt good as they caressed her skin.

From among the hibiscus planted around the perimeter of

the restaurant, lights twinkled like the stars in the inky sky above and lent a sense of peace to the area. That, and the fact that Petey, the pesky peacock Rocky Gatto had rescued and brought to the hotel, had decided not to bother with this celebration and was hanging out down by the bay.

"Let's make this an evening to remember!" said Sheena. giving her sisters, Darcy and Regan, an encouraging smile.

Named after their uncle, the restaurant would, they hoped, bring in enough revenue for them to be considered successful in meeting the terms of his will. With less than a month before their final meeting with Gavin's estate lawyer in Boston, they were trying their best to prove to him that they had succeeded in beating the challenge of turning his rundown hotel into a profitable operation within one year. Winning meant they would inherit Gavin's sizable estate along with the hotel and, more than that, it would determine how they'd spend the rest of their lives.

Sheena brushed an imaginary crumb off her blue linen dress and studied her sisters. Darcy was wearing a green sheath that offset her red curls nicely. And Regan, beautiful as ever, even with the scar on her face that she couldn't quite hide, had chosen a violet, flowy dress that matched her striking eyes. Funny, Sheena thought, how she hadn't really known her sisters until the three of them had been forced to live and work together at the hotel. And when Regan and Brian Harwood, now her fiancé, were in a serious motorcycle accident a few months ago, frightening everyone, they'd become even closer.

"I hope everyone likes what they see," Regan said. "Mo and I did our best decorating the interior with the budget we were given."

"Don't worry. It's gorgeous," said Darcy, giving Regan an impish nudge with her elbow.

"The restaurant is stunning," said Sheena, "and the food is great. We were lucky to get Graham Howard as our chef." She turned as a stream of people headed their way from the parking lot, which was filling up fast.

"Here we go! Make it good," said Sheena softly, prompting Darcy and Regan to roll their eyes at the big-sister moment Sheena couldn't help.

They'd invited county commissioners, members of nearby city and town councils, other government officials, news people, owners and managers of other hotels in the area, and even the governor of Florida to join them for this grand opening. It had been a bold move on their part, but it had already paid off in publicity, even though the governor and some county commissioners had politely declined. The fact that Darcy had been writing a column for a local newspaper helped them. She was acquainted with the ins and outs of generating publicity and had invited several writers of local social columns, travel bloggers, and magazines.

Sheena was soon swept up greeting people and ushering them inside to enjoy drinks and to taste the delicious-looking food displayed in the bar and on a long buffet in the dining room.

The dark wooden paneling on the walls of the main dining room supplied a rich background for the crystal-accented wall sconces that spread a soft glow along the room's edges. Crystal chandeliers hung from the ceiling, casting their own warm light. White linen cloths covered the tabletops. Flickering battery candles sat among tasteful, holiday greenery, adding a pine perfume to the mouth-watering aroma of the hors d'oeuvres being passed by staff.

Upstairs, the large function room held another bar and more food to sample, drawing people through the entire restaurant. The buzz of conversation highlighted the sense of excitement. The crowd was a pleasing mixture of people who, hopefully, would be a source of future business.

Kenneth Cochran, better known as Casey, was a Cornell Hotel School grad and manager of the restaurant. Tall, thin, and wiry, he was a natural at his job with his ever-present smile and alert blue eyes. Tonight, he seemed to be everywhere, overseeing staff, and greeting people. Sheena observed him with satisfaction as guests responded to his attention. If she and her sisters won the challenge, they hoped to be able to hire Casey as the hotel manager to help Sheena, who would remain an active overseer of the property.

Sheena looked up as her husband, Tony, appeared with their two children. Tears stung her eyes when she noticed the effort that Michael, at eighteen, and Meaghan, at fifteen, had put into their appearance. After initially being against her plan to come to Florida, they now embraced their new lives and were proud of all she was doing.

"Hi, Mom," said Michael. His brown eyes, so like Tony's, sparkled. "Okay if I help myself to some of the food?"

She laughed at the typical, teen-age hunger of a still-growing, young man. "Of course. Enjoy."

"You look pretty, Mom," Meaghan said. "Thanks for letting me wear your necklace. It's great with my new holiday dress." She twirled in front of Sheena. Her auburn hair, like Sheena's, swung above her shoulders and brought out the hazel in her eyes.

"You look pretty, too, sweetheart," Sheena said. Her little girl was growing into a beautiful, young woman.

Tony gave her a smile that warmed her heart. His smile had been one of the reasons their marriage had been prompted by the unexpected creation of Michael all those years ago. And though they'd always loved each other, their relationship had grown even stronger during their time in Florida. He kissed her. “See you later. I’m going to mix with the crowd a little. Brian and I are hoping to pick up some new business.”

She gave him a heartfelt smile. Following Brian Harwood’s motorcycle accident with Regan, Tony had agreed to become a partner in Brian’s construction company. As Tony walked away, Sheena noticed Blackie Gatto headed in her direction.

Blackie was Uncle Gavin’s financial advisor and a great supporter of her sisters and her as they attempted to do as their uncle wished by transforming what was a small, run-down, family hotel into the nice property he’d envisioned.

“Welcome to Gavin’s,” Sheena said to him, giving him a quick hug. “I’m so glad you could make it.”

“I wouldn’t miss it for the world,” he replied, lifting her hand, and kissing it in a gallant gesture. He indicated their surroundings with a sweep of his arm. “I think Gavin would be very pleased with this.”

“We hope it brings in enough funds for us to complete our challenge here at the hotel.”

He nodded and settled his gaze on her. “I hope so, too. The downside of borrowing the money from Gavin’s estate to complete the restaurant could be difficult for you and your sisters if you fail.”

Sheena’s stomach curled inside her, but she didn’t want to allow Blackie to see how worried she was. For the sake of her sisters and her family, she had to remain upbeat. With only a few weeks remaining to accomplish everything they had left to do, self-doubt could ruin them.

“I probably shouldn’t warn you, but a special guest is going to appear this evening,” Blackie said mysteriously.

“What? Who?” Sheena said, and turned when Tony joined them.

“How are you, Blackie?” Tony said.

Sheena smiled as they shook hands. At one time, Tony had

thought she and Blackie had something going on between them. With his Italian temper rising, he'd even yelled at Blackie to keep away from her. Now, they all could laugh about it.

"Heard you bought into Brian's business," Blackie said to Tony. "A good investment, if you ask me. The two of you guys can make a real go of the construction business in this part of the state."

"Thanks," said Tony. "Brian is still recovering from his motorcycle-accident injuries, but he's doing more and more in the field."

"Nice to keep it all in the family," said Blackie. He waved to a gentleman in the crowd. "Well, guess I'd better go say hi to a few other people."

After he left, Tony wrapped an arm around Sheena. "You look beautiful, Mrs. Morelli."

She smiled at him. "Thanks. When you entered the restaurant with the kids, I could hardly believe how grownup they looked."

"Just a couple more years and we'll be on our own." Tony gave her a sexy grin that sent a gleam to his dark brown eyes. "It's gonna be great. Really great."

Sheena's laugh came from deep inside her. She loved that Tony still found her so desirable.

Darcy approached them holding Austin Blakely's hand. Engaged now, they were, Sheena thought, a darling couple. And well suited. Darcy tended to be a bit impetuous, and Austin, though not the least bit boring, was a calming influence.

"What's up?" Darcy asked.

"We're talking about the future," said Sheena. "The kids will be gone before we know it."

Tony grinned. "It'll be nice. What's going on with you two?"

"I'm starting to get a little nervous about my wedding," said Darcy. "Looking around at all the preparations for this party, I hope I can get everything done the way I want."

"All I care about is saying 'I do.' I don't need all the fancy stuff associated with it," Austin said in his usual, good-natured way.

"Whoa! We're counting on you two to set the standard for weddings here at the hotel," said Sheena. "It's a big reason why we're going after the wedding business."

"What about Regan's wedding?" Darcy said to her. "Are she and Brian going to get married here? I've asked her, but she says she doesn't know."

Sheena laughed. "She'll figure it out. I think her engagement to Brian is still a surprise to her."

At the sight of the manager of a nearby hotel, Sheena excused herself and went to greet him. They needed as many friends as possible to help pull off the restaurant's success. In truth, they probably should have waited to build Gavin's. Now, all she could do was hope it would prove to be a chance worth taking.

CHAPTER TWO

REGAN

Regan mingled with the crowd, telling herself it would be good practice for when she'd begin filming as spokeswoman for Arthur Weatherman's restaurant chain. After her accident with Brian, she'd been certain Arthur would rescind his offer, but he and his wife, Margretta, had surprised her by keeping to their agreement. She'd always be grateful to them for helping her realize that her beauty was perceived by her actions and how she felt about herself as a person.

Growing up, she'd been considered the "looker" in the family—and the dumb one.

Being here in Florida, working on the hotel, had been the beginning of a whole new life for her, one she'd vowed never to leave. Her gaze searched for Brian Harwood. He was across the room leaning on his cane while he talked easily with a group of people. Even with his injuries, he still looked like a poster boy for Florida tourism with his sun-bleached brown hair and buff, tanned body. Love for him surged through her. Of all the good things that had happened to her, finding love with him was the best.

As if he knew what she was thinking, he looked over at her and smiled, making her feel warm inside.

"I heard you two got engaged. Congratulations!" said a voice behind her.

Regan whirled around. "Nicole! I'm so glad you made the trip!" She gave Darcy's old roommate, Nicole Coleman, a quick hug. She looked fabulous in a red sheath that offset her blond hair. "Have you seen Darcy yet?"

"No. I just walked in." Nicole's blue eyes sparkled. "Where is she?"

Regan pointed her out in the crowd. "She'll be so glad to see you."

Nicole studied her. "I was sorry to hear about the accident, but you look great, Regan." Nicole lifted Regan's hand and studied the diamond ring winking on her finger. "I'm so happy for you. And for Brian too. I had the chance to talk to him when I visited in September. He's a nice guy, and you two are great together."

"Thanks. I think so too," said Regan. She was still surprised sometimes when people told her how good she and Brian were together. For a long time, she'd been sure Brian would be nothing but trouble for her.

As Nicole left to find Darcy, Regan watched her walk away, thinking that life sometimes seemed to be one surprise after another. In this case, she was glad Nicole had suddenly decided to leave her job in Boston, sell her new condo, and move to Florida. She suspected it had everything to do with Graham Howard. It was a good thing for Gavin's because Nicole had promised to help them with publicity for the restaurant, and they needed all the help they could get.

"Hello, Regan," came a smooth, low voice.

Regan turned to find Arthur and Margretta Weatherman standing near her. She felt a smile, still crooked from injuries she'd endured in the accident, spread across her face.

"Hello, Arthur! Margretta! I'm so glad you could come to our opening." She held out her hand, and they each shook it.

"Glad to be here," said Arthur. He glanced around. "I like what you've done here. You and Mo do good work together."

"We can't wait to have you and your business partner get started on our restaurants," said Margretta.

"Thanks," said Regan. She and Mo had bid on redoing six of the Weathermans' family restaurants in their Florida's Finest Restaurants chain. The smile left Regan's face as she suddenly fought tears. "I want to thank you both again for allowing me to be your spokesperson. As you can see, the scar under my chin and onto my jawline is now a part of me, along with a lip that may or may not completely recover from nerve damage."

Margretta, a tall, beautiful brunette, gripped Regan's hand. "We talked about it a lot before deciding, and we're very happy you'll represent us. You're a beautiful woman as you are. It's important for young girls to realize that they don't have to be perfect. None of us is."

"That's why I agreed to do it," said Regan. "It was a scary thought at first, but I'm comfortable with it now."

"We'll be in touch about the filming schedule. Probably next week. We need you to start the New Year off right for us," said Margretta.

"I hear congratulations are in order," said Arthur. "I've known Brian for some time. He's a good man. I'm happy for you." He glanced around the room. "Ah, I see Blackie. I'd better go say hello."

"Thanks again," said Regan. "Be sure to enjoy the refreshments. Graham has done a wonderful job with them."

After they left her side, Regan decided to go check the food displays. As she was walking through the main dining room, she saw Mo talking to a gentleman who looked vaguely familiar. She hurried over to them.

"Mo! I'm so glad you came!" She hugged him and turned to his companion. "I almost didn't recognize you, Kenton! Glad you could join us too." Kenton Standish, a robust man with sandy-colored hair and fine features, was wearing tinted, thick-rimmed glasses that disguised his blue eyes. His ordinary blue blazer hid the muscular, bare chest that women were used to sighing over on his television show. On screen, he played a heroic Scottish fighter. In reality, he was a kind, soft-spoken person who was Mo's partner. Ordinarily, they took great care not to be noticed, so Regan knew it was a tribute to her sisters and her for them to be here in this crowd.

"You look fabulous," Mo said. His brown face softened with affection, and his dark eyes shone with admiration. "Love that dress on you!"

"Thanks. You look pretty dapper yourself," Regan said, admiring the subtly checked gray blazer and the bold, red holiday tie he wore. "Have you spoken to Arthur and Margretta?"

"Yes," said Mo. "They're very excited about what we've designed. I can't wait for us to set our work in motion." He smiled at Kenton. "And then, we'll begin work on Kenton's house."

Regan smiled at them both. "It's going to be so much fun to do that. I've already got some ideas in mind."

Mo smiled. "Me too. Black and white ... like Kenton and me ..."

"... with bold colors," said Regan.

Mo laughed. "Exactly."

Regan loved how closely their minds worked. Since meeting Mo and working with him on a few projects, her whole world had come alive with color and texture, drawing out her artistic side.

"I understand you and Brian are engaged," said Kenton. "Congratulations."

They all turned as Brian approached.

"Here he is now," said Regan, beaming at the man who'd finally won her trust, along with her heart.

Brian smiled and put an arm around her. "Hi, Mo! Good to see you. Thanks for the books you sent to me. It's frustrating to be laid up, so it was nice to have them to read."

"Brian, I want you to meet Kenton," Mo said. "Kenton, this is Brian Harwood."

Brian and Kenton shook hands.

"I understand you're in construction," said Kenton. "I'm wondering if I could talk to you sometime about doing some work on my house. I want to upgrade the kitchen and do a few extra things with it."

"Thanks. Tony Morelli, my new partner, and I would be pleased to meet with you." He handed Kenton a business card. "Give either one of us a call, and we'll set up a time. Now, if you two don't mind, I'm going to whisk Regan away to meet some of my old friends."

"We don't mind at all," said Mo. "In fact, we're here just to congratulate you, and then we're driving to Cyndi and Tom's house for a holiday event."

"Have fun, and say hi to them for all of us here," said Regan. Kenton's sister, Cyndi Jackson, and her husband, Tom, were the hotel's first official guests who'd taken advantage of the hotel's special military discount plan. Since then, they'd been instrumental in steering new guests their way.

As Brian led her through the crowd, Regan gazed at her friends and family, wondering what the coming weeks would bring. The last few had been full of surprises, including her own engagement.

About the Author

A ***USA Today* Best-Selling Author,** Judith Keim is a hybrid author who both has a publisher and self-publishes. Ms. Keim writes heart-warming novels about women who face unexpected challenges, meet them with strength, and find love and happiness along the way—stories with heart. Her best-selling books are based, in part, on many of the places she's lived or visited, and on the interesting people she's met, creating believable characters and realistic settings her many loyal readers love.

She enjoyed her childhood and young adult years in Elmira, New York, and now makes her home in Boise, Idaho, with her husband, Peter, and their lovable miniature Dachshund, Wally, and other members of her family.

While growing up, she was drawn to the idea of writing stories from a young age. Books were always present, being read, ready to go back to the library, or about to be discovered. All in her family shared information from the books in general conversation, giving them a wealth of knowledge and vivid imaginations.

Ms. Keim loves to hear from her readers and appreciates their enthusiasm for her stories.

"I hope you've enjoyed this book. If you have, please help other readers discover it by leaving a review on Amazon, BookBub, Goodreads, or the site of your choice. And please check out my other books and series:

The Hartwell Women Series
The Beach House Hotel Series
The Fat Fridays Group
The Salty Key Inn Series
The Chandler Hill Inn Series
Seashell Cottage Books
The Desert Sage Inn Series
Soul Sisters at Cedar Mountain Lodge
The Sanderling Cove Inn Series
The Lilac Lake Inn Series

ALL THE BOOKS ARE NOW AVAILABLE IN AUDIO on Audible, iTunes, Findaway, Kobo, and Google Play! So fun to have these characters come alive!"

Ms. Keim can be reached at **www.judithkeim.com**

And to like her author page on Facebook and keep up with the news, go to: **http://bit.ly/2pZWDgA**

To receive notices about new books, follow her on Book Bub:

https://www.bookbub.com/authors/judith-keim

Sign up for my newsletter and get a free story. I keep my newsletters short and fun with giveaways, recipes, and the latest must-have news about me and my books. Welcome! Here's the link:

https://BookHip.com/RRGJKGN

She is also on Twitter @judithkeim, LinkedIn, and Goodreads. Come say hello!

Acknowledgements

A writer is always working no matter where s/he is—at a desk, driving a car, sitting in an airport, reading someone else's book, or lying in bed in the early morning hours figuring out a plot twist. Shapes, sounds, overheard conversations, observation of others all play a part in enabling us to create real-life characters. But to do this, one must have support. Uniquely I think, writers truly do support one another on the journey because only they can appreciate the process, the highs, the lows. I especially want to acknowledge a group of my fellow women's fiction writers for their support and encouragement. Thank you, Heather Burch, Betty Lee Crosby, Ashley Farley, Christine Nolfi, and Patricia Sands. I'm so pleased to have met you at NINC 2017 and to have formed a treasured bond with you.

As always, I thank Peter for his hard work in our business and with his editing. I'd also like to thank Lynn Mapp for her editing contribution.

www.ingramcontent.com/pod-product-compliance
Lightning Source LLC
Chambersburg PA
CBHW061558190726
48288CB00007B/2078